A Circle of Empowerment

A Circle of Empowerment
Women, Education, and Leadership

Rita L. Irwin

STATE UNIVERSITY OF NEW YORK

Published by
State University of New York Press, Albany

For information, address the State University of New York Press,
State University Plaza, Albany, NY 12246

Production by Christine Lynch
Marketing by Dana E. Yanulavich

Library of Congress Cataloging-in-Publication Data

Irwin, Rita L., 1955–
    A circle of empowerment : women, education, and leadership / Rita
L. Irwin.
        p.   cm.
    Includes bibliographical references and index.
    ISBN 0-7914-2441-3 (cloth : alk. paper). — ISBN 0-7914-2442-1
(pbk. : alk. paper)
    1. Arts—Study and teaching—Canada, Western.   2. Arts—Canada,
Western—Management.   3. Women art teachers—Canada, Western—
Attitudes.   4. Art consultants—Reporting to—Canada, Western.
I. Title.
NX313.A3W475   1995
700'.68—dc20   94-21387
                                                          CIP

10 9 8 7 6 5 4 3 2 1

Dedicated to my father, Ellwood R. Irwin
and
the women in the Cactus Club
who graciously allowed
me into their lives.

Contents

Preface

There are times in one's life when personal experiences become powerful forces for change. This book represents an opportunity I had to share professional and personal experiences with a group of women who worked together at a fine arts center in a board of education in Western Canada. Even though the experience was framed by a two-stage research study, what emerged was an inextricable bond between people working together. If I am indebted to anyone in writing this book, it is to those women. I would also like to acknowledge research support from the Center for Curriculum and Instruction in the Faculty of Education at the University of British Columbia and my many colleagues, friends and family who also supported me emotionally and intellectually during my academic career.

When I began working on this project, my primary focus was on the role of a supervisor and what she had come to know about educational change in the arts, that is, in the way of practical knowledge. Much of what I learned throughout the data collection and analysis stages resonated with my own experience as a consultant. However, what I had not anticipated learning was how differently power may be conceived: rather than having power over someone else, what seemed to be encouraged was sharing power with others. Embedded within this understanding came a desire to investigate more deeply just how this kind of knowledge may be taught, learned, or shared between two or among more persons. What ensued was an extension of the first study to include the women with whom the supervisor worked.

Although my primary goal was to understand and interpret the practical knowledge of one curriculum supervisor, what soon became evident was the type of leadership that emerged within the community of women: rather than hierarchial, it was circular; rather than competitive, it was cooperative. Power was not conceived as control but rather as empowerment and entrustment. In turn, leadership became redefined to involve a mentorship role where women learned from the practical knowledge of one another in a community of pedagogues.

And so the task of this book is not simple. The role of supervisor is not a role that has demanded a lot of attention in the literature yet it remains pivotal as an interface role between and among groups of professionals. As we take the time to get to know individuals in such a role, we may examine the quality of understanding that has developed in and through time. This quality is worth our contemplation if we are to reflect upon our own abilities as pedagogues and leaders. This is particularly true for women who need to read about and learn from the experiences of other women. Although I believe the message portrayed in this book should speak to men and women alike, I am hoping that women who read the material are particularly drawn to its intent.

Chapter 1 is meant to provide a personal introduction of Ruth, the supervisor, and myself, the researcher. Through doing so, it is hoped that the reader will come to understand some of the historical background that brought each of us to undertake the studies.

Chapter 2 presents the results of a small study which actually came after another study presented later in the book. However, it is presented first in an attempt to quickly situate the reader into the context of the milieu, to recognize the influence the supervisor has had upon her colleagues, and to portray the ever present feminist perspective. The community of women participating in this study are quick to discuss a form of leadership that is at once powerful and empowering.

Over the last twenty years there has been a great deal of interest in implementation and educational change issues. Supervisors serve a critical role during educational change as they act as an interface between and among a variety of professional groups. But little is known about the kinds of knowledge individuals in these positions have and use everyday. Chapters 3 and 4 are designed to share the content and contexts of Ruth's (pseudonym) practical knowledge. Through an interpretation of the findings in chapter 5, one begins not only to recognize the power of empowerment in educational change, but also to recognize the pivotal role of the supervisor in helping teachers to change.

Chapter 6 takes the practical knowledge of Ruth and shows how practical knowledge becomes a pedagogical resource to transform a community of educators. What may be called "charismatic leadership" or "transformational leadership" exhibits characteristics that are associated with mentorship. Mentorship as leadership is seen as an enlarging circle of commitment, collaboration, and caring. Since these principles are set within a feminist viewpoint, one is left to consider reconstructing leadership from a feminist pedagogical perspective.

Chapter 1

A Personal Introduction

In recent years, there has been a gradual realization that researchers bring to their research activity personal experiences, beliefs, attitudes, and biases that will undoubtedly influence how they perceive, conceptualize, and design their research programs, as well as how they interpret and give voice to their findings. In the past, objectivity was heralded as a benchmark for good research activity. Over the last decade, a continuing debate has ensued regarding the so-called division between subjectivity and objectivity. Without raising the issues dealt with in such a debate, let me begin by saying that I have come to believe that who I am as a person, teacher, researcher, consultant, friend, and colleague has everything to do with how I choose to design, implement, report, and evaluate my research activities.

Many of us involved in empirical research would agree that we bring with us to our work all of who we are. However, not everyone would agree with revealing who we are to our audiences. And so in a practical sense, for me to share with you who I am, also reveals my own ongoing exploration of objectivity and subjectivity. In many ways, I am pursuing my own professional growth as I deal with my role in the research process.

Some feminist writers have chosen to reveal themselves to their audiences in a way that provides the reader with a greater sense of connectedness between the researcher and those participating in the research study. They have also presented a background narrative in an effort to provide a greater sense of context: my personal and professional context as the researcher directly influences the entire research process. In keeping with these notions, allow me to share with you, who I perceive myself to be.

Let me begin by saying that I can remember wanting to be an art teacher from the time I was a little girl. This was extremely unusual given that I grew up in a farming community which supported a small rural school of ten grades and approximately fifty-five children. All of my teachers at this school were responsible for teaching the entire curriculum within a multigrade situation. I can remember doing very little art activity. Exceptions centered around projects that involved students drawing pictures that depicted the events of what we were studying. Occasionally, I remember working in groups of youngsters who

1

created a mural based upon a social studies theme. When I was in grade eight, this country school closed down and all of the students were transferred to a consolidated high school in a rural town of approximately 15,000 people. I was able to take one year of art in my junior high school experience. Although there was a wider variety of media experiences in the art program, I remember being bored with the activities or projects that were presented. I also remember being secretly frustrated. It seemed the male teacher I had did not see any artistic ability in my work and in effect ignored me and my work. Needless to say, I never took art again in my public school education.

My desire to be an art teacher was profoundly linked with my relationship with my own mother. I can remember her encouraging me to draw, paint, and create with a whole variety of materials throughout my formative years. These experiences left an indelible impression upon me. For example, I remember looking forward to Valentine's day every year, not because of any school girl romances, but because for the two preceding weeks I could look forward to my mother coming home from the city armed with red, white, and pink paper, felt pens, glue, and scissors. We would rummage through scrap fabric drawers to find interesting textures of discarded fabric, lace, and ric rac. Then without any upset in the running of the home, I was granted free rein of the dining room table. I could create with great imagination all sorts of wild and wonderful Valentine's cards. No designs were repeated and everyone received their own personalized card. This type of artistic activity happened for virtually every special day or event happening at school or at home.

Though my mother was slow to accept recognizing herself as an artist, she in fact was an artist, and she provided a safe environment for me to explore my own artistic abilities. My parents had four children and decided ten years later to have another two children. I was the oldest of the second family. While I grew up, I believe my mother was in a phase in her life when she desperately wanted to discover what she could contribute beyond her immediate home and family. By providing me with an environment which nurtured creativity and artistic expression, she was also providing herself with the courage to become an artist.

I remember watching my mother grow as an artist. As she moved through different mediums, she demanded more and more of herself. Later, as I passed through high school, university, and into my career as a teacher, I watched my mother become an exceptional porcelain artist. Because of all the occasions given to me for artistic expression and to herself as an emerging artist, my mother and I became colleagues in art. She would always seek my advice and vice versa. We were proud of each other and each other's work.

Art was always a field I wanted to explore. Yet there was another side of me that also called for my attention. I remember as an elementary student, with mixed feelings, how I was often called upon to lead small work groups within classroom activities. Although I enjoyed working toward change and improvement, and on occasion fantasized about being influential, I never really wanted to have an authoritarian role. Even though I was uncertain what kind of a leader I might be, I was drawn to leadership positions. I wanted to improve education or education related systems. Perhaps this side of me was also encouraged by my parents, particularly my father. Although I do not remember being actively encouraged to become a leader in a field, I was influenced by the constant leadership activity in which both of my parents were involved: hospital boards, fraternities, church boards, agricultural organizations, and so forth. My father was perceived by our community as a committed and dedicated leader in a number of organizations. My mother usually supported the work of my father although she, too, directed a few groups.

When it came time for me to decide upon a career, I inevitably chose to be an art teacher. Although I was convinced I should become a secondary art teacher, an early experience in my preservice education program made me aware of the great need for specialist art teachers at the elementary level. Until then I must have assumed there was no room for an art teacher in a generalist approach to education. Remembering my own frustrating art experiences as an elementary student reinforced this view.

I considered myself very lucky for my first teaching position gave me the opportunity to provide specialized art instruction to children in grades four through six. I took great pride in delivering a program rich in variety of studio materials, critical appreciation, and historical overviews. But as most educators know, we seldom spend entire teaching days teaching the subjects we love the most. To round out my days, I was viewed as an arts specialist and was scheduled to teach music classes, grades three through six, as well as a selection of language arts and health. For the next nine years, and three schools later, I would be considered an art, music, and drama specialist. Although I had a minor in drama, my musical abilities were subject to limited knowledge of three instruments. Needless to say, I spent virtually all of my professional development energy as a teacher upgrading my knowledge of music.

As an arts teacher I found myself being committed to providing a better arts education for my students than I had received. As a result I was inclined towards leadership which would encourage change and improved arts education. For instance, I was involved at the grass roots level in establishing a fine arts emphasis elementary school in my school district. As the art department head of this school, I was obligated to provide a leadership role. I was also very active in local, regional, and provincial arts education groups who played significant roles in arts advocacy: policymaking, professional development, and public awareness activities.

Early in my career, I consciously decided that after fifteen or so years as a classroom teacher, I wanted to be an art consultant. It seemed like a job that would combine everything I enjoyed doing. It was a dream I had: helping teachers become better arts teachers. Ironically, after seven years of teaching, I was offered a halftime position as an art consultant coupled with a halftime position as an art department head at my school. It would be a role that brought me face-to-face with all sorts of issues facing arts teachers, administrators, curriculum specialists, students, and the community.

Two conflicts emerged for me as I pursued my consulting role in educational change. These conflicts may resonate with the experiences of other neophyte consultants. First, I had been trained as a generalist teacher with a speciality in art education. By accepting the role of art consultant, I was essentially assuming a particular placement in an organizational structure designed to stabilize or maintain certain standards, policies, or affiliations primarily directed from either the local school board or the department of education. Specialized training for this role was nonexistent. The conflict arose as I had to rely on my previous personal and professional experiences and knowledge base without any apprenticeship and/or mentorship for my new role. Yet, the role was different and required me to alter, shift and sometimes reinforce my frame of reference according to particular situations. It seemed to me that I had to acquire a different conceptual framework in which to proceed.

Second, what quickly became evident was the accountability and credibility I needed to embody in the eyes of my clients and public stakeholders. The local and provincial government bodies assumed I would implement the art curriculum guidelines as faithfully as possible. The teachers on the other hand assumed I understood the predicament the generalist art teachers were in, or as with specialists, would realize their commitment to a particular viewpoint, and would adjust my expectations accordingly. The middle ground posed a conflict or contradiction. I could not ignore either position yet as the art consultant I had to reduce the conflicts for myself personally and professionally in order to be effective in my role.

When I decided to pursue doctoral work in education, it was only natural to pursue a research program that involved arts education, educational change, and leadership through the role of the consultant. The work presented in this book represents two interconnected studies, the first of which began as a dissertation. The first study describes and interprets the practical knowledge of a fine arts supervisor. So little is known about what consultants or supervisors know in practice or their personal practical knowledge. Much of that study is represented in chapters 3, 4, and 5 of this book. The data collection process for this study also involved interviewing people with whom the supervisor worked. These interviews led me to consider how the supervisor's practical knowledge and consultative style influenced the practical knowledge of the team of consultants or specialists with whom she worked, regarding arts education, educational change, and working with teachers. The second or extended study is comprised of additional interviews with a group of women who worked closely with the supervisor. The findings of this extended study are presented in chapter 1.

Before moving to the body of this book, let me also say that in doing this research I have come to be more reflective of my own influence upon students, colleagues, family, and friends. I have attempted to stand back at times and watch myself interact with others. Or, conversely, I have been extra attentive to the speech, actions, and silence in others as they learn about life, learning, and teaching.

This manuscript, though intimately tied to who I am as a person, woman, teacher, leader, and researcher is even more reflective of a group of women who work together to improve arts education. The supervisor in the story is the focal point of this book. Let me share with you now how I came to work with Ruth Britten (a pseudonym).

As the art consultant for my school district, I felt that I needed to be connected with other consultants in Western Canada. This connection was often portrayed through meeting one another at conferences, exchanging curriculum resource materials, acting as visiting workshop leaders, sitting on department of education committees, and other networking activities. Given the geographical distances separating me from other centers, this networking seldom included much ongoing conversation.

In preparing for the initial study presented here, I listed those with whom I felt comfortable working, who had a number of years of experience, who had expressed an interest in research, and who had enough interaction with me previously to accept my credibility as an art consultant. After prioritizing these names, one person stood out. Ruth Britten had been a fine arts supervisor for nearly twenty years. I had gone to a couple of talks she had given at teachers' conventions, and though I was impressed with her knowledge, insight, sense of humor, and compassion, I never had the opportunity to discuss any issues with her. Perhaps it was my own lack of confidence that held me back from approaching her or perhaps the right situation never arose. I also learned through a variety of sources that she was highly respected, not only in her own school board, but also across the province. When I joined the faculty of the fine arts emphasis school in my community, and took upon myself some leadership responsibilities for guiding the philosophy and curriculum of the school, it became important to invite an external facilitator who could help us refine our ideas. I suggested Ruth Britten. This day long event would serve as my personal introduction to Ruth. She gave us a good start on the road to improvement towards a fine arts program. Within a couple years, I became the art consultant, and one of the tasks I was involved in was the evaluation of school art programs. Two schools that year were earmarked, one of which was a junior high school. In consultation with my supervisor, we decided to bring Ruth Britten in as an external voice on the team of evaluators. This fine arts program review at the junior high school took several days and would serve as my last interaction with Ruth prior to this study.

When I looked over the list of potential consultants, I just knew there was a great deal to be learned from Ruth's practical knowledge as a supervisor. She was considered an excellent educator, supervisor, and leader by virtually everyone I met. In deciding how many consultants to include in my study, I decided that we had been amiss in the education field; we lacked in-depth description and interpretation of people who were highly respected and admired in our professional circles. In the case of consultants where very little research or training activities currently exist, this seemed to be absolutely important. The arts in education programs are always struggling and whatever can be learned from reading this account will be helpful to anyone involved in educational change.

Before we begin with reviewing the nature of the study, the research foundations and findings, let's turn to a biographical sketch of Ruth Britten. Who is this person I will be talking so much about?

The Supervisor's Experiential World—A Biographical Sketch

Ruth Britten has an impressive scholarly background as well as a varied teaching base from which she can draw in her role as fine arts supervisor. As a young adult she obtained a Honors B.A. (1950) with distinction in philosophy at a catholic university. Following the lead of a truly powerful mentor, a philosophy professor who was a nun, Ruth decided to become a nun herself. Though she would later leave the sisterhood, her life experiences during the subsequent ten years as a nun provided her with numerous anecdotes, stories, and a strong sense of herself in community.

Ruth began her teaching career as an elementary and junior high teacher in a New York catholic school. Before leaving New York, she obtained a B. Ed. (1956) and served as vice-principal for one year. She returned to Eastern Canada and taught in three cities over a nine year period. It was there that she taught grades one to seven art, english as a second language, junior high art, english, science, and acted as department head of humanities in a senior high school. It was also during this period that she left the sisterhood and dedicated her life to teaching and pursuing her own educational challenges. Ruth managed to take additional university drama courses to help her as a senior high drama teacher and also completed an M.A. in english (1967).

After deciding not to marry her fiance in the fall of 1967, Ruth relinquished her teaching assignment in the east and headed west in an effort to start afresh. Upon arriving in Mountainview (fictitious name), she approached the board of education for a teaching position, thinking that was the only system available. Receiving little encouragement, she was ready to try another city when it came to her attention that there was indeed a catholic school system within the same city. Ruth speaks fondly of her initial reception to that district. People were caring, interested in her, and encouraging. And in fact, she was quickly given a choice of two teaching assignments. One was to teach in a high socioeconomic area of the city and the other in a low socioeconomic area. She chose the latter, for she believed she could provide the pupils with more insight and instruction; she also thought they would be more receptive to her teaching. The assignment was difficult in that it was split between two schools: one where she would teach junior high art and mathematics and the other, art in grades one to six.

At the end of the first year in Mountainview, she applied for the advertised position of Fine Arts Supervisor, a position that had been advertised the year before but left vacant because of a lack of qualified candidates. Receiving the position was perfect for Ruth, and being the first one in the role, she quickly sought to establish it according to the job description. In one of my field diary entries (FD or field diary #7, page 46), I reflected upon asking her about her early days in the job and how she proceeded:

> At the start, she looked at the context of change by visiting all schools. Even in her interview, she said she would have to get a feel for the culture and political reality first before defining a theoretical model. For her to effect change, she needed to know where the teachers were coming from, what needed to change, and what needed to remain. She also did an overview of the facilities and then drafted a plan of action. For example, with developmental drama, she hired someone from a local theatre group to give two demonstration lessons at every school. Ruth attended many of these and listened at the side and corrected perceptions made by the teachers. Then when in-services were held, people knew what drama was all about. People couldn't talk about it without some context and the quickest way to learn about it was through demonstration teaching.

After assuming the position of supervisor, Ruth also launched a longitudinal study at an elementary school in which she taught a grade three art class every week until those in the class were in grade six. As part of her study, she also had two control groups at elementary schools of similar socioeconomic backgrounds. One of these groups received no instruction from Ruth and one was taught only in the sixth grade, but received the same instruction as the experimental group. The purpose of her research was to determine whether a sequentially developed program in art made any difference toward idea formation and had any carryover from one year to the next. To determine any differences she used the Torrance Tests of Visual Thinking as well as the verbal form, and the MacGregor Perceptual Index. In addition, she also kept anecdotal records and heuristic interpretations. At the end of the fifth grade, she completed a battery of tests in order to record the entry behavior for grade six and found the results to be statistically significant in favor of sequential instruction (FD 57, 319).

It was during the last year of this longitudinal study that her program superintendent suggested she submit a proposal for a fine arts center that she had envisioned at an initial meeting of all supervisors in 1968, where everyone was encouraged to design five year plans for their own departments. If money were no obstacle, where would they take their programs? The government was offering school districts special funding for projects that would benefit children in a way that was not already being offered. Ruth submitted her initial plans for creating a research and demonstration teaching center for the fine arts and put forth a proposal where selected classes would be invited over time to come to the Centre. Though her superintendent thought her plans were the most visionary of those submitted, the government rejected her proposal because of the primary focus on teachers rather than students. Ruth rewrote the proposal stating that a fine arts center would be established to offer students and teachers alike an intense involvement with art, drama, and music. This proposal was accepted for implementation for the fall of 1973 (FD 57, 320). Because of this sudden development and windfall of funding, Ruth regrettably was unable to complete her initial longitudinal study, leaving the final testing and documenting unfinished.

The Fine Arts Centre would consume most of her energy for the next nineteen years. Ruth speaks of those early years with great enthusiasm for it marked significant efforts to change students, teachers, principals, parents, and central office staff notions of arts education. The 1950s and 1960s had marked two decades of a child-oriented perspective, a movement devoted to child development theories, creativity, and self-expression. The 1970s and 1980s as we now realize, introduced and have subscribed to a more discipline-centered orientation, one which commits itself to sequentially developed programs. The 1990s, though still disciplined-based in orientation, are dealing with issues related to child-centered and culturally sensitive curriculum initiatives. The Fine Arts Centre would help to establish these new notions. A full complement of staff assisted Ruth. Two specialist teachers in each of the fine arts areas, an art and a music consultant, a project manager, and a secretary manned the Centre, besides Ruth. It was a luxurious time. She maintained that number of staff until 1981 and ever since then, with a new slate of people on the administrative council, she has steadily lost staff members. When the special government funding supporting the project was finally taken away in 1987, as a consequence of budget cutbacks, Ruth lost four staff members, a very hard blow to the Centre (FD 57, 322). No one remains from the first year although Ann, the art specialist, joined Ruth in the second year of the Centre operation (FD 12, 63).

It might seem that Ruth had enough to do running the Centre, but she in fact continued to pursue her own studies. In 1973 she received a B.F.A. with distinction in visual arts and in 1978 she completed a Ph.D. Her dissertation looked at the religious symbolism in the poetry and painting of the pre-Raphaelites, an obvious interdisciplinary study between three of her personal loves: religion, english, and art history. Her scholarly achievements were honored with the following academic awards: Kappa Gamma Pi (International Catholic Scholastic Award) in 1950, and two Killam Scholar Fellowships in 1966 and 1977. In 1981, she was honored by receiving a Provincial Achievement Award from the Minister of Culture and the Premier of the province. It reads:

> Dr. Ruth Britten was responsible for undertaking an extensive research study on art education within Mountainview Catholic School System. Her findings indicated that sequential developmental programs in the arts would have a most positive effect on student learning. This research formed the basis for the establishment of the Fine Arts Centre in 1973. Under Dr. Britten's direction, the Centre serves as a nucleus for exploration in the fine arts: allows for specialists to team with classroom teachers in providing demonstration teaching in music, art, and drama for elementary school children: and, serves as a major influence for excellence in education. For her leadership in arts education, Dr. Britten was elected a Fellow of the Royal Society of the Arts.

Her teaching experience did not end when she became a supervisor. Instead she regularly taught demonstration lessons in her school system, also taught art methods courses in education, and art history courses in fine arts as a sessional instructor at the local university over an eleven year span.

Her professional leadership record portrays her as intensely active with the Canadian Society for Education Through Art, and in the provincial Arts in Education Council. She was editor of the provincial journal in her subject area, and provincial conference chairperson, as well as being instrumental as a curriculum designer for recently developed secondary art guidelines. Her leadership with a local museum, a regional arts foundation, and the city of Mountainview Centennial Celebrations should also be noted.

Her resume lists numerous speaking engagements over the last fifteen years wherein she has spoken in several Canadian provinces and one American state. In the one school year alone, she gave four keynote addresses and one other main address to such groups as the Catholic School Trustees Association, a Religious and Moral Education Council, an Arts Education Council and two area Teachers' Conventions. Other years she spoke to such groups as the Western Canada Administrators, Early Childhood Educators, Art Therapists, Museum Educators, and teachers of the Gifted and Talented.

Ruth's publication record, though not a priority to her, spans a wide array of journals and magazines. Since the completion of her Ph.D., Ruth has actively pursued a second career as an artist and is proud of her two recent one-woman shows in which all items were purchased. She hopes to be a full-time practicing artist following her retirement from the profession.

Ruth's latest accomplishment has been the establishment of a fine arts alternative school (grades 4–6) based on the Mead Model. The school board and parents have been so pleased with the program that a junior high extension of the program has also been instituted. Ruth and her committee are constantly adjusting the intentions, logistics, and design of this program.

This biographical sketch portrays the exceptional nature of Ruth Britten as a fine arts supervisor. Gaining access into her lifeworld might not have been possible had I not known her previously.

Let me end this personal introduction by relaying one last anecdote. In the process of gaining access for the study, I wrote to Ruth requesting her participation. I waited for a reply for approximately six weeks at which time I decided to phone her for an answer. I was prepared to proceed with a multiple case study if she declined. To my delight, she agreed. But one sentence which she said to me, stays with me even today. She said with earnest enthusiasm, "Of course I'll help a woman earn a doctorate!" At that time I had no idea I was entering a study that would eventually force me to deal with feminist issues. In fact, even as I completed my first study, I only briefly described the obvious women's issues, concerns, and beliefs held by Ruth. But as I moved on to include the women in the extended study, I realized that I had been fooling myself. In describing and interpreting Ruth's practical knowledge, I saw all of the subtleties and complexities of one person's guiding notions. Once I extended that to include the collective group, what was once perhaps too subtle to recognize, became almost the essential ingredient for success. The group of women worked together in a way that recognized the stability of practical knowledge but also made it dynamic through a collective social and historical process. Chapter 2 endeavors to situate the influence of Ruth's practical knowledge with her colleagues and how her leadership impacts them as educators. What is crucial is how her charismatic and transformational form of leadership strengthened the sense of community within the Fine Arts Centre. It also acted as a pedagogical tool to teach leadership and through the belief of all involved, everyone became leaders.

Chapter 2

Charismatic and Transformational Leadership Within a Community of Women Arts Educators

In the first chapter, I shared with you a personal introduction to the work presented here: some may prefer to view this as a form of personal ground. It is my hope that this background serve as a reference or starting point. Your partial reality may be quite different from mine, or resonate with some of my experiences. Before introducing the role of supervisor as an individual involved in educational change and the literature dealing with women in leadership, let me begin by setting the stage for the necessity for research which captures the life experiences of those who are involved in transformational leadership.[1]

Yvonna S. Lincoln (1989) has argued that the field of educational administration needs more case studies and ethnographies of exemplary leadership in order to hear the stories of individuals who struggle for empowerment. We need to listen and respond to these stories in an effort to encourage and nurture transformational leadership. Case studies are especially important because they provide us with examples of what transformational leadership actually looks like, insight into the qualities of the individuals who are transformational leaders, an understanding of the struggles to achieve empowerment, and finally, vicarious experiences of transformational leadership through stories or narratives. Elevating these examples allows for opportunities to find one's voice in the midst of many competing voices. Lincoln not only argues for case studies and ethnographies in educational leadership but she also outlines five strengths of narrative. The first strength lies in the communication of meaning. Through narrative, all phenomena are situated within a context and as such allows us to intimately examine and interpret the situation in detail. The second strength is value laden: case studies do not deny the moral dimensions of leadership but rather provide an opportunity to discuss the moral dimensions of leadership. The third strength is in the portrayal of not only the narrator's voice, but also the voices of those involved in transformation. This naturally leads to the fourth strength that presents the lived experiences and perspectives of participants.

Through the vicarious experiencing of empowerment or oppression, communities of understanding and change may be created. Finally, another strength of narrative is the implicit ability to consider and examine possibilities for the future.

> The narrative embodied in case studies thus provides a necessary complement to the possibility of transformation and transformational leadership. Discourse which personalizes the political rather than distancing the political from individuals has the power to alter relations of power. Until discourse is recaptured, however, transformational leaders, especially those who already exist as marginalized (e.g., women) or oppressed (e.g., persons of color) will have some difficulty in finding or helping to create the democratic communities of caring and freedom in which they can reside and work safely (Lincoln 1989, p. 180).

The following discussion of Ruth as a transformational and charismatic leader of women arts educators provides an example of a narrative of one individual's attempt to provide for and instill a sense of empowerment within her professional community. The narrative provided in this and subsequent chapters should provide a venue for each of the above strengths to be felt by the reader. Before we begin, let us take a brief look at the role of a curriculum supervisor during educational change efforts.

AN INTRODUCTION TO THE ROLE OF SUPERVISOR

In recent years, research has shown that the study and practice of educational change is concerned with reform (Fullan 1993; Schubert 1993). This reform typically takes on two characteristics: intensification versus restructuring. Fullan (1991) suggests that intensification is any move toward greater specificity of teaching and learning outcomes. In practical terms, this would be apparent through greater use of standardized tests, increased monitoring of teaching performance, and mandatory curriculum materials (Corbett and Wilson 1990; Wise 1988). Restructuring on the other hand, involves a move toward collaborative work cultures, school-based management, teacher leaders as mentors, and radical reorganization of schools and teacher education programs (Harvey and Crandall 1988). Although these two extremes are philosophically contradictory, both are strong contenders in the school culture.

One district-based role that is designated to help teachers and administrators with educational change and implementation of new subject-specific provincial or state curriculum guidelines is that of the consultant or supervisor (other titles may include coordinator, resource teacher, director, specialist). Numerous studies in the past have supported the necessity of this role in supporting staff development activities while providing individualized assistance in solving curricular problems (see for instance, the Rand Studies, Berman and McLaughlin 1978, and the DESSI study; Crandall and Loucks 1983; Huberman and Miles 1984). These studies pointed out that teachers need specific kinds of assistance that cannot be given through a generalist approach. Ironically, supervisors and consultants are a threatened group of facilitators during tough economic times. Unfortunately, they have received limited attention in educational research.

In Canada, John A. Ross and Ellen M. Regan (1990) have recently studied experienced and inexperienced curriculum consultants in Ontario and found that experienced consultants knew more about what kinds of effort as well as how much effort was necessary to bring about change. For instance, experienced or expert consultants were more likely than novice consultants to see themselves working with systems *and* individuals, while being focused and tenacious in their efforts. Further research (Fullan, Anderson, and Newton 1986) also suggests that consultants have come to appreciate the need for skills in the content and process of change. They also need to recognize the dilemma between scope versus intensity (Fullan 1991). Balancing the numbers of people with the depth of assistance is a constant dilemma for any consultant. Perhaps experienced consultants or supervisors are more likely to have acquired more implicit theories to guide their practice.

Tetsuo R. Aoki (1984), Terrence R. Carson (1984), Basil Joseph Favaro (1984), and Louise M. Berman (1984), have chosen to investigate implementation and educational change through in-service and consulting from a cultural perspective. The authors are concerned for the individual, and particularly, the teacher-consultant dialogical relationship. Through dialogue, teachers receive respect and dignity as individuals with credible ideas, regarding curriculum development and implementation. This perspective would support terms such as "colleague" or "co-participant" to describe the nature of the relationships between teacher and consultant. Prior to the work of these authors, supervisors and consultants were often characterized according to managerial roles who fulfilled certain functions and skills (for example, Madey 1980; Mann 1982). The latter viewpoint perceives supervision from a management perspective; the former, from the teachers' perspective. Although authors have often viewed the role from either one of these positions, Carson (1985, 1988) suggests that both are involved. He studied teachers and consultants during the implementation of a new social studies curriculum and discovered that "the concept of curriculum implementation emerges dialectically—as being both help and control, or improvement and increased management" (1985, p.10). This dialectical orientation between help *and* control, empowerment *and* power, informs the study of Ruth Britten. For Ruth as a supervisor, she is placed at the interface between these two perspectives, and thus, her role becomes a political play between teachers and administration. Current research fails to take an in-depth look at how consultants or supervisors perceive their role, especially as one resolves the dialectic between the two opposing roles. This concern will be addressed in detail in chapter 5. However, for the moment, let it also be recognized that very little research describes and interprets the influence of a supervisor on or with her community of specialists and consultants who in turn help teachers.

One way to examine the insider's perspective, is to study the experiential knowledge gained by a supervisor in her work. This is particularly important considering that the Ellen M. Regan and Carol F. Winter study (1982) revealed that consultants have no specific training or experience preparing them for consulting other than their initial training and classroom experience. Matthew Miles, Ellen R. Saxl, and Ann Lieberman (1988) also found that consultants receive little or no training prior to or during their tenure as consultants. The assumption is made that consultants are expected to use whatever expertise may have contributed to, or has been conceptualized from, their life histories, or personal teacher knowledge.

Over the last decade, qualitative researchers have sought to describe and interpret just what teacher knowledge or "practical knowledge" might look like and how it is constructed (Clandinin 1986; Connelly and Clandinin 1985). Considering that supervisors come to their roles with a teacher's practical knowledge, one may ask how that practical knowledge might be altered given the change of roles: the interface between administration and teaching. Also, if a group of women consultants and arts specialists are supervised by a woman supervisor, how might their practical knowledge be influenced by hers? Furthermore, how might her form of leadership as a supervisor be characterized within this community of women educators? The main content of this chapter represents a description and interpretation of such a community. Through in-depth and semi-structured interviews with five women consultants and arts specialists, the findings illustrate a charismatic leadership style encompassing four themes: visionary qualities, communicating a vision, creating trust and commitment, and empowering others. These themes also frame how the supervisor taught leadership to her colleagues through her practical knowledge. In particular, each consultant and specialist shared some of the supervisor's practical knowledge constructions. These in turn influenced the consultants and specialists as they worked with teachers in arts classrooms. The study suggests that the women in this study valued making connections and working cooperatively while being led by a leader who provides mentorship by teaching leadership.

In the in-depth case study of the fine arts supervisor (see also Irwin 1989; Irwin 1992) presented in chapters 3, 4, and 5, much is learned about the everyday practical knowledge of a leader in arts education. Essentially, the study found that she is concerned with educational change that stems from a dialectical process between personal and institutional viewpoints: she sought to empower teachers to become more actively involved in their own personal and professional growth while also presenting her authority, expertise, and standards for practice for the good of the whole school district. More importantly, she emphasized the powers of motivation, persuasion, and participation to guide her role as a teacher of teachers, and through the mentorship which ensued, these powers were used to guide the practice of teaching leadership. This chapter looks at another level of understanding: it looks at situating her knowledge within her immediate community of consultants and specialists. I have chosen to portray this description and interpretation first in an effort to uncover Ruth's sometimes conscious, and but more often, unconscious feminist view towards leadership. In so doing, we may come to understand her personal practical knowledge in a deeper way.

Without detailing the practical knowledge of Ruth (which will be presented later), let it be stated that Ruth is interested in the dialectical *power of balance* rather than the authoritarian view of the *balance of power*. The power of balance (an effort to reconcile opposing contraries) was found in her practical knowledge which she used to transform power. William R. Torbert (1991) discusses various aspects of transforming power. Transforming power calls for individuals to transform their interests into the interests of the group as all members support a particular goal. Transforming power thus invites mutuality where both sides are guided by an active awareness of the project that is at stake. Transforming power is a continuous process that is fully aware of the immediate and timely richness of the moment. Transforming power is at once humble to the interests of others yet actively challenging systems that are not aware of what is at stake. And some say, transforming power will empower all who come within its influence, even those who oppose its influence.

Achieving the power of balance is not an easy task. Feminist educators have recognized the contradictions found in women's experiences as educators. "The contradiction between authority and expertise, on the one hand, *and* nurturing and femininity, on the other, is central to the experience of women teachers: exploring this contradiction reveals that,…teachers are always gendered subjects" (Brisken, n.d. p.7). Whereas stereotypes, which suggest that intelligence and authority are masculine traits, parallel stereotypes suggest that nurturance and biased authority are typically feminine traits. Women who attempt to address these contradictions recognize that an overemphasis toward either extreme will only result in a lack of the power of balance. An emphasis upon having power over others, which breeds authoritarianism, regulation, and control, will only diminish the other person(s). However, it should also be recognized that an over emphasis upon sharing power with others, which instills confidence in student or colleague expertise and experience, will only assist individual women to abdicate their expertise and authority. As Susan Friedman (1985) suggests: "In our eagerness to be non-hierarchial and supportive instead of tyrannical and ruthlessly critical, we have sometimes participated in the patriarchal denial of the mind to women" (p. 206–207). When we have done this, we have oppressed the authority in ourselves that we have sought to nurture in our students and colleagues.

One strategy, which deals with the conflicting elements presented above, is explored by Linda Brisken (n.d.). She suggests that an additional paradigm may be constructed to share power while claiming authority. The additional paradigm would extend the sharing of power to a view of "teaching leadership." Carolyn Shrewsbury (1987) suggests that "leadership is a special form of empowerment that empowers others...[T]he goal is to increase the power of all actors, not to limit the power of some" (p. 12, 8). Teaching leadership recognizes that the teacher has expertise that she is willing to teach, and she may teach through non-authoritarian practices. Teaching leadership would implicitly and explicitly address the teaching and learning of individual and collective power. Brisken and Shrewsbury both advocate that teaching leadership should be the goal of all teachers.

Other theorists also advocate teaching leadership. Howard Gardner (1990) has suggested that "teaching and learning are indistinguishable occupations, but every great leader is teaching and every great teacher is leading" (p. 19). For James M. Burns (1978), Warren Bennis (1985), Howard Gardner (1990), Bernard M. Bass (1991), and Peter Strodl (1992), successful leaders and teachers would depend upon trust through dialogue, wherein an emphasis is placed on communication among individuals. Thomas J. Sergiovanni (1990) adds that "the successful leader is also a good follower, one who is committed to ideas, values, and beliefs" (p. 25). Although teaching leadership was assumed to happen by the above theorists, Brisken (n.d.) and Shrewsbury (1987) recognize that teaching leadership is both an explicit and implicit act. One is left to consider, however, what teaching leadership might look like and what power relations would exist among participants if sharing power *and* claiming authority are emphasized.

As we situate the concept of teaching leadership in the context of Ruth's practice as supervisor to the consultants and specialists in the centralized school district Fine Arts Centre, we may begin to question what kind of influence she may have had on her colleagues. This may be particularly informative for women, as all of the educators in Ruth's immediate circle are, coincidentally, women.

The research problem for this study is concerned with understanding the influence of Ruth's practical knowledge on the practical knowledge of those with whom she directly works. The research questions are as follows:

> 1. What evidence is there of a transfer or negotiation of Ruth's practical knowledge constructions with the apparent practical knowledge of her colleagues?

2. How may Ruth's form of leadership be characterized within the community of women educators?

Through in-depth, semi-structured, and open-ended interviews, the current study seeks to describe and explain the influence of the supervisor's practical knowledge on the practical knowledge of all of Ruth's Fine Arts Centre staff: two specialists (teachers), two consultants, and one teacher with whom she worked. The study is particularly critical if we consider that all involved are women arts educators. In no way does the literature reviewed nor the findings of the study suggest that charismatic and transformational leadership is a uniquely women's notion. Rather, feminist literature supports the findings of the study and therefore offers a lens in which to frame an understanding of the influence of Ruth's practical knowledge upon her colleagues.

WOMEN AND LEADERSHIP

An understanding of women's moral development (Gilligan 1982), women's ways of knowing (Belenky, Clinchy, Goldberger & Tarule 1986), women's academic lives (Aisenberg & Harrington 1988), and women's ways of leadership (Helgesen 1990) has led the way to appreciating the feminine principles by which many women live. These principles are typically perceived as integrating professional and personal lives, acting responsibly in the world, and pursuing work which is driven by care and love. Ruth Britten carries these principles into her work with teachers and consultants. She connects with people through a sense of community or a "web of inclusion" (Helgesen 1990, p.41), an interrelated structure that radiates from a strong central point. Thus, everyone involved contributes to the whole group. But it is more than that. Her conviction to make positive educational change and her passion for people, learning, loving, and the arts, illustrate her intensity and her search for excellence. The power of her personality and her practical knowledge becomes the strength of empowerment created by love, commitment, and mutual trust. The act of empowerment foreshadows the power of her practical knowledge to influence another's practical knowledge.

The literature on leadership abounds with male authors detailing the characteristics of male leadership. If we accept the following as a guide to proclaiming Ruth's charismatic authority, faulty connections would exist. To begin, Thomas J. Sergiovanni and Robert J. Starratt (1983) suggest that by using expert power "many supervisors gain the support of others simply because they are admired as people" (p. 110). Similarly, Wayne K. Hoy and Cecil G. Miskel (1978) suggest that power "is the ability to get others to do what you want them to do" (p. 77). Whereas power may be interpreted in a number of ways, authority implies legitimacy, and thus, authority is a legitimate kind of power. Perhaps then, Ruth exhibited an exceptional kind of authority. Max Weber

(1947) suggests that "charismatic authority rests on devotion to an extraordinary individual who is a leader by virtue of personal trust or exemplary qualities" (cited in Hoy and Miskel, 1978 p. 78). Ernest House (1977) described charismatic leaders as those "who by force of their personal abilities are capable of having a profound and extraordinary effect on followers" (p. 189). If this were true, Ruth's charismatic authority and expert power would increase the impact of her practical knowledge on others through the use of prescribed power and control. It would also mean that as a leader she would be concerned with finding or creating followers who would seek to learn and reproduce what she knows. In many ways, this example embedded in the traditional leadership model would be based upon the reproduction of self, that is, the reproduction of the leader. Followers would try to become like their leaders. This type of following may be found in some leadership courses where little attention is given to determine the strengths of the novice in an effort to form the basis of a leadership style based upon those strengths. Rather, predetermined and specified criteria are often outlined and deemed necessary for success as a leader.

However, the above portrayal of charismatic leadership does not correspond with the beliefs of the women in this study. Charismatic leadership provided by Ruth was based upon a collegual model. She and her staff criticized the use of the term "follower" in traditional leadership models and preferred to use the term "colleague." Ruth once said:

> "I don't want followers....I want colleagues who can argue with me, work with me from their point of view. I want that collegial [colleagual] exchange.... There are some charismatic figures who do indeed take the minds of their people and turn them into followers and what happens when that's over, when the charismatic figure moves off the scene, is that there is no dream left because they never developed one of their own" (during telephone interview).

Charismatic leadership for Ruth was based upon a "presence," a "presence of energy," and an "exchange of energy" which mobilized both parties to rejoice in what was possible. Her charismatic leadership helped her colleagues to realize their potential as women: they believed in their abilities and had confidence in themselves. Helen S. Astin and Carole Leland (1991) also found that women leaders spoke of having a presence. It was a way in which to empower themselves and others to feel energized toward projects. It was a productive form of power which created a sense of optimism and support for each other within the group. For instance Ruth said: "I want to make them feel confident about their own beliefs and convictions. I want to release people to realize their full potential. I don't ever want followers."

For this woman, charismatic leadership was based upon an "energy" and a "presence" that encouraged an exchange of energy—the will and deep belief in self and others. It requires a pedagogic moment to reach inside another and to help him or her see their potential. Teaching leadership would simultaneously empower and grant authority in a mutually appropriate fashion.

Bruce J. Avolio, Bernard M. Bass (1988), and Jill Graham (1988) argue that the most effective leadership, or transformational leadership, fosters follower autonomy rather than automatic followership. This capacity for independence, and indeed empowerment, was found in all the women interviewed in this study. The commitment to be viewed and to view others as colleagues sharing power instilled in the women a profound sense of motivation and commitment to the extraordinary vision set out by Ruth and her group. These women considered themselves as colleagues having autonomy within the arts community rather than automatic followers of Ruth. The function of being a colleague rather than a follower is significant to this and other studies dealing with women in leadership positions.

Although the literature on charismatic leadership and transformational leadership are sometimes discussed separately (Schweitzer 1984), they are more often discussed in relation to one another. James M. Burns (1978) suggested that two forms of leadership exist: transactional and transformational. Although a lengthy discussion of transactional leadership will not be addressed here, let it be said that while transactional leaders attempt to maintain the status quo by attending to the follower's needs, the transformational leader attends to three factors: charisma, individualized consideration, and intellectual stimulation (Bass 1985; Bass, Avolio, et al. 1987). Charisma is pivotal to transformational leadership. Charismatic leaders encourage trust and commitment in a vision, develop emotions between and among members of the professional community, and often act as role models and mentors to other members of the organization. Transforming leaders are also concerned with paying attention to individual subordinates or followers. They attempt to understand and share concerns, issues, and needs. They also attempt to encourage subordinates to seek further professional development and enhancement. This in turn leads to intellectual stimulation. Transforming leaders endeavor to rethink old problems in new ways while encouraging members of the organization to critically analyze issues and problems for themselves. In essence, "transformational leadership is development oriented for the purpose of change" (Kirby, Paradise, et al. 1992, p. 303), and it is "an approach that allows humanism to be an integral aspect of the definition of leadership" (Jordon 1992, p. 62).

Within educational leadership literature, Kenneth Leithwood (1992) says that administrators should be concerned with three goals: "(1) helping staff members develop and maintain a collaborative, professional school culture, (2) fostering teacher development, and (3) helping them solve problems together more effectively" (p. 9–10). These goals are achieved with transformative leadership which espouses a form of power *through* people rather than *over* people (see also, Dunlap and Goldman 1991). This form of facilitative power develops collaborative communities in which leadership is community oriented (Foster 1993), and which in turn, may develop communities of leaders. William R. Tierney (1989) suggests that transformational leadership may exist among individuals who are concerned with the advancement of democracy. Leaders empower their followers to take charge of their lives. William Foster admits that "leaders exist only because of the relationship attained with followers, and this relationship allows followers to assume leadership and leaders, in turn, to become followers" (1989, p.29). Although some authors writing about transformation leadership are women, no mention is given to a gendered notion of transformational leadership. In Ruth's practice, the women did not view themselves as followers. Each were leaders and colleagues. The feeling of autonomy for each individual within the collaborative community was essential to the reciprocal nature of leading between leader and colleague. It is a community of leaders.

As stated earlier, charisma is a pivotal factor in transformational leadership. Some authors believe that charisma is an inborn trait or gift which becomes apparent when "followers" form strong emotional ties with the leader, and more specifically, with the vision of the leader who is present (e.g. Avolio and Bass 1988) or the leader who is absent (Rosenbach and Hayman 1989). Others are beginning to question whether charisma is a gift or a relationship (Hunt, Baliga, et al. 1988; Boal and Bryson 1988). Although most authors discuss how charisma can be used for positive and negative ends (e.g., Schweitzer 1984), this study did not find any evidence of negative means for negative ends. If one begins to consider charisma as a qualitative relationship among people (rather than a gift), then we may begin to recognize charismatic situations or actions. Kimberly B. Boal, and John M. Bryson (1988) consider two types of charismatic leaders: (1) those leaders who obtain charisma by using extraordinary vision to communicate with their followers, and (2) those leaders who obtain charisma by way of a situational crisis that calls for charismatic qualities (see also, Bevan 1989). According to this criteria, Ruth was not involved in a situational crisis, but her vision for the arts in education may have been perceived as bold and consistent with the beliefs of many arts specialists. In essence, she became what Michael Fullan suggests for school principals: "a leader of instructional leaders" (1992, p.20).

The literature addressing most forms of leadership fails to address women's perspective on charismatic and transformational leadership. Dorothy Cantor and Toni Bernay (1992) discuss the leadership style of female political leaders in their book entitled: *Women in Power*. Many of the political women they interviewed believed in risk taking. They combined listening to others ideas, concerns, and intentions with their own well-developed beliefs and sought an appropriate direction that involved taking risks. This ability to take risks was often viewed as charismatic and courageous in nature. In turn, this often created a transformational leadership style that motivated others to demand more of themselves. Although Cantor and Bernay did not directly pursue the notions of charismatic and transformational leadership, in many ways, the leadership style of the women they studied was transformative in nature.

Cantor and Bernay (1992) draw on the work of Anne Statham (1987), who found that women tend to use a communicative style which is often oriented toward specific tasks or persons. Men, on the other hand, are often more interested in an agency-oriented style, which is concerned with image development and autonomy. Until recently, communicative styles have been discouraged while agency styles have been encouraged. The communicative styles of the women in these studies were seen to motivate others to accomplish more than previously expected for the collective good. Judy B. Rosener's (1990) research of corporate women's leadership styles is also consistent with the findings of Cantor and Bernay. She found that "the women respondents…described themselves in ways that characterize 'transformational' leadership—getting subordinates to transform their own self-interests into the interest of the group through concern for a broader goal" (p.120). More specifically, she found that they believed charisma, hard work, communication, and contacts characterized their leadership styles. For instance, she found that these women worked from an interactive leadership style that encouraged participation, shared power and information, and endeavored to enhance the self-worth of others while also energizing others. Rosener was quick to mention that her research pointed out that women were more likely than men to use an interactive leadership style, however, this need not be the case. Men *and* women can be transformational leaders.

The above review of literature situated in the context of Ruth's leadership style and in the community of her Fine Arts Centre (combined in-service center and library), points to a need to interpret leadership in context. Within this context exists shared values, beliefs, and norms that are held together by strong affective interactions among group members. Particular affection is found between Ruth and each of her colleagues. Leadership in this context is an example of transforming power being mobilized through charisma. It also sets the stage in beginning to understand how one is a leader while also teaching leadership within a group of women.

BEING A LEADER WHILE TEACHING LEADERSHIP—
THE FINDINGS OF THE STUDY

The following two quotes given by Ruth should resonate with much of the above mentioned characteristics and ideas. Particular attention should be paid to Ruth's need for connectedness, personal and interpersonal growth, as well as her understanding of what makes people powerful and her own central role as a mentor in the process.

"Now empowering other people means giving them a chance to make their special contribution. It's very simple. That's all I mean by that. Your contribution may be a particular insight, a particular talent, a particular energy, a particular loving way to be with people. Part of my job is to see to it that I can create the conditions so that you can give. And giving is what makes people powerful, not taking...one needs to be able to receive what another offers so that there isn't any violence in giving and receiving. Giving and receiving is a very powerful cycle. Taking and refusing has a sense of force in it. And force and violence draws you inward upon yourself and so who you really are can't get out" (Irwin 1988, p. 131).

Ruth found herself in a hierarchy that demanded "leadership," yet in her own way, she found a way to be a leader while teaching leadership to her immediate circle of specialist teachers and consultants. They would in turn use their increased understanding to go out and work with other teachers in a leadership role, and given the interests of the teachers, teach leadership again. Much of this occurred implicitly and explicitly through mentorship. Ruth recognized that women had few role models. More importantly, she believed that she mentored those who wanted to be mentored. In this way, she was not only using expertise in a leadership role, but also she was acting upon being a role model as a guide to teaching leadership (see also Powell 1988, p. 185–187). The nature of what she was and could teach were intimately tied not only to the explicit knowledge of being a leader, but also to the tacit nature of her practical knowledge. The nature of that which is to be learned is inseparable from her as a person and therefore cannot be extracted (i.e. into instructional materials) from the person who embodies it. Mentorship, therefore, becomes the foundation for teaching leadership. Through mutuality, both involved grow from working together, yet Ruth would always take the final responsibility to ensure continued dynamic and appropriate action.

Ruth uses the content of her practical knowledge to provide specialized leadership and guidance to her colleagues. She also uses the contexts of her practical knowledge to situate her leadership and to situate the teaching of leadership with her colleagues. The practical knowledge constructions (rules, principles, and images) which Ruth came to rely upon over the years are sometimes assumed by her colleagues. These specific constructions often portray the quality of understanding that holds the community of women educators together as a cohesive unit. More specifically, Ruth uses her practical knowledge as a form of mentorship. The charismatic and transformative nature of her practical knowledge in turn creates a dynamic leadership style.

In order to understand how Ruth may influence the practical knowledge of women around her it is necessary to situate her leadership in the context of her colleagual community. Jay A. Conger (1989) suggests that there are four stages or dimensions to charismatic leadership: sensing opportunity and formulating a vision, articulating the vision, building trust in the vision, and achieving the vision. Although variations of these dimensions may be found in Ruth's behavior and leadership style, the following grounded parallel themes better describe her particular foci: visionary qualities, communicating a vision, creating trust and commitment, and empowering others. Rather than stages, these are seen as themes in her leadership style. These themes replace the underlying patriarchal notion embedded in Conger's dimensions and offer a woman-centered view of charismatic and transformational leadership. Although Conger limited his work to the description of male charismatic leadership, the themes that are described and interpreted here are more indicative of a combined charismatic and transformational leadership style exhibited by Ruth within her community of women arts educators. One is left to consider if there may be a difference between male and female charismatic and transformational leadership styles. Further research should examine this possibility.

Each of these themes will draw upon text from the interview transcripts of the five women involved in the study. In doing so, one may begin to see the influence of Ruth's practical knowledge on the practical knowledge of those with whom she works. That is, each of the participants used some of the same or similar practical knowledge constructions as Ruth. Although it is difficult to tell who created these constructions originally, each person attributes what they have learned to their role model. Embedded in the interviews are specific examples of the transference or negotiation of Ruth's practical knowledge with that of the other person. In some instances, it is obvious that Ruth's specific practical knowledge has been accepted as a basis for action by the respondent. In other instances, adaptations have been made as individuals gradually learned that their own prior knowledge would not serve them as well as the guidance provided by Ruth. Sometimes these adaptations took several years to be fully realized. Once these new rules, principles, or images were integrated with the practical knowledge of the individual, an elevated feeling of competence and confidence guided each woman in her practice. As with most mentoring relationships, "the mentor exchanges wisdom for the protégé's creative energy" (Murray 1991, p. 54). As competence and confidence grew, energy between Ruth and each of her colleagues also grew. The "energy" and "presence" of this community could be instantly felt as you entered the Fine Arts Centre. Some believe that "power" and "energy" are words that can be used interchangeably (Starratt 1982). Perhaps one feels a type of power upon entering this community.

The following material will explore the character of Ruth's charismatic and transformational leadership style. Simultaneously, one should recognize aspects of how Ruth's practical knowledge helps her teach leadership. One theme which emerged calls forth a combined sense of imagination and strategy. Some may call this combination a form of "strategic vision" (e.g. Bennis & Nanus 1985). In the context of this study, Ruth is viewed as having visionary qualities, which she also uses to teach leadership.

Visionary Qualities

"For teachers, I would think that...she has a vision. She has a good overall vision of where the arts are going, of what they should be doing in schools... her academic background is her biggest strength because she can always back up the practical with the theoretical. And I think that makes the teachers feel justified. [They know] where they are coming from. They know that they're coming from something that is valid" (Karen, drama specialist).

Ruth's personal and professional experiences in the field afforded her heightened sensitivity toward the needs of teachers. Her professional and academic background encouraged her to use and trust her own imagination while recognizing relevant theoretical discourse. In short, she had a vision: the arts are an integral part of every student's development and teachers must provide opportunities for that development to happen. The vision is simply stated. It is essentially a product of her personal experiences and abilities while taking advantage of contextual opportunities. From this ideal vision, Ruth could rely upon her comprehensive understanding of subject matter and her broad exposure to innovations in educational change to determine specific relevant initiatives for her school district.

Ruth's practical knowledge holds numerous rules of practice, practical principles, and images (Irwin 1989; 1992). While these themes or constructions are embedded in her language some are also embedded in the language used by those interviewed in this study. It would appear that some of Ruth's practical knowledge has become part of her colleagues practical knowledge. An apt example is the practical principle: "give more to a few rather than a little to a lot" (Irwin 1988, p. 109). Two music consultants and one drama specialist teacher used this phrase or a rendition of it while they discussed their own initiatives toward educational change. Moreover, this theme is directly connected to other themes found in Ruth's practical knowledge. For instance, the practical principle, "when dealing with adult professionals, no one changes another person's behaviour...all you can do is make them want to change" (Irwin 1988, p. 95), puts the prior principle into another perspective. Consultants may provide opportunities for all teachers to become involved, perhaps enticing them to change, however, the real issue is working intensely with those who want to change. One of the music consultants described it this way:

"At the beginning...I thought that I was going to be able to get to all teachers, to [do] all in-services, however, Ruth told me only to go with the teachers who were willing to commit themselves. They're the ones who want to learn the most, so that's what I've been doing rather than trying to [get to] all of them out there....I think you can only change the people who want to be changed" (Barbara, music consultant).

This was reinforced by Karen, the drama consultant, when she said "you don't necessarily need a background but you definitely need somebody who is willing to commit. That's why we started the client program so they actually had to sign a contract."

Ruth had a vision of bringing arts education to students. This difficult vision evolved to become laden with humanistic values. Her practical knowledge interpreted this vision by defining specific principles to ensure teacher commitment to the cause. These principles also ensured greater depth of understanding among people regarding the subject matter. Implicitly, the practical knowledge themes that her consultants and specialists assumed, took on a far-reaching effect in that they became guides to their everyday behavior with teachers.

It is not enough for Ruth to have visionary qualities. The words or metaphors chosen to describe her vision, along with the manner in which that vision is communicated, takes on a special kind of power and energy.

Communicating a Vision

> "She is very interested in living...with kids and their learning, and that's what comes through...when she does speak at conferences...she definitely makes an impact on people...some call that charismatic...she is able to really give something to people that they can take away" (Judith, music consultant).

When talking to teachers informally or on more formal occasions, Ruth was able to tailor her language to different audiences. In every instance, she supported what she was saying with concrete examples and stories. She also learned about the beliefs and experiences of others through dialogue. In essence, she was building connections through dialogue with her colleagues in the field (Surrey 1987). In this way, she provided contexts to justify a collective vision. Often embedded in these stories were images or metaphors that elevated certain values that were basic to an overall mission.

Since her role as supervisor was to bring about desired change in her school district, the following practical knowledge images are critical to her working relationship with teachers. These metaphorical images are used to provide vividness and clarification of what she is trying to accomplish. In doing so, they appeal to the emotions, intellect, imagination, and values. They immediately trigger insight in the listener, and often, even a change of attitude. They seem to have become a part of the practical knowledge of others working with Ruth.

Three key images found in Ruth's practical knowledge (Irwin 1988) were also identified by several of the women who were interviewed. These were, the "parable of the sower of seeds" (p. 79), "change is slow" (p. 190), and the "collegial [colleagual] model" (p. 155). The "parable of the sower of seeds" was an image used by Ruth to describe the efforts of consultants in helping teachers. The following excerpt from an interview describes the transfer of this image to her art specialist teacher:

"Actually, it's a little like the parable, if you scatter the grain, some fall on fertile soil, others fall between rocks and don't germinate. You present, you provide support, and that doesn't mean that all are going to flourish within it, but those that do become art educators. Those teachers and classes would really be like the grain becoming tenfold and the children would have a much richer art education" (Ann, art specialist).

The drama specialist uses a similar image when talking about what she has learned about educational change while working with Ruth. "I would say that foremost I have learned that you can't plant seeds on desert ground. There has to be some kind of fertility there. There has to be an interest...even if you can possibly have it, some kind of background" (Karen, drama specialist).

Ruth recognized that neophyte consultants and specialists wanted to see change happen in a short period of time. However, she knew it would take a long, long time. One consultant and two specialists who had been with Ruth for a number of years all commented that change is a slow process. One such instance is given below:

"Teachers have to be ready for change...you have to prepare them for it and it's not just one time...by preparing that means sitting them down and talking to them and that's taking up their spare and after school time, which is so important to them. I guess I learned that I just have to be patient. It will take time but we'll get there" (Barbara, music consultant).

The "collegual model" image represented everyone involved in Ruth's arts education community. It was circular in format with Ruth in the middle. Collegiality was a prime concern for her and therefore, this model penetrated everything she did.

"Talking about Ruth's strength, she offers you collegiality. She allows you the space to literally make mistakes and very few administrators would do that....It means our input is valid, taken into consideration, worked upon...not that we run our own programs but we pretty much design our own programs with Ruth's input" (Ann, art specialist).

Ruth believed "you can only teach what you have passion for. If you have no passion for a subject then you're not going to do well at it" (Irwin 1988, p. 91). Conger supports this by saying that charismatics are essentially "meaning makers...they ensure that the vision is well understood, that it is convincing, and that its ideas spark excitement" (1989, pp. 92–93). However, Ruth believed that people would follow her passion, find their own passion, and together define a vision.

To provide a solid foundation, Ruth built trust and commitment among those with whom she worked.

Creating Trust and Commitment

To create trust and commitment among her colleagues, Ruth convinced them that she could transform her ideal into reality. Charismatic authority is interactive: it depends on reciprocal faith yet is dynamically focused by the leader through a commitment to a particular moral order (Sotirin 1987). With her wealth of practical knowledge in hand she would persuade others that she had the prerequisite skills necessary to achieve such a vision or goal. In this way she appeared to be an extraordinary individual with an extraordinary commitment to her vision. "The legitimacy of charismatic leadership involves a dialectic between the extraordinary and the everyday" (p. 24). Perhaps this is why her colleagues appropriated some of Ruth's practical knowledge. Her colleagues could benefit from the integration or coming together of the meaningful and the mundane, the sacred and the commonplace. It's also worth considering that Ruth's practical knowledge allowed her colleagues to experiment and develop their own practical knowledge centering upon their own life experiences. Through mutual trust and commitment each could grow professionally. The women appreciated Ruth's democratic form of leadership (Kushnell and Newton, 1986).

More specifically, a relationship between Ruth and each of her colleagues emerged that recognized that Ruth, as the supervisor, had more power in the hierarchy than her colleagues, and yet each woman trusted herself symbolically to Ruth. Some feminist theorists refer to this as "entrustment." "The relationship of entrustment is one in which one woman gives her trust or entrusts herself symbolically to another woman, who thus becomes her guide, mentor, or point of reference" (The Milan Women's Bookstore Collective 1990, p. 8). Ruth's colleagues trusted her even though they had less power in the structure of the organization. In this instance, mutual trust is compatible with unequal power.

> "You have the sense that you were doing what you were supposed to be doing and she trusted you totally to do your work in terms of your speciality...as a professional, as a teacher, it was just left to you. In that respect, I felt able to grow and develop...given the freedom to do whatever I wanted to do in my area. I did explore and I did try different things" (Karen, drama specialist).

> "You know she's taught me how to get to this level and I think...she'd be the ideal [school] administrator because I think she would bring out the best—she has brought out the best in me" (Barbara, music consultant).

Earlier in this chapter, Ruth described her mentorship abilities. She spoke of community, the power of giving and receiving, and the sense of responsibility among people learning together. In the following excerpt, it becomes apparent that Ruth uses the power of persuasion to encourage self-confidence in others. Having done so, she ensures mutual trust and commitment.

"I really feel like she has this ministry of being a supervisor because her role, as I see it, is to help us develop and become better people and teachers....I really feel called to teaching. My whole job is to love, encourage, and keep my students interested. Now maybe that's the inspiration Ruth gave me because she never said, 'Kathy, do it like this'...She's a politician and a poet. And she's an artist all the way. She can sell you on something even if you don't know how to do it or can't. She will sell you motivationally. She gives you the best P.R. job; it makes you feel that you can do anything and that's a real talent" (Kathy, art teacher).

As a charismatic, Ruth presents herself as not seeking personal gain but rather demonstrating a profound concern for the needs of her followers. This concern, encouragement, and devotion soon become interpreted as her confidence in their abilities. This interpretation leads to an integration of each other's practical knowledge and in turn, the teacher or consultant models mutual trust with others.

Ruth has high expectations of those with whom she works. Colleagues come to believe they are fulfilling their own potential as human beings when they meet her high expectations. "She makes an assumption that people will do their best and so you rise up to that. It's interesting for me to watch how she gets that out of people...how to get excellence out of people" (Judith, music consultant). Through her constant dedication to her cause in combination with her personal and professional achievements, Ruth is able to instill trust and commitment from her colleagues. This would still remain elusive, however, if she did not understand how to direct and motivate their energy.

Empowering Others

Much of the above has been integrated with the idea of empowerment. Empowerment is often manifested through successful accomplishments (Malin and Teasdale 1991). As leaders structure goals for initial success by their colleagues, a sense of accomplishment builds confidence and in turn generates greater commitment to the community effort (Matlin 1987). Empowerment is also manifested through persuasion. Ruth would often bring her colleagues to believe they were capable of achieving what they previously considered unrealistic. Her persuasive abilities were also charged with playfulness and emotional appeal. There were occasions when she held meetings or gatherings away from the Centre in order to create a deeper sense of community. Finally, Ruth was most often able to empower others through her own demonstration of confidence. Her own passion and confidence for her work was inspiring and empowering for others. It is also congruent with her image of "people follow passion."

Empowerment is at once a relational and motivational construct (Conger and Kanungo 1988). Not only must the leader share power through dependence and interdependence, but one must also inspire a sense of self-determination. To achieve this, a charismatic leader must instill great and persistent energy in herself and with those with whom she leads. In so doing, she must make her colleagues feel powerful and confident in their abilities. Often, this means she must act as a role model. As Ruth demonstrated confidence in her own abilities and by participating in some of the same tasks or projects as her colleagues, Ruth modeled the outcomes of personal empowerment, which in turn, encouraged others to desire empowerment for themselves.

All leaders must play a teaching role, however, with charismatics this role is often more intense. In many ways, they carefully guide their colleagues. At others times, they carefully set up challenges as learning experiences, through the powers of persuasion, participation, and motivation, Ruth is able to empower others to fulfill their own goals while fulfilling the vision she has for the school system. The following quote is a fitting conclusion.

> "She's a powerful person. It's her own great faith and belief in people and I would say it's her generous heart in loving people that has carried them to higher levels than they've ever striven for. She's given people vision through her own vision....In my image of her, she is one of the true Christians, a real shepherd, a real leader...she gives you friendship without asking for it" (Kathy, art teacher).

CONCLUSION

In summary, the four broad themes characterizing Ruth's charismatic and transformational leadership style create the dynamics of attraction, motivation, empowerment, and performance. They are: visionary qualities, communicating a vision, creating trust and commitment, and empowering others. Communicating a vision that appeals to many teachers establishes her credibility. Providing intellectual justification for her vision appeals to far-reaching needs such as high expectations, commitment, and mutual trust. Creating trust and commitment within a community of educators demands unyielding dedication. Finally, empowering others is absolutely essential to the success of the supervisor and the community as a whole. Great and persistent energy is needed to achieve the vision.

Each of the above themes relating to Ruth's charismatic and transformational leadership style also influence the practical knowledge of those with whom she works in two ways. First of all, some of the actual supervisor's practical knowledge constructions (rules, principles, and images), become part of the practical knowledge of her colleagues. Second, the dynamics or content of the supervisor's practical knowledge influences the ability of the colleague to extend her practical knowledge in ways she has never done before. In essence, the practical knowledge of a charismatic fine arts supervisor has the potential to provide a great impact upon the practical knowledge of teachers and consultants.

Implicit within this discussion has been the view of women mentoring women. Although some may suggest that mentoring can be structured (Murray 1991), this study suggests that mentorship or teaching leadership is a deeply empowering activity carried out through the content and dynamic of the mentor's practical knowledge. It also suggests that women value making connections, working cooperatively, allowing for intuitive insights, and playing with ideas, while being guided by an individual who will not only provide this backdrop of professionalism but will call for higher expectations and greater standards (Kuhnert and Lewis 1989). In this particular study, the intense bond between leader and colleague, or mentor and mentee, paved the way for an undercurrent of personal and spiritual growth. Phrases spoken about a "real shepherd," "faith," "loving people," "true Christian," and the "parable of the sower of seeds," all suggest a deeply conscious spiritual affiliation. One is left to contemplate the inner power of her practical knowledge and the charisma she exudes as a women, as a leader, as a teacher, and as a mentor. One is also left to contemplate if charismatic and transformational leadership styles between or among men and women differ. This study, unfortunately cannot answer that question, but it does beg the question.

The next two chapters will take an in-depth look at the practical knowledge of Ruth. Although the themes generated in this chapter are embedded in the description, attention is now given to the particulars of Ruth's beliefs, values, and assumptions, and how they are made manifest through the implicit and explicit constructions found in practical knowledge.

Chapter 3
The Basis and Content of Ruth's Personal Practical Knowledge

Current research fails to address how consultants or supervisors perceive and characterize their role(s) especially as they endeavor to resolve the demands of administration and teaching. This is further exacerbated if we recognize the assumption that consultants are expected to use their personal teacher knowledge with little or no knowledge of administration. In recent years, qualitative researchers have sought to describe and interpret what teacher knowledge or "practical knowledge" might look like and how it is constructed (Clandinin 1986; Connelly and Clandinin 1985). If we consider that supervisors come to their roles with practical knowledge gained as a teacher, one might ask how that practical knowledge would be altered as they take on some administrative roles. This becomes even more important if we consider the trend, because of budget cutbacks, to return consultants or supervisors to classroom practice. One could ask of such supervisors how well-suited their practical knowledge was for their return to the classroom.

To examine a supervisor's practical knowledge, it is beneficial to acknowledge those research studies describing and interpreting what a teacher's practical knowledge might look like and how it is constructed. Freema Elbaz (1981, 1983), for instance, sought to describe through a case study method, the content of one teacher's practical knowledge, the orientations from which that knowledge was derived, the structures upon which the knowledge was constructed, and lastly, the cognitive style of the teacher. By undertaking such a qualitative approach, Elbaz was able to portray the multiple expectations demanded of a single teacher through lenses that focused on the intricacies of a practical knowledge previously unarticulated. Case studies such as hers illuminate the reciprocal relationship between theory and practice, means and ends, rather than the technical rationality of a linear progression from means to ends. Her use of imagery reinforced the contention that "practical knowledge is not just content, nor is it only structure—it is a contextually relative exercise of capacities for imaginatively ordering our experience" (Johnson 1984, p. 465).

In the past, the view of what constituted valid knowledge was seen as being theoretical, one held primarily by experts. The experiential knowledge of professionals was generally not acknowledged as being valid even though such eminent thinkers as John Dewey (1938) equated knowledge with experience. Instead, professionals were viewed simply as possessing experience. Using this assumption, a supervisor's experience could be downgraded to a description of factors observed in decision-making, which portrays the individuals functions and skills in a fragmented way (e.g., Havelock 1973; Butler and Paisley 1978; Crandall 1977; Nash and Culbertson 1977; Leithwood 1982). However, if experiential knowledge were to be accepted then specific factors could not be delineated out of the context of situations or events (Sternberg & Caruso 1985). Rather, the content and relevant contexts of all previous situations or factors would be regarded whenever new situations arose. It therefore becomes important to understand what the content might look like for supervisors as well as perceiving what contexts influence the use of that content within given situations.

Practical knowledge research has offered the educational community a micro-look at the personal practical knowledge of individual teachers. In doing so, we are reminded of the incredible complexity of human experience that is simply unattainable through reductionist models and linear analysis. However, what practical knowledge research is unable to do is suggest whether or not other participants in education, such as supervisors, who are first teachers and later assume second roles, retain or adjust their conceptual framework of personal practical knowledge. Given that supervisors are granted a certain level of autonomy and acquire unique experiential knowledge in their roles, it becomes important to understand the influence of past experiences. To date, supervisors' roles have been conceptualized according to behaviors suggesting that the prescription of certain roles, functions, and skills would improve their effectiveness. On the other hand, their roles are viewed in dialogical relationship to those of teachers. In contrast, the study reported in chapters 3, 4, and 5, addresses the view of supervisor as an active participant in educational change which is informed by classroom and administrative experience. The purpose of this study is to describe, characterize, and interpret this role with an emphasis on the unique knowledge used by a supervisor in her work. The study addresses the differences between teacher's and supervisor's practical knowledge by examining the personal practical knowledge of a fine arts supervisor during ongoing curriculum change in the fine arts within a school district. The guiding research questions are:

    1. what are the content areas of the fine arts supervisor's personal practical knowledge?
    2. in what contexts may these content areas be found?
    3. how is this practical knowledge constructed?
    4. what consulting style(s) appropriately describe the fine arts supervisor?

The purpose of the study is to describe, characterize, and interpret one supervisor's practical knowledge using ethnographic techniques over a four month period. In so doing, presumably the field may better understand the dialectical interface between administration and teaching. We can also learn how one person resolves the "tensions" between the two while at the same time encouraging and facilitating educational change, as found in one's own theories-in-action, or rules of practice, practical principles, and images. Doing so may offer a useful perspective on fine arts (or other subject areas) curriculum implementation or change initiatives. The Appendix describes the methodological foundations of the study and provides a detailed review of data collection techniques and analysis.

THE NEED FOR A DIALECTICAL PERSPECTIVE

Supervisors are viewed within school districts as curriculum experts, dealing with theory and practice as they implement new innovations. Often, they are identified with specific subject matter expertise. Supervisors also need to be proficient in understanding and facilitating change processes. These theory and practice areas present dialectical relationships that must be resolved within the personal practical knowledge of the individual supervisor.

The following review will take an in-depth look at the dialectics of supervisory practice found in opposing curriculum orientations and in the relationship between theory and practice. This is meant to provide a rationale for studying the dialectical nature of personal practical knowledge and implementation issues. Although there is a paucity of descriptive and interpretive field research on consultants and supervisors, the role of supervisors during implementation and educational change will be explored. Alternate views of consulting will be delineated so that we may later come to understand Ruth's style as a supervisor.

Opposing Curriculum Orientations

Reconceptualists William F. Pinar and Madeleine R. Grumet (1980), and Tetsuo R. Aoki (1983) have described how "curriculum" as a field of study and concern came into being as an administrative activity. Apparently, Denver Superintendent Jesse Newlon decided that an administrator in the central office needed to be attending to the curriculum, particularly in specific subjects and within specific schools, while addressing the curriculum needs of the district overall.

If one conceives of curriculum as an administrative designation one would also begin to consider the implications of a management orientation. This management orientation is clearly reflected in Ralph Tyler's (1949) development of an instrumentalist ends-means model. Many early curriculum theorists followed a similar orientation. In his rationale, Tyler systematically delineates the educational purposes of the school, the appropriate selected learning experiences, and the organization and evaluation of those experiences. It is this essentially ends-means rationality that has permeated much of the twentieth-century educational thought and practice even though it seriously neglects the contextual meanings individuals and groups create and hold for themselves in a situation-oriented world.

Aoki (1983) is critical of the instrumentalist curriculum, or as he refers to it, the empirical analytic orientation, because it fails to acknowledge the experiential world as the source for theory development. He puts forward a situational interpretive orientation, which reflects a reconceptualist orientation. "The central interest is in the communicative understanding of meaning as given by people who live within the situation. The rules for the understanding of meaning are constructed actively by those who dwell within the situation" (p.14). The essential activity is dialogue within a community of people and the form of knowledge is rooted in situational meaning. Reconceptualists are concerned with describing and interpreting the meaning-making derived between individuals within a given situation as a result of that experience being transformed through dialogue. The quality of lived experiences is of primary interest to reconceptualists.

The reconceptualist orientation or the transformation orientation, as John P. Miller and Wayne Seller (1990) refer to it, has received limited support in a predominantly instrumentalist educational system. With transformation as its goal, it lies in opposition to the instrumentalist goal for transmission.

To the supervisor or consultant, these theoretical tensions in curriculum theory become practical dilemmas. As government bureaucrats apply instrumental action, teachers, principals, parents, and students remind her to interpret a situation on its own merit. The practical dilemma is heightened if we consider the implicit conflict that arises when ones tries to transfer the skills of a classroom teacher into a managerial role: facilitation and control are not one in the same. Theorists who subscribe to one orientation or viewpoint may be seriously criticized by practitioners such as supervisors or consultants who are faced with opposing orientations regularly in practice. An alternate curriculum orientation has emerged that deals with this concern.

The Relationship of Theory and Practice

The above tensions are presented to the supervisor as she tries to resolve the practical conflict between her knowledge of what is presented in the intended curriculum and what is actually happening in classroom practice. In order to understand this tension, we need to understand the difference between the nature of theoretical and practical knowledge.

Joseph J. Schwab (1969) believed that educational research needed to recognize the relationship between theory and practice before it could impact upon the field of education. To him, theoretical knowledge is limited to, or claims to be, universal statements that can withstand scrutiny across situations and across time. Practical knowledge on the other hand, guides situational action through contextual decision-making. In contrast to theoretical knowledge, practical knowledge is not necessarily applicable across situations or across time.

As long as theoretical knowledge is viewed as superior to practical knowledge, Schwab believed the field of curriculum inquiry could not make a significant contribution to educational practice. Theory simply cannot account for the complex decision making found in teaching. If theories are usable, they can only be applied to very specific situations.

Schwab's theory/practice distinction initiated several decades of reflection upon the practical world of teachers. Although this reflection was ultimately critical for the well-being of the field, it also caused an arbitrary division between theory and practice, thereby suggesting that teaching and learning could be viewed as either theoretical or practical rather than an integrated whole where theory and practice work together. Later, I will discuss the work of Elbaz (1983) who acknowledged the autonomous decision making authority of teachers in adopting, adapting, and/or developing curriculum materials for specific classroom practice; a view previously discouraged by those interested in mastery of intended learning outcomes.

Richard McKeon (1952), a philosopher, is also concerned with the problem of relating theory to practice. Although many interpretations may be found when discussing the relationships between theory and practice, McKeon applies the following terms: logistic, problematic, operational, and dialectical.

The logistical method devises formal systems of theory on the model of mathematics. Rational solutions to practical problems are sought through the application of theory to practice. The professions of engineering and medicine both apply scientific laws to practical problems. Curriculum specialists might use this method to develop knowledge which would control what and how theory is applied to practice. For those educators interested in promoting change, planned models for change would be applied to practice (Bennis, Benne & Chin 1961).

The operational method is characterized by knowledge that is derived through the process of translating theories into action which can be verified through practical results. Curriculum specialists who subscribe to this method are concerned with needs assessments and user opinions statements. The literature dealing with change agentry (or linking agent) would be consistent with this view of theory and practice (Havelock 1973).

The problematic method is used to resolve situational problems. Within this method, theory and practice are closely related, as knowledge is viewed as entering practice through practical problem solving. Knowledge is therefore modified according to the parameters of the particular problem. This method may be found in curriculum change literature when mutual adaptation between opposing forces is considered necessary (Berman & McLaughlin 1978).

The dialectical method regards theory and practice as inseparable since "action, like thought, consists in reconciling contraries in dynamic organic wholes" (McKeon 1952, p. 84). Teachers using this method seek to resolve oppositions in theory, in practice, and between theory and practice. Theory would not be considered absolute and would change according to the shifting exigencies of the practical world. Practice is therefore theory-in-action. If theory and practice were not working together, then theory would be viewed as insufficient for the practical situation. The curriculum field has only recently begun to accept this view towards theory/practice. The work of Freema Elbaz (1983), Michael F. Connelly, and D. Jean Clandinin (n.d.), and Clandinin (1986) are apt examples of this method.

Aoki (1984) also distinguishes between "theoria" and "praxis" in order to understand the common dichotomy separating theory from practice. Theoria "is a way of knowing in which a subject comes to know through a contemplative non-engaged process, as a spectator as it were, guided by the telos of theoretical knowledge itself" (p.10). Praxis, on the other hand, "is a way of knowing in which the subject within a pedagogic situation (like a classroom) reflectively engages the objective world guided by the telos of ordering human action. Here, theory and practice are seen to be in dialectical unity" (p.10). Praxis seeks to integrate the whole person from an ethical viewpoint within a political context. Theory becomes both informative and reflective toward practice. Knowing, therefore, becomes derived experience. Aoki uses the dialectical method as he discusses implementation as situational praxis (Aoki 1984).

Over the last twenty-five years, many educational reform movements have been guided by the logistical method, with occasional use of the problematic and operational conceptions. If we apply the research reflecting a dialectical relationship between theory and practice in regard to teacher knowledge, one may question what form practical knowledge might take in the minds of consultants or supervisors.

Personal Practical Knowledge

Research describing the supervisors' role during educational change portrays an array of complex activity. This notion is consonant with studies (Clandinin 1986; Elbaz 1983) in the area of conceptualizing the role of the teacher. Research on teachers has often tried to reduce the complexity of the classroom to a few simple factors. The teacher is viewed "in isolation from the substance of what she teaches, that which gives much of its meaning and direction to her work" (Elbaz 1983, p.10). Seymour Sarason (1981) maintains that researchers need to consciously seek an understanding of the teachers' point of view. Purely objective fragmented renditions of classroom life ignore the need to study holistically the practitioner-in-action. In essence, descriptive and interpretive studies of teachers and other professionals in education may begin to illuminate how educators construct a blending of theory and practice.

Much of the problem attached to studying practical knowledge is a result of its tacit nature. Robert J. Sternberg and David R. Caruso (1985) consider practical knowledge as "procedural information that is useful in one's everyday life" (p. 134). Therefore, practical knowledge is determined through the context in which the knower lives. Because of the tacit nature of practical knowledge, it is difficult to teach through direct instruction. "The procedural nature of practical knowledge means, almost a priori, that it is knowledge acquired by doing, not just by listening or reading" (p.143).

This problem is exacerbated in that much of practical knowledge is held unconsciously. The only way to teach such understanding is through the process of mentorship or apprenticeship. In this way, tacit instruction will teach for tacit knowledge.

It is also important to recognize that "one's ability to acquire tacit knowledge on the job will be a key factor in one's success or failure as a teacher" (Sternberg and Caruso 1985, p. 148). In essence, the more practical knowledge a person has, the more able one will be to adapt to situational needs successfully.

Practical knowledge is important in everyday life and ironically, often disregarded as a form of knowledge. Elbaz (1981, 1983) questioned this popular conception. She believed that teachers held a form of knowledge or practical knowledge unique to themselves. Through the use of a case study method, she proceeded to describe the content of one teacher's practical knowledge, the orientations from which that knowledge was derived, the structures in which that knowledge was contained, and lastly, the cognitive style of the teacher. The findings of her study suggest that the content of a teacher's practical knowledge focused upon knowledge of self, subject matter, curriculum development, instruction, and the milieu of teaching (Schwab 1969). Furthermore, the orientations permeated across the various content areas of the teachers' practical knowledge and were viewed as multidimensional viewpoints: situational, personal, social, experiential, and theoretical. Elbaz interpreted the structures (or how the personal practical knowledge was held in active relationship with the world) through three forms. Rules of practice are those specific directives defining what to do or how to do it in particular situations. Practical principles bridge rules of practice and images through some specificity yet with more personal expression. Moreover, they are often moralistic in that they provide reasons for certain actions. Images are the most broadly conceived and are descriptive yet metaphoric statements which act as guides to the everyday continuum of practical knowledge. Images seem to combine the teacher's feelings, values, needs, and beliefs towards specific issues. Under close observation, rules and principles give direction to instructional knowledge while images guide all other aspects of practical knowledge. Lastly, Elbaz' final characterization of the cognitive style is based upon Alfred Schutz (1962–1973). In this way, style is conceived as a quality which finds unity in an individual's lived experience or, in this case, practical knowledge in use. Elbaz described all of these aspects for a teacher involved in a curriculum development project.

Elbaz (1983) began to question how teacher educators conceived of previous experiences influencing teacher knowledge. She used the notion of image as a way of rethinking how past experiences could have guided a teacher, thus analyzing how practical knowledge was constructed. Michael Connelly and D. Jean Clandinin (n.d.) have pursued the notion of image as a kind of knowledge that connects the past, present, and future in a meaningful way. Images are created from imaginative processes that bind together a person's diverse experiences in order to create personally significant and practically useful patterns which act as guides for making sense out of future activities.

In Clandinin's dissertation (1983), the notion of relationship is used to account for the unity she sensed in her participants' lives but which was not completely rendered in the images of her participants. Subsequently, Connelly and Clandinin (n.d.) have used the moral philosopher Alasdair MacIntyre's (1981) notion of narrative unity to develop this further: "ongoing life experience creates the narrative unity out of which the images are crystallized and formed when called upon by practical situations" (p.14). This narrative unity or continuum within a person's experience portrays life experiences as meaningful because of the unity they achieve for the person. Those life experiences form personal practical knowledge for the actor.

Recounting stories of experience touch the mind of the reader or listener in unpredictable ways and in turn yield new understanding and awareness. Educators are beginning to use stories or case studies (Connelly and Clandinin 1990; Schon 1991) as a way of reflecting upon and transforming practice. Stories offer educators a way to communicate the particulars of their experiences while also allowing for their varying interpretations of events (Holland 1989). Donald E. Polkinghorne (1988) calls us to recognize that narrative is a form of language that relates the meaningfulness of individual experience within the unified and contextualized experience of language as a whole. Through narrative, language organizes experience. Narrative also has transformative potential in that the narrator gives significance and meaning to particular events. Stories and narrative, therefore, become interpretations of experience. Finally, stories and narrative have the "capacity to define and create community" (Holland 1989, p. 74). As educators share their stories, common values are expressed and the potential for collective action as a community of educators becomes possible. Educators are able to socially construct meaning through the use of telling stories, reading each other's stories, and critically analyzing the essential characteristics of the stories.

The significance of this body of literature to the field of curriculum inquiry is great. Teachers are not mere delivery agents of intended curricula, for they are thinking, feeling, striving human beings holding a unique form of practical knowledge. This study considers the instrumentalist approach to curriculum implementation and educational change as problematic. Supervisors are not mere delivery agents of intended curricula either. Rather, they hold a unique form of personal practical knowledge for their role as supervisor. In addition, the field of education needs to hear the stories of an individual supervisor as she recalls her experiences within her role. In doing so, teachers, administrators, and other supervisors may be better able to understand the significance and meaning of her role. The following description endeavors to portray the intricate practical knowledge of Ruth Britten as a fine arts supervisor.

THE FIVE CONTENT AREAS OF RUTH'S PRACTICAL KNOWLEDGE

The content of Ruth's personal practical knowledge may be best viewed as a knowledge of content that is different from the seemingly superior knowledge possessed by experts. Ruth, for instance, has knowledge of music, though that knowledge is quite different from that of a professional musician, for her knowledge is used in different ways.

In talking about the content of Ruth's practical knowledge, five categories are used as found in Schwab's (1969) commonplaces of practical knowledge. They can be similarly found in the practical knowledge literature outlined by Elbaz (1981, 1983): knowledge of self, subject matter, instruction, curriculum development, and the milieu. Elbaz examined the teacher as a curriculum developer. Here, Ruth is portrayed as instrumental in curriculum development but also implementation.

Knowledge of Self: Mentor, Colleague, Christian, Artist

Ruth has a knowledge of herself in the role of supervisor as she is: influenced by mentors and is a mentor, colleague, Christian, and artist. Each of these aspects are addressed separately.

In the role of supervisor. Ruth feels particularly well-suited to the role of fine arts supervisor. It is an image she has of herself perhaps as a result of her interest in the three art forms of art, music, and drama, as well as her energy and enthusiasm for working with others. But also, "she feels so many circumstances led to her taking the job, and she loves it" (Field diary #49, page 283. From now on, field diary will be referred to as FD.). More importantly, it is an expression of all her talents and personal energy.

> "You know, I'm in a job that suits me. I was lucky, I mean in my career, I was lucky that I got this, because it's a job I enjoy doing. I find it challenging, and I

find it interesting....I have been at it twenty years and I am not anywhere near the end of my years....I have always made a contract with myself that when the day comes that I cannot approach it with enthusiasm any more, then I will give it up. And that hasn't happened yet" (Interview #2, page 13. From now on Interview will be referred to as Inter 2, 13.).

Ruth is deeply committed to her team of fine arts people who presently include an art specialist, a drama specialist, and a music consultant. The ending to the previous school year was fraught with major political decisions that found Ruth losing all of her fine arts team, a total of seven staff. Through constant articulation of district needs framed by the new provincially mandated fine arts curriculums to be implemented, Ruth was able to regain three of the original staff. The struggle to maintain even that amount was difficult.

As influenced by mentors.   Ruth's knowledge of herself as a supervisor is also embedded in a history of an understanding of herself, a way of viewing herself as a woman in a man's world, and as a woman capable of doing anything she chose to do. Her mother was a powerful mentor in establishing this viewpoint.

"And of course my mother was tremendous. She was so full of the joy of living. She used to tell me when I was little, you have to be like a cork, Ruth. You can't sink a cork. You can push it down in the water, but it will always come up. You have to be like a cork. She gave me to believe when I was a tiny, tiny, little girl that there was nothing I couldn't do if I wanted to. She was a true feminist. When I was in grade three, she used to talk to me about going to college. You see this was in an age when most families would educate the boys but the girls would probably get secretarial courses or something....But my mother was a great influence. She thought I was perfect and that gave me great confidence. I knew I wasn't...but somebody thought I was and that gave me courage" (Inter 14, 13).

Ruth had other mentors, including a university philosophy professor. Each of these people influenced her life in a unique way and each is still remembered today for his or her contribution.

"In my youthful fervor, when I got out of university, I met this amazing philosophy teacher. She was a nun. I had this vision (laughs), this image of myself in a monastic setting, the eternal scholar, not unlike the medieval monks with their manuscripts, and I thought that I would serve the world doing what I did best. It was a very idealized situation. Now you must remember that I was young and it was in the early 1950s. If it had been in the 1960s, I probably would have gone with the hippies. I had that streak in me. But this was five years after the war and many men had been killed during the war; there was a great flurry of religious fervor at that time. We asked many questions. Where are we going? What does it all mean? How can we best serve our fellow man?

And in this youthful idealism, I thought, I'll become a nun....It was not at all what I thought it would be. I ended up in New York, in the inner city, teaching and working, working at the Rust Institute with people who were sick...to help young people who were crippled. It was just nonstop working. But I realized that kind of life could not call out of me what I thought I could do best, so I left" (Inter 14, 7– 8).

The philosophy professor influenced her thinking in many ways. Ruth recalled her saying that "every decision you make will influence the next and one must be careful that poor decisions do not become a habit" (FD 61, 335). Ruth recalled these teachings fondly as illustrated below.

"She was such a powerful teacher that sometimes she would say, 'I will be in my classroom tonight at 6:30 if anyone wants to come. And there would be standing room only. She was wonderful. She never gave you answers. Her whole class was questioning, reflecting, arguing, and putting holes in arguments, because one has a tendency to speak in cliches when one is young or certainly to speak in universals. She taught me a lot. She was really the one who trained my mind. I took logic and psychology with her....She trained my mind in so far as it's trained. She taught me the skills of reason. And then I had another classics prof. Wonderful, just wonderful. With her I studied Greek and Roman literature and another course in the humanities. Then I had Roger Purdue at the university who was very good. So I was lucky...in the course of a lifetime, you know, most teachers are ordinary" (Inter 14, 12).

Ruth's image of herself has changed considerably since those early years. She had once imagined herself at a university teaching art history or art education courses, but after having assumed this role, discovered that as the years went by and other opportunities came up, the salaries at the university level were much less than she was prepared to accept. Her decision to remain a supervisor was not a difficult one however, since her role as supervisor had come to mean so much to her (FD 5, 38).

As a colleague.   Ruth's knowledge of herself is also framed in relationship to others. "Teaching is an extremely complex enterprise...and you know we have tons to learn, we don't do enough colleagual work" (Interview 1, 16). She feels a certain need to guide her group of teachers not only through specific curriculum content changes, but also through their coping mechanisms, their views towards living. She operates from a practical principle of "we go as far as we can, but on the way we're going to have a good time."

"As I say to those who work with me, 'let's all relax. We do what we can, we go as far as we can, but on the way we're going to have a good time. We're going to enjoy life.' Because I think in being happy and cheerful and just enjoying things, again the energy is outgoing." (Inter 14, 9).

Ruth also views herself in relation to men in the workplace. She generally believes that men see offices as a status symbol. She, on the other hand, sees an office as a place to work. It was not a status symbol for Ruth, a place to honor herself in her position (FD 33, 182).

The knowledge of herself as a supervisor is also framed by her own knowledge of other fine arts supervisors. While Ruth spoke with a counterpart in the city's public school system, her colleague made a reference to a memorandum she found dated to 1971 in which the issues addressed today were also addressed at that time. Ruth was quick to point out that in her role, a full circle would nearly be complete: "I came in just before the climax and rode the crest and now it's on the downward swing" (FD 54, 298). The role varies according to circumstances within a district and therefore, all the consultants and supervisors she knows across the province, have quite different working conditions, ways of reporting, job descriptions, and internal structures, than that from which she works (Inter 2, 15).

As a christian.   The spiritual dimension of Ruth's knowledge of herself is not obvious even though she works in a Catholic school district. But it permeates everything. Phrases, caught in the midst of explaining the power of the arts, or the human spirit, or the community of human beings to which she belongs, stand out and cannot be ignored. They are penetrating, value-laden, and full of guiding notions in living life to its fullest. After talking to her about her Catholic beliefs, I recorded this in my field diary.

> It is fundamental to her whole nature. She says that the most fundamental teaching of the church is "love your neighbour." It is very difficult but it is the most fundamental virtue....She then talked to me about her conception of Catholicism....She said that God was everywhere and within each of us. As for ritual, it was an expression of 2,000 years of beliefs, of the arts, of the greatness of God—all in a celebration of the human spirit in community (FD 56, 323–333).

In talking about the dynamics within the group of supervisors, Ruth talked of how they had worked together for a long time and had come to support one another's subject areas. My field diary recorded this: "She feels they work together well because they have a common sense of values, Catholic values, that is, they have as an operating principle, 'love of fellowman.' Because of this, they can speak out in trust without fear of reprisal" (FD 2, 15). The image of "love your neighbour" appears to be a potential institutional operating or practical principle.

On another occasion she reinforced her image of "community" being derived from her Catholic background.

> The community idea she felt came from her Catholic background of loving your neighbor whether they were weak, strong, rich, or poor. Everyone comes

together to praise God. So fellowship is strong though she struggles with it at times because she is a solitary-liking person (FD 22, 123).

The image of community may also be linked to the power of the arts to shape the human spirit in community.

"What I am going to deal with this morning is the essential nature of music and its power to shape the minds of the young. This is a power as a vital subject in the curriculum and in its recognized potential to shape the human spirit in community" (FD 4, 1).

As noted elsewhere, her role in her image of community could possibly be referred to as "mystical." A community is a group of people growing and sharing together, but her role has some sense of being charismatic, perhaps evangelical. This is aptly revealed in an interview with a junior high art teacher, who had tears in her eyes at the end of the interview.

"So she would come in and ask, What do you need? Ruth was always at the service of the teachers. I really feel like she has this ministry of being a supervisor because her role, as I see it, is to help us develop into becoming better people and teachers...she just encouraged and loved us through it all.... This will sound strange. She's a real woman of God. She has led me through her ministry and her faith" (Inter 8, 5–14).

When asked if her experience as a nun had influenced her role as a supervisor, Ruth could not answer, but she did reflect upon how it influenced her as a person. Over time, she has integrated this into her practical knowledge to produce a rule of practice, "I don't take myself all that seriously."

"It made me very wary of pure idealism. It made me much more hardheaded than I ever was or might ever have been as a result. You know, I am very cautious about embracing causes and ideals that have no foundation. I was going to say no foundation in rationality, but I'm very wary of authoritarian positions. That sounds like a contradiction and you're going to ask, how can a person be a Catholic? The authority in the Catholic Church does not press upon people. The major tenet in the Catholic Church is number 1, you are free. You commit freely or you don't commit at all....I'm very cautious about going into organized authoritarian structures. It also gave me a more realistic assessment of myself. I don't take myself all that seriously. In talking to you, I often sound like the guru of the Western world, but in actual fact I have just thought these things out over all of these years. I don't pretend to have all the answers" (Inter 14, 8).

"The parable of the sower of seeds" was referred to by Ruth as a parable that aptly portrayed what she does within her school system regarding change, but she does not consciously pursue it (FD 46, 260). It is an image also well-grounded in her religious beliefs. References to this parable are found in The Holy Bible under St. Matthew, St. Mark, and St. Luke. The following quote is taken from St. Luke chapter 8 verses 4–15.

> 4. And when much people were gathered together, and were come to him out of every city, he [Jesus] spake by a parable: 5. A sower went out to sow his seed: and as he sowed, some fell by the way side; and it was trodden down, and the fowls of the air devoured it. 6. And some fell upon a rock; and as soon as it was sprung up, it withered away, because it lacked moisture. 7. And some fell among thorns; and the thorns sprang up with it, and choked it. 8. And others fell on good ground, and sprang up, and bare fruit a hundred-fold. And when he had said these things, he cried, "He hath ears to hear, let him hear." 9. And his disciplines asked him saying, "What might this parable be?" 10. And he said, "Unto you is given to know the mysteries of the kingdom of God: but to others in parables; that seeing they might not see, and hearing they might not understand." 11. Now the parable is this: The seed is the word of God. 12. Those by the way side are they that hear; then cometh the devil, and taketh away the word out of their hearts, lest they should believe and be saved. 13. They on the rock *are they*, which, when they hear, receive the word with joy; and these have no root, which for a while believe, and in time of temptation fall away. 14. And that which fell among thorns are they, which, when they have heard, go forth, and are choked with cares and riches and pleasures of *this* life, and bring no fruit to perfections. 15. But that on the good ground are they, which in an honest and good heart, having heard the word, keep *it*, and bring forth fruit with patience.

There is great consistency between the ideas found in the Bible and in Ruth's beliefs.

> "I say I'll do what I can *now* and then I'll be off the scene and then somebody else can continue. Now, one of the things, as in Scripture, I plant the seed and apply the waters, but God gives the increase. You plant the seeds, but then you don't stay on the scene to congratulate yourself on the flowering of these seeds" (Inter 2, 16).

After the interview, Ruth said she sees herself aligning with the parable of the sower sowing seeds. She sees herself scattering seeds of change everywhere. If the seed takes, that is, if teachers choose to take advantage of an opportunity for learning, then she will nurture them. She does not take responsibility for their growth though. The teacher is left in charge of her own change (FD 19, 114).

A moral dimension deriving from her Christian beliefs permeates much of Ruth's expression of self. Two key components emerge. One is her attention to protocol in her role as supervisor. It is a way for her to express her loyalty to the organization, and through modeling, instill in those around her, loyalty to her as their leader. It is a rule she follows in her practice. She even said she could not tolerate disloyalty (FD 61, 337). The second is her sense of right and wrong applied to situations. There are many times the two go hand in hand.

Ruth spoke about following protocol. She does not go beyond the proper authority. She believes the system has a life of its own which is to be stable, or to maintain order. She therefore works within that structure. It has worked for her. People trust her as a result. She was two of many who survived a major upheaval in the central office/school board several years ago (FD 2, 12–13). A junior high teacher states:

"She is so professional. I have never, ever, ever, heard her contradict, condemn, insult, or take down another person even if that person were wrong or were perceived wrong or there was a misunderstanding. There would never be any backbiting or any small talk, either. In my image of her she is one of the true Christians, a real shepherd, a real leader. She gives vision to people" (Inter 8, 14).

On another occasion, this became even more obvious to me. She states a practical principle that "people come before the program."

It was very obvious today how morally upright she is. She told me she will not lie, cheat, judge anyone, nor be mean or deliberately hurt anyone. Her practice is that people come first—the person before the program....Her instincts tell her to be mean or vicious but "I would diminish myself if I did that." Over time she has come to realize what she can reasonably accomplish and how to maintain her moral standards. She says she will not sacrifice her principles for anyone. She maintains a loyalty to her leader just as she expects from those she leads. This is particularly obvious in her attention to protocol....One phone call that interrupted us today was from someone with whom Ruth had an appointment to see yesterday, but in Ruth's hurry she misread her calendar and left for her school visits just prior to that time. A secretary covered for her saying she didn't think Ruth was feeling well and so therefore went home early. Ruth denied this in the phone call and explained to the lady what had indeed happened: the bottom line was she forgot. Ruth told the truth though it would have been easier to stick to the original, third-party story. However, it was important to her to remain truthful (FD 23, 134–137).

As a rule of practice, Ruth seeks to be "loyal to my leaders" but she has trouble accepting her superintendent of curriculum:

Unless they talk and he keeps her informed, she has a tendency to dislike him. She feels loyal to him because he is next in line. It would be no good to speak to trustees or other superintendents behind his back. She said she cannot pretend. If she is irritated, she must be up front. She said this is something she does as an administrator. In her personal life, she accepts these things and is not so bold. She feels she does this when she is in a position to effect change. At times when things are givens, like time constraints with secretaries, or peoples abilities, then she is accepting, especially with subordinates....People who are subordinates are powerless in the hands of powerful employers. She does not feel she demands power (FD 13, 64–65).

"The right and wrong way to proceed is often tied to the placement and responsibilities of the people within the organization and their power base. I try not to be cynical. Now like everybody else of course, I have my moments but I won't take advantage of those who are in a less powerful position. Those who are in a more powerful position are fair game for everybody, they really are" (Inter 14, 11).

As an artist.   Perhaps the best introduction to Ruth as an artist is to hear her express the power she perceives in each of the art forms.

Interviewer: "You have spoken to me this fall about the power of music and the power of art. I was just wondering if you could explain to me what you mean by power when you say it that way?"

Ruth: "I think that it takes you out of yourself. It causes you then to become greater than yourself because I think that energies turned inward are narrowing....A person without horizons is diminished. You look inward and you feed upon yourself and your own worries and so on and you become diminished. The arts take you out of yourself. There is no way that you can be dedicated to music without having music claim you and so with art and so you're drawn out of a self-centered narrowing approach into a broader world that is powerful because it reflects a biological reality. There is some evidence that shows that the most successful compositions and indeed the whole principle of the golden mean has the same ratio as the DNA molecule which is the foundation of our life. There is some evidence to indicate that the biological rhythms of our very existence are reflected in an intellectual and orderly way in music. So in many ways those are external structures of what we are internally. Consequently, I think they enlarge our existence, and that's what I mean when I say 'they are powerful.' We need something we can keep at arms length" (Inter 14, 1; Irwin 1992, p. 114–115).[1]

The "power of art" is an image that motivates Ruth to continue with her own art. Often, Ruth shares her knowledge as an artist with teachers and students. The following excerpts are taken from an informal observation of Ruth teaching a grade five class about what it is like being an artist and the necessity of keeping a visual journal.

"Today I'm going to talk to you about being an artist and not as a supervisor... recently a book came out showing Picasso's journal...he is probably the leading artist of the twentieth century....The artist captures in his notebook what he notices...if you draw well you have a grasp of the communication of images others may not have...little we do has not come to us through images....Many of my colleagues and I who are artists have a visual journal.... I always have a visual journal with me...take note that I write notes to myself (looking through journal)...this finally became a painting of a thistle, but it was based on my series of notes. A lot of what young people do is intellectual. There is nothing wrong with that but you won't grow unless you start fresh every time....In your visual journal you need to record your experiments so you record what you learn....An artist learns as much from failure as with success...you learn in critiquing. Don't be afraid of failure" (Informal observation #3, page 1–4. From now on this will be referred to as IO.).

She acknowledges images as a form of communication and also as a way of learning, of organizing knowledge. The rule of practice, "don't be afraid of failure," is furthered by her belief that "we can only grow if we start fresh every time." In this way, it becomes a practical principle.

Ruth is very excited about her involvement with art and spoke fondly of her weekend painting excursions, never as a hobby, but rather as a necessary, regular, if not daily experience (FD 5, 31). Her commitment was evident when she did not follow her school district's centennial choir into a major city wide celebration, which would have meant many Sunday rehearsals (FD 5, 36). Summer long holidays are also spent painting. This past summer Ruth painted twenty-five watercolor paintings, ten of which were completed and ready for exhibition. Later she analyzed all of them for why they were or were not successful. In so doing she tried to discover where the powers were coming from in the objective matter (FD 6, 46). This power was derived from discovering something within the subject matter that captured her.

"I'm really not painting the things that I see. I'm painting the feeling of what I see. What captures me is the light, the mysterious effects of light on spaces so that there's a fair amount of abstraction but the forms are recognizable....I don't just sit down and whip off a painting. I do studies of forms in sketchbooks. I'm a very methodical person and I do studies of the kinds of forms that I might eventually use in paintings" (Inter 11, 1–2).

Though Ruth is proud of the fact she's had two private shows in the last two years that have sold-out, she does not consider it a priority in her life.

"Talking about my art is quite different from talking about my work. You see, it's a very private dimension of my life....I would keep on painting whether I sold any or not, I'm not doing it for that. I'm doing it to explore something about the world that I see, how I react to it as something about light. I don't see nature as something to be copied. I see nature as something very vibrant, very dynamic, constantly changing, very mysterious and sometimes threatening" (Inter 11, 3).

The professional aspects of marketing one's art is an area that frustrates Ruth. Yet she realizes her potential.

"I get irritated sometimes with myself because when I go to galleries and see the work there I know that what I do is better than much of the work I see...but then it really doesn't matter to have shows and do all that, because I'm not earning my living at it. It's just something I like to do" (Inter 11, 12).

Her experience as an artist had an impact upon her teaching career in different ways.

"Being a painter has given me great insights into the process of teaching painting, by trying to practice it myself. I recognize how incredibly complex it is and how much there is to learn. And the self-discipline it requires...so when I go around to the schools and I'm in classes and I see kids talking and fooling around and wasting time and listening to music and tossing off paintings, it irritates me. I think they're being shortchanged" (Inter 11, 7).

Although there are some similarities between the way she views herself as an artist and as a supervisor, there are also distinct differences.

Interviewer: Do you think there's any relationship with how you work with your paintings and how you work with people in your job? Is there any kind of relationship there or is that stretching it?

Ruth: I don't know. People are something else. I don't think so.

Interviewer: Maybe I should say working with ideas rather than people?

Ruth: "Yes, I think ideas, yes. I'm sure working with ideas is what I like to do best of all. I like to work with ideas whether those ideas are in art or other areas of expertise, for example, in my office. I don't like to take something set and say 'this is the way it's going to be forever.' I don't see anything mechanical about learning. I think it's a great adventure and I believe that everything you learn changes you. A person learns something new and puts it together in different ways. So exploring ideas at work [my office] is different than exploring ideas in a painting, for in a painting the painter is in one way limited by the medium yet challenged by that medium. Whereas ideas at work, are explored through people who have their own agendas. Whereas painting, which comes

> with the painter, has it's own qualities and what he/she tries to do
> is push the limits all the time in order to get ever greater possi-
> bilities out of the material. The painter is always trying to see
> more, to say more, to make the painting more dynamic (Inter 11,
> 11).

The key practical principle that emerged here is about "learning is a great adventure and everything you learn changes you." This inevitably falls in line with her notions of subject matter knowledge.

To summarize, in her "knowledge of self," Ruth was guided by an understanding of herself in the role of supervisor. In particular, she felt she was well-suited to the role of fine arts supervisor. Ruth recognized she was strongly influenced by mentors, and recalled these individuals fondly in her accounts. Her knowledge of herself was also framed in relationship to others, encouraging everyone to enjoy themselves while working. As a christian, she held the images of "love your neighbour," "community," and "the parable of the sower of seeds." Each reflects her love and respect for others. As an artist she centered upon an image of the "power of art." It not only motivated her own art-making activities, but also it was used to motivate children to participate in their art-making.

Knowledge of Subject Matter: "You can only teach what you have passion for."

Ruth has a knowledge of subject matter that portrays her expertise, as a specialist, and her interest in all aspects of learning, as a generalist.

As a specialist.   As indicated in the biographical sketch of Ruth, she is highly specialized in art production, art history, and has considerable ability in the criticism of art objects, as well as in the field of art education itself. She has chosen to keep up-to-date by maintaining an active involvement in these fields. Aspects of this knowledge are demonstrated on various occasions, for instance, when she delivered a talk to a group of curators and museum educators, she said:

> "One thing that happens when you bring children to a gallery show is
> surprise...if your expectations are entirely defeated you will ignore it...
> children must have preparation for approaching art. Seeing, then, is active and
> that's what we have to keep in mind. Also art has meaning...if we believe
> meaning is accessible it will add to the inquiry of talking about it...not
> everything in a work of art is accessible to everyone...we do a disservice to
> children to assume they get a lot out of it. A child's mind is all information...it
> will never equal the insights of an adult mind....Art is the evidence of thought
> made visible...making a piece of art may seem effortless...but you have to
> honor conventions of representation, something of the world, know something
> of participation...if we accepted a work of art is ultimately experience of a
> mental event then we can get at that even by working through it ourselves...if

we understand the cultural context then we can enter the work...we are given a clue to enter the painting because the artist has something in mind...which is the key idea to hang onto. The power of art resides in the image...image connected to a mental event...as educators we deal with not just the image but to the intention of the artists" (Formal observation #3, page 2–4. From now on this will be referred to as FO.).

The power of art not only resides in the image, but it is also a way of communication. During a phone call from a student in the teacher education program at the university, Ruth said: "images are an authentic way of communicating...having art in the curriculum is a significant way of finding meaning and of communicating" (FD 19, 113). In talking with a grade six class, this view was also evident.

Ruth: "Now what artists are drawn to is not that they just like it, but that they are drawn to relationships like dark and light. Now for me to send a message to you I must speak in words. What do you do?

Student: ...make sentences.

Ruth: "After you've made sentences then what do you do?

Student: ...make paragraphs.

Ruth: If you are going to communicate through images, what do you have to be able to do? We have to draw images. You can't make pictures if you don't put things together...I put down as much visual information as possible like dark and light, texture,...sometimes just a line, where I record a specific line (FO 2, 2).

She also sees art as a difficult process, with many decisions to be made continually regarding what to keep, alter, or delete; the use of color, the use of skills, and the process of framing. It is a complex decision-making process (FD 1, 5).

Ruth understands that secondary specialist arts teachers tend to identify themselves with their programs and with products. When one secondary drama teacher was on sick leave and while a substitute teacher had to bring her drama group to performance, Ruth requested that the drama teacher still be named as the director of the production, not so much for ego gratification but as an expression of herself before the students and the community (FD 46, 256).

Ruth uses much of her specialist knowledge with other specialists in the field but also with generalist teachers. In helping them with their students, she refers to her knowledge of child development in art, particularly the perceptual development of children (IO 4, 1). She couches this with her understanding that children often learn how to draw by copying masters or any other visual imagery they are in contact with and does not dismiss this, though she is quick to point out that the learning should not stop there but become a starting point for further independent learning (FO 2, 4). And in fact, "in a very real way you can only draw what you love…you must be moved," a practical principle to be followed, implying a significant relationship between thought and feeling. It is further developed below for teachers, as "you can only teach what you feel passion for."

As a generalist.   Having taught all levels and all subjects at some point in her career, Ruth believes she has a grasp of the difficulties facing the generalist teacher because she had been considered one herself for a time. Having this experience in her background, she can use it as a discussion entry point with teachers.

Ruth said that you only notice what you know and your tastes change as you come to know more. And it is not necessarily what you like that is good art (IO 11, 2). She has difficulty with current trends toward the teaching of generic teaching skills. They essentially conflict with her rule that "you only notice what you know." It is a rule that becomes a principle on occasion, as it is extended by "you can only teach what you feel passion for."

> "The very principle which I espouse is you cannot teach what you do not know…you cannot argue with that. All supervisors have that problem with people who do not know anything about the subject they are teaching but at least in some subjects they have a language to start with.…There is no such thing as a generalist…you can only teach what you feel passion for" (IO 9, 4).

Ruth, in talking about her own teaching experiences, felt passion for language arts, mathematics, art, and drama. However, she was quick to point out that knowing everything about a subject does not necessarily imply that one is passionate about it (IO 9, 4).

As Ruth interacted with a junior high non-art specialist teacher, she suggested that the teacher needed to take at least three university art courses: one in design, one in art history, and one in drawing. Apparently, with the budget cutbacks there was a freeze on hiring and so non-specialists were being put into areas they were not trained to teach. It would be a struggle to instill a passion for a subject in someone untrained in art and Ruth quickly pointed out to me that she would actually prefer there were no programs in secondary art rather than having bad programs (FD 46, 254).

On the other hand, Ruth's art specialist, Ann, when asked what significant event or situation or statement Ruth had made, which in turn had made an impact on Ann's practice at the Fine Arts Centre, acknowledged Ruth's ability to be patient with elementary generalist teachers and identified another of Ruth's rules of practice:

"The point she made when I came on staff: 'don't ever take anything for granted with teachers, because when you're trained as an art specialist you sometimes have a tendency to aim high....If they need a recipe to begin with, it's a start'" (Inter 6, 1).

Ruth talked about this in a more personal way as she spoke about developing in-service programs for teachers.

"We had some in-service activities last winter where we had fifty-five teachers come out. Because, you see, they recognize that what they are going to get from us will translate into more enjoyable classroom work for them. We don't hesitate to give them a lesson plan, we don't condescend nor do we treat them insultingly by assuming a level of knowledge we know they don't have because that's also hypocritical. I always say to teachers, do not feel the least bit diminished because you don't know this. How could you possibly know this?" (Inter 1, 11).

In summary, Ruth's knowledge of subject matter may be seen from two perspectives. As a specialist, she exhibits a knowledge of expertise in her fine arts subjects. As a generalist, she relies on her experience teaching all subjects at many levels to provide credibility to her work with generalist teachers seeking help in the implementation of new curricula.

Knowledge of Instruction: "The Art of Teaching" and "People Follow Passion."

Ruth has knowledge of instruction which may be classified under nine headings: the learning cycle, passion in teaching, students, adult learners, teacher of teachers, teaching teachers, teachers, artists, and the art of teaching versus the science of teaching. Each of these contributes a unique way of knowing.

The learning cycle.   Ruth has an operating theory of how people come to learn. Much of it is rooted in the theoretical literature she reads, and also in everyday common application.

For the last twenty years, a lot of work has been done on brain research, but the brain, while it is undoubtedly the organ of thought, is not the mind. Those are two different categories. Mind and brain are not the same thing. We know a lot about the structure of the brain, we know a lot about its electrical and chemical events. The mind is still mysterious. And so we mix those two categories at our peril. I'm sure you have heard much nonsense about teaching to half a brain....I'm going to do this for the left side of the brain, I'm going to do this for the right side. When was the last time you were aware that you were switching from one half of the brain to the other?...You know it can't be done....I've always felt it flies in the face of common sense, it certainly flies in the face of experience...while it is undeniably true that different powers reside in each of those hemispheres, it is also undeniably true that the mind operates as a unit. You have many, many minds (FO 4, 9).

Ruth goes on to ground these statements in the work of Robert Ornstein, a cognitive scientist, and Howard Gardner and Evelyn Mayer who are psychologists writing about different forms of intelligence and the psychology of the arts respectively.

The learning process, she believes, is always contextual. In fact, "a curriculum is always a context for thought" (FO 4, 8). Her rule of practice, "you only notice what you know," is tied to her understanding of the learning process, and furthers another rule, "it's the learner who learns." To facilitate this, she has a practical principle that, "the teacher has to be the coach so that the student can master the curriculum."

> The learning process as it develops has to always remind us that learning is always contextual. We are always noticing what we know and consequently the curriculum shapes our consciousness of what is valuable and what might be. You only notice what you know...that's what we're all about in education. We want children to know more so they'll notice more (FO 4, 10).

Ruth's theory of learning can be outlined as follows:

> I believe that as we learn we go through a cycle. And it's a cycle of teaching as well. And in this cycle there are four stages: experience, intuition, logic, and encoding....I believe that teachers can organize their classes and materials so that all of these stages can be managed, and the important thing that we have to remember is that it is the learner who creates the condition which will make active learning possible. There's no other way. Now, as teachers we forget that at our peril. It is the learner who learns. Parents remember that only if the child is a raging success. If he or she is a failure it is because of something we do. But, we shape our own minds....So our task as teachers is to try to make conditions so that the young people can enter an experience consciously and actively. And one of the essential elements in experience is play....Another step now in the cycle of learning is intuition. This stage is variable and often invisible because the young are not given to rushing out into the street like Archimedes calling "Eureka." We have to just sort of sense when they are with us and when they have insights....The next stage is logic...Logic that doesn't have a foundation in an intuitive thought is meaningless. I mean anyone can spout off a trilogy....On the other hand, an intuition that does not get expressed logically, goes nowhere...Encoding is making your thought visible, and there's where the teacher's skill and experience comes in...and in encoding, the teacher has to be the coach so that the student can master the curriculum. The teacher's task is to help them make their thought visible" (FO 4, 11–14).

Ruth applies this learning theory to the placement of the arts in the total curriculum. In an article she wrote on the creative potential of the child in the classroom environment she says:

> If we push our exploration of creativity back a step further by considering making as a primary means of problem solving—a form of communication through which we receive, use, and share information through the process of making—we realize that the categories of symbol systems we use to organize and communicate thought are limited to five: word, number, gesture, image, and sound. A part from these, used singly and in combination, there are no other ways of encoding information. Every piece of knowledge, every idea, must be expressed through these encoding systems. While the focus of any endeavor might be on word, number, gesture, image, or sound, the underlying harmony of all these encoding systems working cooperatively allows us to give form to our ideas, allows us to arrive at new conclusions, to invent and communicate new patterns, and to devise new solutions to problems (Document 1, 7).

Ruth feels the arts, including literature, should be the core of education because to gain access to them one must learn the act of contemplation. A person may learn techniques and skills from teachers, but the quality of the relationship between the process yielding a meaningful product depends upon contemplation (FD 1 15–16).

Ruth believes that after grade six, students can be taught through discrete subjects but before then they should be taught through the various modes of learning (FD 4, 24). She was always quick to argue for the arts in education, but was also realistic about how much one could expect of the system and how soon. For instance, if we expected all students in high school to take an arts course, it would mean more studio space, more supplies, and so on (FD 2, 14).

Education to Ruth is really an operation to change minds. The teacher in developing this change, assists the learner's mind in collecting, modifying, and transforming ideas. But it is the learner who shapes his or her own mind. "A human mind controls its own learning. Teachers feed that, but we learn, we shape our knowledge, we build community, we share vision, we sing. Teachers make intellectual adventures possible and teachers are sustained in their practice by this conviction, that what we do as teachers changes minds…and what we do as teachers makes a culture and a community possible" (FO 4, 16).

To truly make learning significant, Ruth portrays experience as having a sense of design, an artistic nature if you wish. "Now if we want to make experience significant, we try to capture the essential element of tension, release, and recurrence, to make a structure that mirrors these internal events and so allows us to participate intellectually in a phenomenon that marks our very existence, and indeed the existence of all that surrounds us" (FO 4, 5).

Passion in teaching.   Ruth adamantly believes in her practical principle that "one can only teach what one feels passion for."

> If school boards are going to ask teachers to teach music and they are not qualified to teach music then the school board has the responsibility to help that teacher become qualified. If you ask people to do, just like I said, all you know is what you know? You can only teach what you have a passion for. If you have no passion for a subject then you're not going to do well at it. Because it becomes a very mechanical operation (FO 4, 12).

Ruth believes that passion for subjects is what makes a teacher's or consultant's style successful, for it is passion that people are drawn to and will follow (FD 6, 47). It is an image of "people follow passion." She feels lucky to work with people of the arts, because they are very often passionate about the arts, and because of that passion are strong, independent people. Unfortunately, there is usually only one or two on staff and so they need extra support from her (FD 2, 18). Even her associate superintendent of curriculum said, "She has a passion for what she does and in turn that passes on to other people" (Inter 12, 1).

Students.   Much of Ruth's knowledge of students is derived from her constant classroom experience and exposure in fine arts classrooms. Often when talking with teachers, she guides them through how to diagnose the stages of artistic development of the child as well as suggesting possible strategies for student growth in art.

> "At grade four, students are coming out of their carefree modes and are entering into a more rigid drawing style. They have good proportions, and a good feel for composition....Yes one can praise them for many things. But one can encourage them to try more. Now, what is interesting is, they have organized their shapes in a very sophisticated way (overlapping)....On this side of the building, the only overlapping is over the building. However, these horses are still on the baseline so they haven't dealt with foreground and background yet. The gate is in the center and it is very dark, which draws attention to it. Now I would ask the students, on what parts do you want the greatest attention? If it's the center, then that's where I'd put the darkest dark and the lightest light. Often, I'll take kids at a distance so they notice dark and lights....With kids in art I do not use words like right and wrong...rather there is a very powerful organization of elements....I wouldn't have them change anything on their drawing but our dialogue would cause them to think for future drawings" (FO 1, 4).

Causing the learner to take responsibility for his or her own learning is evident in Ruth's demonstration lessons given for teachers within their own classrooms. In the following excerpt of a grade six lesson on the use of visual journals, Ruth suggests a way of proceeding.

"There's a recipe for self-discipline for long years of study...number one, keep a visual journal...there's a book just published on Picasso's visual journal...in a visual journal, put down at the start your observations...do pages and pages of one simple thing until you can draw it from memory...now when you come to do a painting first, select from your journal, second, decide on the pattern of shapes. This is important because if you just draw things, you'll just draw an apple for instance, so what...there's no pattern there...third, decide on patterns of dark and light, four, make a color plan...okay four steps to making images. This will help you if you have recorded things in your visual journal" (FO 2, 3).

Ruth has knowledge of student behaviors and needs, not only in her subject area, but also in other subjects. She prides herself in knowing something about each discipline area taught within her school district and about current issues regarding student learning. In describing gifted children for instance, Ruth said: "The essence of giftedness is that they can see patterns in anything they can work through" (IO 9, 4). However, whenever an opportunity arises, Ruth points out overlapping features between disciplines or how the arts contribute to an overall education. In one meeting, a fellow committee member elaborated on a problem situation in which some school children watched a skating practice and were disappointed the rehearsals lacked a polished performance. Ruth pointed out that it was a lot like watching rehearsals in the arts which work on specific areas and show the determination and hours of hard work and practice that have gone into creating a piece of work. She also pointed out that it was "process-oriented" leading to a product and that kids need to learn more about this in education (FD 34, 188).

Adult learners.   One of Ruth's key practical principles she uses to guide her practice is "when dealing with adult professionals, no one changes another person's behavior....All you can do is make them want to change" (Inter 3, 3).

"You must convince adults that you are going to give them some insights into one area of their task but they themselves have many more insights into areas that you are not touching upon. Like they have to have the sense that they have the power to change. However, you cannot present it in such a way that you are going to change them. That is impossible. The only way that change can happen is if the person decides to change. Nobody on earth is going to change me if I decide I'm not going to change. You see, it's that moment of conviction. I have to see the possibilities for myself" (Inter 2, 7).

Ruth understands the special needs of the adult learner. In speaking in reference to adults in a system-wide choir and a number of people who have worked for her in various positions such as consultant or specialist over the years, Ruth demonstrated an understanding of the time and personal change involved for adult learners.

"To really make an understanding of your own and to achieve it, takes at least three years, which is why it is so difficult to deal with school policies that whip people in and out of these jobs, that give people short-term contracts for consultative work or short-term contracts for supervisory work. People who deal with teacher education need to have, some stability to design programs that are long-range. It takes longer for an adult to go through this series because, it seems, adults have so many built-in defenses. They have adult expectations of their performance. They haven't got the knowledge, they haven't got the skills, so their performance might be at grade 3 or grade 4. It makes them very unhappy and terribly self-conscious, which is why, of course, we recommended years ago to stop putting everybody together....They don't mind trying if they know they are all at the same level; adults are on the defensive. However, after so many years of refining those programs and having them in place, we don't ever suffer for lack of turnout. People do come out for art. For none of our in-services are one shot affairs. They are all long-range" (Inter 1, 9).

Assuredly, "working with adults for me, is much to be preferred than working with children. I love children, it isn't that. I like to play with them" (Inter 2, 14).

Since Ruth is being asked more and more to speak to adults at conferences, she has acquired some knowledge of what she can offer in such a situation while also addressing the needs of an audience. A practical principle of "concrete terms are necessary for things to become real" is often used.

Ruth believes abstraction left without concrete examples in images, analogies, or metaphors leaves the reader or audience frustrated.

Concrete terms are necessary for things to become real, understandable, and tangible. Ruth talked about how she prepares a speech, runs through it, and then prepares notes to speak spontaneously from—so that it appears as if she does not read a speech, but creates it from the top of her head. She said, "Since I know my script, I treat it as a theatrical performance" (FD 11, 57).

After one of her speeches, Ruth told me, the key to success was to make something difficult look easy, and so she would rehearse her talks until they reflected her written word, yet they were spontaneous enough to appeal to the audience (FD 24 139).

Teacher of teachers.   At one point in our discussions, Ruth talked about her view of teaching as an art and on another occasion, told me how she viewed herself as a teacher of teachers. I asked her if she could describe to me how her work with teachers or administrators might be artistic.

"I think that when I said 'teaching is an art,' I was talking about the ability to woo knowledge. I think a learner structures his/her own learning; giving people information is the very basic and least effective way. It is necessary, mind you,

> I'm not denying that. But that is only the starting point. People to whom I give information are at my stage zero. Once they have some information, I want them to take action. The action might be something very simple like, 'this looks interesting. I'd like to know more.' They make the next move. So when I say 'I see myself as a teacher of teachers,' what I see myself as, is in that realm, the art of making people want to learn what I have to offer them. I want the teachers to be eager to participate in fine arts programs. I want them to want to make art; I want them to love to make music, I want them to enjoy doing drama, and I want them to become highly motivated to seek out opportunities on their own and with us. Therefore, I try to influence through motivation rather than through command, and also through example. I am not afraid ever to demonstrate to a teacher what I might be encouraging her to try" (Inter 1, 7–8).

The image of "the art of making people want to learn what I have to offer them" has to do with her ability to encourage others to woo knowledge.

Ruth is also governed in her role by a strong image of "community," one which follows the principle that "whenever people come together they have a responsibility then for one another." It is an image that includes the notion of teaching each other, and for Ruth, the image of "mentoring." In describing how she feels as a mentor to her staff and other teachers, she says:

> "A very strong feeling that...um...I hesitate to call it mystical, but...I think that when people come together they have a responsibility then for one another...like in a normal course of events the people who are in your department become part of your community. A community to me is people sharing and growing together so that when someone comes on my staff for any reason or teachers come on my committees or whatever, I then have a sense of responsibility that while they are with me we should both grow....everyone has something to give and consequently to take. So I try to keep that going" (Inter 1, 15–16).

The image of "community" and the image of "mentoring" are called from the practical principle of "when any two people come together, both should grow."

Teaching teachers.   In many ways, Ruth's knowledge of the adult learner is derived from her experience and knowledge gained through teaching teachers. However, the needs of the individual teacher are often more idiosyncratic and thus Ruth's influence on the teacher more unique. She is quick to accept the starting point of anyone, before she begins to seek ways in which they might grow.

> "I learned years ago that there is always something there in the first place...I do not despise that mind-set...I start there so thoughts can encompass more insights" (FO 3, 5).

In one particular situation, two junior high teachers, neither of them trained at all in art, were assigned to a junior high school. One was a first year teacher and the other a second year teacher. Upon meeting with them, Ruth immediately asked their backgrounds and tried to bridge their understandings of their specialities with the visual arts. One said language arts and the other physical education. Ruth suggested that the physical education person might best understand some of these ideas through the ideas of movement and grace in dance and sport. The language arts teacher might best come to understand these concepts by relating them to poetry (IO 1, 2).

Consistently in her teaching of teachers in their classroom milieu, Ruth would answer questions, give numerous examples or suggestions for practice, and if the teacher needed it, a specific plan of action, which would also include another visit from her after a certain amount of work was complete. "I want to caution you. The very day you feel your enthusiasm draining, phone me. Because even a phone call can help, but I can come to the school and help too" (FO 1, 6).

As a rule of practice, she only encouraged teachers "to do a little at a time when implementing a discipline-based program," and this rule led to another, "do anything you can to cause them to reflect upon their practice."

> Just do a little at a time when implementing a discipline-based program...for years, junior high people did fun and games in art. Ruth tried to lead into what they were doing and then talk about what could be taught and learned in art...forcing them to make a statement of goals. They would work on iden- tifying learning outcomes. "We get this all the time in art where teachers say, 'what are we going to do on Friday?' Try to get at outcomes and respond to sections in those books...do anything you can to cause them to reflect upon the outcome of their teaching (FD 14, 81).

It was apparent that she did not expect teachers to work from the curriculum until they had a basic knowledge of art. Ruth talked with the teachers and, through dialogue, helped them to understand the similarities and differences between art and other subjects, as a way of creating meaning for the outcome of their teaching.

> The two (junior high art) teachers raised the question that they were actually teaching two different grades and could they both use the same ideas. Ruth said yes. Her concern was that "you begin to learn processes before working directly on curriculum." Another teacher expressed concern about working through the curriculum, so Ruth asked her how she proceeded through language arts. The teacher spoke about reworking writing before proceeding. Ruth said: "The same thing happens in art, it is just the knowledge of art that is different. The artist's task is to compose this field so that everything in it has a reason for being there and so that the audience takes on the feeling the artist

wants. In two-dimension you organize tones, patterns, colors…this may seem complicated, but we'll take our time while working through it" (IO 1, 3).

In this particular situation, Ruth came back later and taught a lesson for each of these teachers. For the physical education teacher, the lesson went very well, but there was great concern for the language arts teacher and her class.

> The kids were receptive and disciplined. Ruth moved through steps describing foreground, middle ground, and background, drawing different amounts of each, and showing examples through the use of reproductions. Finally, she talked about value scales and how to use contrast effectively in landscape drawings. The students made value scales and thumbnail sketches of landscape areas. The teacher made notes, asked questions, mingled with students and corrected some students who stepped out of line. The next class, with the other teacher was to be a repeat lesson in terms of subject matter, but there was definitely a different quality to the class. Ruth struggled to keep their attention. Boys were rude to girls. Some were ignorant to Ruth and many didn't do the assignment. The teacher didn't introduce Ruth properly, sat at the back of the room chewing gum (which the students were not allowed to do), never corrected the misbehaved students, never took notes, and generally did not exhibit any energy. Ruth was very frustrated with the second lesson. It was a flop for her because the students were not prepared to learn. The differences between the two teachers' behavior was almost extreme…later we talked about the incident. Ruth said, "if they were her students, she'd ask them if they believed there was a tomorrow. If so, they shouldn't live just for today. Therefore, they should develop habits today that would hold them in good stead for the future." In this way, Ruth felt she was causing them to reflect…. Ruth has little tolerance of irresponsibility at any age. She expects people to think about their actions, to reflect upon how they impact others, and to contemplate how they are themselves influenced by others. She believes in thought. She expects teachers to reflect upon their practice (FD 41, 224–227).

Ruth not only wants teachers to reflect, but students as well. The above incident was couched with an underlying anxiety that every time she gives a demonstration lesson or a workshop or even a speech, Ruth's reputation and her authority through expertise, are on the line. She always reflects upon her own intentions and behaviors before and immediately following the lesson. Self evaluation and recognizing teacher evaluations of her performance seem to be a way of life. "Every single thing we are going to do, we rehearse in our heads. Yesterday, as I was coming out on the plane, I could see myself standing here doing this. I was rehearsing in my head. When you go to work, you rehearse in your head, when you make your lesson plans, you're rehearsing in your head… our heads are full of rehearsals" (FO 4, 7).

Ruth takes evaluation in her stride and works to create an atmosphere of reflection with teachers. During a Continuing Education course offered by the local university, Ruth and her art specialist team taught a class of twenty teachers. While referring to the structure of a lesson, Ruth remarked about the importance of causing teachers to experiment and to record what it was they were noticing. In this way, she was teaching for *her* rule of practice, "you only notice what you know" and through teaching, causing them to notice more.

> "It's always important when teachers are experimenting and you are leading them through a series that you call their attention to noticing effects. They should keep a journal of their experiments. So tomorrow night, I will say to them, have your pencil out and under these experiments you write down what you are noticing so that when you guide the children through this lesson, you can give them sequences that will cause them to change" (Inter 2, 2).

Ruth realized that even though she might teach teachers through in-service activities, she could not assume that they would teach children the "what and how" of what she gave them.

> "The next week, when I saw one teacher who had attended that workshop, she called me aside to see her repeated lesson, I was horrified....The teacher had divided up the tasks between the rows...row one to make pumpkins...row two to make something else...she had reduced the lesson to following directions.... I had a hard time understanding what had gone wrong until through asking the teacher questions. I decided the teacher had reduced the decision-making of the children...It was a revelation to me what she did with what I thought I taught. We don't often get the opportunity to see what teachers do" (IO 2, 6).

Ruth is very aware that instructional improvement will not happen quickly, and holds an image of, "change is a slow process."

> "Instructional improvement is not a superficial process. It requires considerable time and effort. It's an assumption that you make on a job like this....I don't say now my goal this month is instructional improvement and then next month I'll work on time and effort (Inter 3,3).

Ruth also has very specific notions or practical rules that direct her in how to cause teachers to improve their instruction. While talking about an educational administration course she team-taught (with the public board music supervisor) at the university on the role of a music supervisor, it is noticeable that many of her assumptions of the supervisor's role are grounded in the rule of practice, "do anything you can to cause them to reflect upon their practice."

> Goal-directed behaviour is more efficient in achieving instructional improvement than behavior that is not focused on specific outcomes, that is, goal-directed behavior both for the person directing the program and those

receiving the instruction. That's why in our client program we sat down and we made a contract with the teacher. This is what we would like to accomplish, this is what you'd like to accomplish, this is what we're going to do together.... Many times in a consultant's work you will run around and visit a teacher, and put a finger in the dike and go onto something else and so on....People have to have a direction to change. They must have some notion of what's possible and what's desirable and then they'll go. And then another assumption that we could make is that objective recording and descriptive reporting of teaching data are more useful for instructional improvement than subjective evaluative statements—such as, I like this, I don't like this, or the kids have a good time and so on. The supervision should have some way of objectively recording and descriptively reporting teaching data, for example, the teacher entered into this activity and asked these questions and this many children answered. But there must be a way that the supervisor can say to the teacher, if you do a classroom observation, at the end of the class, this is what you did. That's descriptive reporting. The teacher is usually smart enough to say that's not really what I wanted to do....

Again I always like to ask teachers where they think the trouble might be so that I have a focus for being there in the first place....They want me to tell them what they might tackle, but in this case, the teacher, the lesson was so over-directed. You see, she had even asked the students to bring a toilet paper roll. And one child brought in a paper towel roll. Now he couldn't use that. Also, she had the art paper precut for whatever it was she was going to do. So every time an alternate was suggested by the child, it was suppressed, because the teacher had a very rigid program. Her intent was honorable, but the means by which she produced the object, the means by which she got there was destructive to the initiative and enthusiasm of the kids. So what did I do in her case, in that classroom observation? I simply wrote each direction as she gave it in one column, and a student response in another column. When we finished, what we had to look at together was two columns. One column of her directions, and in another column, clustered at the start, alternate suggestions which gradually tapered off to nothing. The result was an objective record before her eyes, stating what happened in this class. In very little while, she came to realize that the children had all subsided, working quietly, working busily, and doing their own work, but not taking any more risks. And, of course, taking risks is what causes enthusiasm about things, because a feeling of control is present. There was a very good post-conference with the teacher, because I had the objective record to show her. So I asked her, "What do you think is happening here? What is the one thing that appears to be going on?"

She laughed, and said, "By the looks of this, the one thing that is going on in my class is that *I* am giving directions.

I said, "you've got it. The one thing that is happening is that your students are following directions. Now there's nothing wrong with following directions but if that's all that is happening then that might present a problem..."

Teaching, as an intellectual and social act, is amenable to intellectual analysis. That's an assumption that we can make. Now many times teachers accept it as a social act and many times they don't think about it. But it is an intellectual act. As I said in my Kodaly talk, "experience is a mental event, teaching is a conscious activity, and you get to the point where you're operating off intuition, however, that still means it has to be rooted in some understanding of what it is you're doing, so you can always analyze it. The act can always be analyzed. Teachers must do this themselves, but that's one of the roles of a consultant and a supervisor. A consultant must be able to analyze what's happening so that he/she can give support where it is required" (Inter 3, 5–7).

Further to this, Ruth felt that "supervisors demonstrate leadership most effectively as a participant in the process of educational growth" and that "professional practice is action guided by implicit or tacit theories—intuitions— and by explicit or scientific theories supported by research" (Inter 3, 9). Professional practice could not be just a hit and miss affair, but had to be grounded in theory.

Teachers.   Ruth's knowledge of adult learners and the teaching of teachers is represented by her particularized knowledge of individual teachers and types of teachers. For instance, in reference to the staff at the alternative fine arts school, Ruth said, "Those teachers would be good in traditional schools but good teachers in traditional schools may not work well at that school" (FD 14, 76).

Ruth's practical knowledge of the individual teacher, is often very particular.

She took the opportunity to tell Marlene how she had become so much stronger every year. Barbara (music consultant) verified Ruth's message. Ruth continued saying that you just have to believe in yourself, your strengths, to know what you do well and to know what others do well also. To not be afraid to acknowledge yourself for doing something well (FD 29, 160–161).

Ruth believes that "everyone has a rhythm" and that rhythm influences one's motivation, energy, and life within one's teaching role. It is an image she holds of individual teachers.

Some of her people like Barbara, her music consultant, keep getting better every year because that's her rhythm. Some on the other hand have lasted at the Fine Arts Centre only two to four years because they had done all they could or wanted to in that role for that time period. They needed a change and so they moved on (FD 16, 101).

Artists.   Since a few of Ruth's secondary art teachers see themselves as artists first and teachers second, she often has to remind them that there is a curriculum to be used (FD 2, 10–11). The new secondary art curriculums for instance, are designed around drawing, composition, and historical/critical components. To approach classroom instruction from a purely media emphasis, would defeat the purpose. Going deeper than this, she is also on occasion reminded of the differences between artists and art teachers. Ruth suggested the following:

> Artists are not always good art teachers. They are engaged in art at a highly professional and intuitive level and they find it hard to articulate that to others. They tend to dismiss education in art not realizing their entire practice is an education in art. It is hard to do collegual work with them because they say that we should just give kids stuff to work with. They do not realize intuition only comes through knowledge and discipline (FD 6, 45).

Ruth believes that the task of educators is to make understanding and enjoyment accessible and so there can and should be guidance given to viewers in a gallery experience that would assist the viewer in understanding the context from which art was produced. "Remember I said there is no innocent eye...the audience has to have some preparation" (FO 3, 4).

> Everything we do rests within its context in history...context penetrates purpose...you must realize your time in history influences how you not only make but interpret...we need to teach children not everything is possible all the time... (FO 3, 2).

Artists and curators, gathered at a local museum, took exception to Ruth's philosophy, since they believed that a piece of art speaks for itself regardless of the context from which it was made and therefore no biased preparation for instruction should be given ahead of time. They were frustrated with her views and she with theirs. Colleagual work with this group of people was difficult given their fundamental differences in philosophy.

The art of teaching versus the science of teaching.   Ruth explained how she hired her Fine Arts Centre staff in the past. "She auditioned them because she felt if teaching is an art then auditioning through teaching was the way to go, so she always viewed her staff in a teaching situation before hiring them" (FD 12, 62).

Ruth has definite notions about the differences between the art of teaching and the science of teaching. After leaving a one-on-one teacher meeting she spoke of thinking only of the teacher and not herself, especially since she had taught all subject areas. She elaborated further on the guiding image of the "art of teaching."

Ruth believes she knows the art of teaching. The science of teaching is knowing the "what" such as rules, vocabulary, content, and regulations. The art of teaching is approaching science in a more integrative fashion while allowing for flexible application of the rules. Art works from the intuitive sense. No one can teach the art of teaching or intuitive teaching. As a supervisor she was trying to bring out the art of teaching in a teacher. If you just send a recipe, they won't change practice. Practice must meet the intentions in all teaching and learning (FD 6, 40).

> During the span of the study, several supervisors including Ruth became quite concerned about the "Super Seven," which were the seven guidelines derived through the effective schools research, that were being applied by the personnel department, administrative council, and all principals, toward the evaluation of teachers. The package developed several years before, addressed specific behaviors the teacher should exhibit in any given lesson presentation. The curriculum department supervisors were not included in the development of this package, yet they were constantly putting out grass fires as teachers across the district were discovering the impact of such a policy. Even though Ruth's associate superintendent of curriculum believed it should not be carved in stone, it was obvious that it was becoming that way. Ruth remarked that the Super Seven was a technological view of teaching and that it did not look at the management of ideas and suggested that it be removed (FD 48, 268).

Ruth talked about the problem in the school board's evaluation procedures, especially the Super Seven, which only looked at the presentation and not the ideas within a lesson. She went on to say that if Keegstra (who was dismissed from his teaching post because of promoting racism and discrimination toward Jewish people) were evaluated, he might have been rated very high on presentation, but he did not manage ideas well. On the other hand, it could be that teachers who work on ideas may in fact be better teachers but are being told that they are very poor according to the Super Seven. This really concerns Ruth, as she sees it wherever she goes (FD 50, 284). Ruth strongly believes the Super Seven is not a recipe, and the "teacher is not a technician" (FD 48, 268). Her fellow supervisors felt the same way and as a group, formulated a committee that would take their views to the administrative council and the principals. The thrust of this meeting talked against the rigidity of the model, since:

> It did not allow for inductive learning, process, learning through surprise or discovery. Essentially, the present model assumes a lock step approach, with the full class moving altogether. It denies apprenticeship and the teachable moment....Ruth felt the Super Seven is based on a behaviorist model, which is now out-of-date...Ruth stated that an artistic teaching situation gives analogies, in order to provide images for learning. "The image you use captures your imagination and that is what the art of teaching is all about." The Super Seven is good only in certain contexts. Implementing this defeats the purpose. This may improve poor teaching but it will downgrade good teaching....Good teachers are demoralized by this (FD 55, 305–307).

In summary, Ruth has a "knowledge of instruction" that is grounded in a definite theory of learning. This was evident in her work with students, teachers, and artists. The theory is also grounded in a recognition for the necessity of "passion" in teaching, and the need to understand the difference between the art and science of teaching. Much of this knowledge overlaps with Ruth's knowledge of curriculum implementation as the next section outlines.

Knowledge of Curriculum Implementation: "Enlarging the Circle of Professionally Developed Colleagues."

Ruth has a knowledge of curriculum implementation in relation to her administrative role in implementation, the client program model, networking of secondary teachers, the fine arts center role in implementation after budget cutbacks, understanding curriculum development, the fine arts alternative schools, and evaluation of curriculum implementation. Each of these will be addressed in turn.

Administrative role in implementation.   A fellow supervisor perceived Ruth "as being able to be avant-garde in terms of change" (Inter 0, 1). Whether or not she is, Ruth's knowledge of herself as a supervisor encouraging teachers to change is based on a great many beliefs about the nature of the human spirit, the relationship between peers, and between generalists and experts, and on the nature of change itself. It is important therefore to describe how she views herself and her consultant gaining access of entry to teachers and their classrooms, encouraging them to take the first steps toward change, and finally committing themselves to change. She begins the process of change through acknowledging her practical principle "when any two people come together, both should grow."

> "You take the person out of the classroom and ask them, now you are going to be a consultant which means that you have to now change teacher behavior, you have to get out, meet your population, organize your population. You see, you just can't drift around a school district going here and then there, you have to organize the population. You have to have some sense of what their needs are, you have to be able to motivate them to seek you out since you can't possibly go into their territory uninvited. You can but you won't get very far. So it has to be a mutual contract....Now, it's very difficult to work with a peer when you're in an advisory role because you automatically set yourself up as an expert. *I know what I'm doing and I'm going to tell you what to do so you will be a better teacher.* These ideas are submerged in this contract, but you must convince these teachers that you are going to give them some insight into one area of their task, but they themselves have many more insights into areas that you are not touching upon. They must have the sense that *they* have the power to change. You cannot present it in such a way that you are going to change them. You can't do that. The only way that change can happen is if the person decides to change. Nobody on earth is going to change me if I decide

I'm not going to change. You see, it's that moment of conviction. I have to see the possibilities for myself. I have to say, yes, I could do that, and yes, that would be better than what I'm doing now. So, as a consultant, you are a person whose job is to improve instruction in a specific area by causing a teacher to become a better teacher. Then you not only have to know your subject area, but you also have some insight into what is possible for that person to do. And that person has to see in you trust and support. She must see the desire in herself to make the change and that change will indeed make her better in what she is already doing. Now because of that you come across people who first, do not want to change....They are comfortable with what they are doing, more or less. They see no need to change their behavior. They do not value what you have to tell them. They're not terribly interested in the arts. They have lots of support for that, because the arts are not presented to them the way language arts and mathematics are. So, they feel, well, I can let that go. Now when you come across people like that, there's no need to waste a lot of time. If you sense that the person is not going to change, then I move on.

I have over twelve hundred teachers in the district. There's no way I can deal with twelve hundred people, but I keep sending out invitations to them constantly. Here's this program, here's this opportunity, come on and join us and you'll have a good time and you'll meet some interesting friends. Come to this in-service and we'll get what you need and we'll get you started and you'll enjoy doing this. You'll love teaching children this way—trying to entice them into making that commitment because they've got to make that commitment to us. One of the most successful things we ever did was run that client program. In the client program, they actually signed a contract where all the different duties were spelled out. But a part from giving information, which I do through newsletters, it's then their move. I do not track them down" (Inter 2, 6–8).

Her understanding of change is furthered by another rule:

"What I can't change, I don't bother dealing with. Give me the people who will take that one step with us and I will take them as far as they can go. If they won't take that one step, I'm not interested in having them there by force and I don't deal with them....I talk to you and give you information and then I say, when you're ready to make a step in this, give me a call and I'll be back. If they never call, I don't lose any sleep over it. If they call, then I'll go back and keep working with them and gradually we'll get them into our net. But if we don't, I don't worry about it. There's no way I could deal with that many people so it's a very slow process....I give a lot to a few...but my few is getting more all the time" (Inter 2 17).

Ruth mentioned to me that she has an operating principle of "give more to a few rather than a little to a lot." To encourage people, she uses the powers of persuasion, motivation, and participation" (FD 12, 63).

When I interviewed a senior high principal, who had known Ruth for many years, he commented on her strengths as a supervisor, helping teachers to change.

> "First of all, I think she is very much a people person and, therefore, teachers are comfortable in working with her. She has a great understanding of human nature, and is able to present a problem in the form of a challenge with a guarantee for a lot of assistance from her office or her position. I think when Ruth had the Fine Arts Centre as a facility, that provided a tremendous opportunity for teachers to experience both as a professional in in-service work and as a teacher, taking groups of kids to the centre to really see how it is done. The hands on kind of things. So, I think Ruth Britten is a person who didn't tell people how to do it, she actually demonstrated it. She's a very skilled person herself in many ways, through her demonstrations and the demonstrations put on by her staff. Teachers were taken by the hand, at least for those who needed that kind of assistance through the early stages, and then were given those kinds of demonstrations. Both the teacher and the student and *I* think any supervisor who is able to bring teachers along this way, has a great deal of success and is well received by the teachers themselves and certainly by the students" (Inter 13 1).

The client program model. Much of Ruth's knowledge of curriculum implementation is derived from her twenty years in her role as supervisor. Probably her most well-known strategy is her client program (Document 2). This program was developed during the early years of the Fine Arts Centre primarily for the elementary generalist teacher, although teachers with some background in fine arts education also participated. Essentially, it was a three year program in which a generalist teacher could potentially become a specialist and offer workshops in the arts.

Ruth would begin by offering information about the client program to all the elementary art teachers in the district. If they decided to participate, a contract was written up between the teacher and a Fine Arts Centre staff member and according to their level of expertise, would enter at level one or level two. The first level was a general in-service program of thirty hours over the span of one year. The Centre staff would work with these identified clients on an individual basis regularly throughout the year. Often, the teacher would bring her class into the Centre on a field trip, where the Centre staff would teach them for a full day. Later, the Centre staff member assigned to the teacher for the year (in the chosen subject area) would teach demonstration lessons in the teacher's classroom and review the progress of the teacher since the last visit, as well as help prepare the next unit of work. By the end of the first year, the teachers were often able to teach one unit without assistance and were proficient in lesson planning. Understandably, they would be very familiar with the concepts in the appropriate curriculum guide. Those who were not yet comfortable with this level could choose to repeat the first level. Those who were successful, were given a certificate for completing level one.

Level two was another set of in-service activities spanning thirty hours which focused on enabling the teacher independently to write up one unit plan and a year long-range plan. The Centre staff members continued their one-on-one involvement with identified teachers and their art classes. Again, upon successful completion, the teachers were granted a certificate.

Level three appeared to be for those teachers having no grave weaknesses and who were competent workshop leaders-in-training. Many of these teachers would assist the Fine Arts Centre staff with workshops or would be responsible for some on their own, while the Centre staff would offer support or make suggestions for improvement. Peer coaching was often used. Having completed this level, and receiving the certificate, teachers would then become "network leaders" who would in turn take on clients of their own at other schools. Often, they would also serve on advisory committees and work on special projects during the year (FD 5, 28–29).

Sharon, Ruth's drama specialist, spoke of the client model evolving into this final form. At one point, the specialist teachers had difficulty with some teachers treating them as substitute teachers rather than demonstration teachers for the in-service training of the teacher herself. After grappling with why these teachers were doing this and how the Centre staff could change it, the idea of drawing up a contract emerged. This caused a shift in attitude. It was a growing process for everyone, not only the teachers, but for the Centre staff and for Ruth (Inter 5, 13).

Ruth has applied her acquired knowledge of teacher change to other aspects of the Centre work. For instance, the growth of the teachers' choir was gradual but deliberate.

"Now we have discovered through our client program that it takes three years to turn a generalist teacher into a teacher who can successfully teach in the classroom. The first year is very much on the level of fundamental knowledge with very basic skills. You may have noticed that last night in our choir. This is our third year for the choir. All right, Barbara now has a class that meets before the choir meets for learning to sight read. Now, that is growth for those teachers. The first year we had the choir, if we had said come at 6:30 P.M. and we'll teach you to sight read, we would have had no one. They were at the level of beginning information. Barbara is at the point now where she is able to introduce harder songs. She is breaking the group up into sections, sharing some of the conducting with people who are section directors, and then bringing the choir altogether. She has enlarged the possibilities for the members. Those who have been in the choir now for three years and, who come to us as raw recruits are doing very well. They are beginning to read music, therefore, they will be able to take those skills back to their classrooms. To really make an understanding of your own, takes at least three years" (Inter 1, 8–9).

Often when Ruth speaks of her implementation plans, she speaks as if the client model were still in operation and so there were times I was confused as to exactly what was or would be happening. But as the months went by and the new model took on a life of its own, less mention was made of the client model. Ironically, few teachers complained of its absence at the beginning of the school year. As time went by, more were coming forward, assuming it would still be in place even though there were fewer Fine Arts Centre staff to act as resource people (Inter 5, 14).

The networking of secondary teachers.   The secondary art teachers were organized as one group with a designated chairperson who assisted the Centre staff in organizing four in-service activities during the school year. Often these were run by the Centre staff but on occasion guests or the teachers themselves would make presentations. As a way of strengthening the networking of these individuals, these in-service activities were held in various art classrooms in the district. In that way, teachers could see what other teachers were doing and the type of facilities in which other people worked.

The secondary drama teachers were organized in a similar fashion, except that the junior high and the senior high teachers often met separately for their in-services. It was necessary to provide the junior high teachers with a great deal of background knowledge in "developmental drama," since it was an extension of the optional elementary drama program, but quite different from the senior high tendency toward "theatre in education" (FD 45, 248). It was also a reflection on a current problem that many teachers teaching junior high drama are nonspecialists teaching a specialized subject area (IO 9, 2).

The secondary music teachers came from a variety of program strengths such as band and choral, and the corresponding subgroups. Therefore, each subgroup designated a chairperson who in turn joined a music executive. Each subgroup determined their in-service needs for the year, and, after being allocated a certain amount of money from the executive, decided which clinicians they could bring in. Since the needs of these teachers were so specialized, the clinicians were hired to work with specific teachers within their classrooms.

The fine arts centre role in implementation after budget cutbacks.   With the severity of the budget cutbacks, and thus a reduction in the Fine Arts Centre staff, Ruth was forced to abandon much of her client model and adopt a different model. But much of her practical knowledge regarding the needs of teachers as people first and teachers second, remained intact.

> "As a result of the change it meant that in September we would be faced with an entirely new model of delivering our services. That was a major challenge....I had managed to salvage the music consultant, who is invaluable to me, an art specialist, and a drama specialist, so that I had one helper in each department for a total of four. However, we have no secretarial back up except the one in the central office. Out on the site we don't have any. Because the

Fine Arts Centre was in operation in the district for thirteen years, we have a long and appreciated history of service to the district, so I did not want to lose the name and I didn't want to lose any of the facilities either. I felt attached to that name; there was a certain level of expectation between the teachers and the Centre. I felt we'd be in a better position to face all those changes than to start all over again. At one point they were going to move us out of there completely and simply give the traveling teachers a space, which you know limits it to teacher operation and, in that case, our identity would disappear. Then we would become service persons and not a service group. So in June we chose to celebrate our accomplishments in our Centre rather then mourn....by hanging an exhibit of children's art, and of young people's art. After painting the halls, rearranging the furniture, fixing up the room—we had new signs made for all the doors, sorted out office space, gave the three people who were left bigger spaces to work—we hung the exhibits in the halls at the Centre. When everyone returned in September, there was an atmosphere of optimism and possibilities and the place looked good; it looked professional....We were going to get on with what we had. We decided we were not going to mention that this was all we had left. Here we are. Here's the works.

Then, we had all these new programs underway so that as soon as this happened—that the money was cut—I then moved to put the elementary art on a three-year implementation cycle, which then allowed us to get the necessary resources. I pulled Ann, our arts specialist, to work only on that project. Now I say *only* with some chagrin because in fact she had twenty-one schools, which is a big job....To make a change for Sharon, who also did elementary and some secondary, we looked at piloting the new drama program at junior high and senior high, so that she would also have a new project to which we could dedicate some resources. And then of course Barbara, who handled everything in music, she had a lot of projects within programs and the centennial choir and so on. We had, upon our return to work, a new program in place. It was already to go. I had the schools selected, the resources all ordered, the books already for the drama, the music, which had been ordered in the summer for the choir, was all sorted out. Everything was ready to go. We spent a fair amount of time over the summer, I want you to know, getting all that stuff in hand, getting it checked off, even to buying a new and smaller coffee pot that would be much more attractive and makes twelve cups. Rather than have that great demarcation that a lot of people have. The whole atmosphere was, this is a new and exciting program. We've all got different things to do this year, so let's get on with it.

I changed our meeting date to Monday morning. I built in one-on-one meetings every week, which I decided to do for the time being, until such time as I saw that it was just not accomplishing its purpose. I built into our monthly meetings, the last Monday of every month, work on some professional development....I had ordered some tapes in July to get a start on this. I bought a video camera, which I will learn to use, so that we can tape some model lessons in order that we can improve our skills. Whether or not we know we survive into the future, the fact is we can't operate now on an uncertain future. I can't say: well chances are we're going to lose all the money this year, and so chances are none of us will be doing this next year at all. That doesn't matter. My whole philosophy about working with people, with professionals, is that we come together for a certain time so we should all grow" (Inter 1, 3–5).

Ruth set out with a tone of optimism and controlled the mood of the group with whom she worked, attending to the major changes caused by the cutbacks. She handled changes in resources, facilities, budget allocations, and even attended to the details of the operation in order to ensure a positive psychological viewpoint by her staff. All of this, she recognized, would need to occur in order to maintain and mobilize the continued trust for her and the Centre staff gleaned through the historical context of the Centre. In a sense, she was looking for some stability in the change. When stating her philosophy as, when any two people come together they should grow, she is uttering a practical principle that falls in line with an assumption she made visible in her supervisor's course: "supervisors demonstrate leadership most effectively as participants in the process of educational growth" (Inter 3, 9). Having said that, there come many implications from her way of helping teachers through curriculum and other professional change. She cares for staff members who have left her Centre and looks out for them personally and professionally. She has purposeful intentions and sets out to provide opportunities for teacher growth. Much of this is brought into focus by her image of an "enlarging circle of people who are professionally developed," and involved in raising the level of fine arts instruction in the district.

"The other thing I did, too, was reorganize all our constituent groups so that I've got this year an elementary teachers' group working with Barbara, the music consultant, on evaluation. In secondary music, we have formed a secondary music executive and that will put teachers in touch with Barbara once a month; they organize their in-service plans. Our resources are limited so we want to make sure now that what in-services we offer are going to be effective and that they are not going to be all over the shelf. We have the elementary art teachers, who are organized for the moment, around the liaison teachers who are in the implementing schools. We have identified one person in every school who is our contact. And Ann is helping out with that group and is doing very well. The whole implementation plan was designed colleagually with Ann. The plan is out in the schools, principals have it, and they know what to expect. I was talking to a principal just a moment ago, and she was telling me how delighted she was that her liaison teacher came back and gave all the lesson plans to all the teachers and the teachers all tried that first lesson plan and were thrilled with themselves. So when Ann goes back to do her workshop at noon next week, she will be very favorably received. It's a good strategy. It's working. Then, the secondary drama, Sharon has taken on the junior high drama as an identifiable group and the senior high drama. In secondary art, each of those have a chairperson. And the chairperson from each of those groups will be put together with the remnant from the Fine Arts Centre, plus the teachers from the Centre who are now out in the field. I didn't want them to just disappear...you want them to still feel ownership and you want them to have opportunities to contribute...and so we formed the Arts Council...that has a very specific goal. You never just form a group, for the sake of just getting together...I presented it to them as a challenge not as a task. I want them to feel that they may make a contribution and that contribution they make will be valuable. But they are under no pressure or coercion to produce something, because classroom teachers are just swamped. I think what I have tried to do in this job with all those teachers is to make them feel that they are indeed my colleagues and that I am working with them to better their lot, and not to add to their burdens. I do that by making them feel welcome, by not judging where they are, particularly where they are at the moment, by putting their in-services into discrete groups....Try to make opportunities like that for teachers....It enlarges the circle of people who are professionally developed and involved in raising the level of fine arts instruction in the district" (Inter 1, 5–7).

Emerging from this text, are the rules "I never just form a group for the sake of just getting together"; "make them feel they are indeed my colleagues;" and the image of an "enlarging circle of professionally developed people involved in fine arts instruction."

The Arts Council was a way for Ruth to involve more people from across the disciplines in a concerted effort. In her opening letter to them, she stated:

The purpose of the Council is advisory. In spite of the elimination of many of our resources, we still hope to maintain the interest and energy that is invested in our Fine Arts program. With you, we shall explore alternate delivery models, directions for in-service, provision of resources, etc. We shall also involve you in the review of new curriculum resources: monographs, new texts, and so forth (Document 4).

Not only does Ruth try to support teachers in the field, but she supports her Fine Arts Centre team. For instance, Sharon, the drama specialist, had spent much of her time previously with elementary drama teachers and was this year cast into the junior high realm. She was worried how teachers would perceive her. Ruth said: "Don't do that to yourself, or you will limit yourself" (FD 14, 79). Ruth seems to have an understanding of the human potential once people believe in themselves.

Several years previously, the curriculum department managed to convince the administrative council and then the school board that whenever there was an introduction of a new curriculum, the central office should allocate enough money for each school to purchase class sets of required texts by the department of education. Therefore, even though Ruth had suffered cutbacks in human resources, she had not yet suffered cutbacks in textbooks as resources. With any of the newly implemented curriculums such as the elementary art, she made sure the schools on the three year implementation cycle received student and teacher texts in the adopted series. Naturally, the schools were pleased to receive these texts (Inter 11, 1).

With Ruth's fine arts team actively helping specific groups of teachers implement new curricula, she took it upon herself to handle any incoming calls from those not on the implementation cycle (FO 1, 1), (FD 3 19). For instance, during the study, she helped elementary and junior high teachers new to art, by visiting them during preparation periods or at noon hours, walking them through various aspects of the curriculum. Often, these sessions included the introduction of available resources appropriate for the level of the teacher's expertise. Ruth would bring these up, point out specific portions of the texts or visuals, and leave the teacher with the materials, suggesting that three or four weeks later, she would return and discuss the next best sequence to follow (FO 1, 5), (FD 4, 22), (IO 4, 3–4).

When I left Ruth, she was talking about beginning work on an art chart that would detail the elementary art curriculum in a simplified way, on one large poster sized sheet of paper. The system's instructional media center could produce it in sufficient quantity for each elementary art teacher. She envisions that it could be hung in the classroom for quick reference on a practical level (IO 5, 2).

Understanding curriculum development.   In her province, curriculum development committees are made up of people from across the province and from across educational roles. The elementary art curriculum document suffered major committee problems and was eventually contracted out to be written by a specialist. Ruth obviously has a practical knowledge associated with curriculum development and how it relates to curriculum implementation. Though the present curriculum covered the emerging trends in art education, that is, the productive, critical, and historical methodologies, it was done so in an impractical way for the generalist teacher. In order for such a teacher to be able to use the document, much resource help would be needed.

Ruth herself has actively contributed to the development of the provincial senior secondary art curriculum and resource guide. Her role as supervisor gave her unique insights and she was careful to point out that often "curriculum designers treat their curriculum as if it were the only subject being taught" (IO 6, 4).

Fine arts alternative schools.   In 1985, an elementary fine arts magnet school was begun in a vacant inner city elementary school. After much groundwork by Ruth and others in the curriculum department, in the course of which they visited several fine arts schools in Canada and the United States, the philosophy of the school was based upon Ruth's theory of learning and the five symbols systems (word, number, image, melody, gesture) derived from the current literature on the different ways of knowing and intelligences (Gardner 1983). The structure of the curriculum was based upon a specific magnet arts school in Connecticut: The Mead School (FD 14, 75). Research based on this model discovered significant growth across all discipline areas as a result of fine arts instruction.

The school would house only grade four through six, and the curriculum would integrate certain themes across all subject areas. Ruth refers to these as energizing concepts. Each theme developed internally by the staff is one reporting period long, with four themes per year. As much as possible, all five channels of communication or modes of learning are accommodated in all subjects. The thrust for a unit comes from a different subject each theme. The staff all have an arts background, except for the principal, who was chosen by the personnel department. The principal and Ruth have worked closely together, and over the three years, the principal has grown considerably in her appreciation of fine arts programs, and has advocated the necessity of more alternative schools like this one (FD 14, 74).

Students were not auditioned as an entry requirement, even though many alternative fine arts schools have chosen that orientation. The philosophy committee wanted to be careful about allowing only "talented" children to participate, since they believed some children, who were not achieving in the regular school, might actually achieve more under these conditions. To date, entry has been on a first-come first-serve basis, with preference given to families with children already attending the school. The school houses a variety of children from across many backgrounds, but the tendency has been for well-educated parents and low-socioeconomic parents to send their children: the former for reasons of enrichment and extension, and the latter, for hope not found in the regular schools. Classes have many talented students as well as many behavior problem students. Nevertheless, after the first three years of operation, Ruth, the school staff, and the parents have noticed considerable changes in the students, and now realize the hardships many of the students suffer as they reenter the regular school system in junior high. As a result, the parents have lobbied the school board for an extension of the philosophy into junior high and possibly later into senior high.

During the duration of this study, several meetings were dedicated to the junior high extension of the philosophy of the elementary fine arts school. Though the intentions of the committee, the school board, and the parents were honorable, the committee faced major difficulties in applying the Mead Model to the junior high school concept with the department of education's regulations regarding core subjects, allotted time for core and complementary subjects, and the consequent rigidity such requirements would introduce. Given the present structure, students would be able to take only one fine arts course during their entire junior high experience, from a broad list of: art, drama, dance, band, and choral programs. Some of the regulations would simply have to change if the school could actually be different. No resolution was found before I completed the study (IO 9, 1–12).

Evaluation of curriculum implementation. Annually, Ruth evaluates the implementation of the Fine Arts Centre offerings to the teachers, but it is done more as a needs assessment than as a teacher evaluation of the Centre staff. Ruth said that at the end of the year she'll send out a questionnaire regarding how the teachers felt about the implementation and how well they felt they could proceed on their own (IO 11, 1).

Ruth was quite adamantly opposed to the personnel department's concern for submission of workshop leader evaluations sent in anonymously by teachers. Another principle is expressed below as she feels this type of evaluation is ethically unprofessional and believes the only true evaluation of her program and her team can occur after a year's work (FD 55, 305).

> "Now those blue cards, I won't use them. The blue card system says excellent, very good, good, fair, poor, and the teacher gets to circle that, and then it says comments and the teacher gets to make comments. I don't hold to that operation because workshop leaders who work long and hard and put in many hours of preparation to put this thing together are in fact then many times being graded on performance. How do you think this went? Well good, she certainly had a lot of ideas. That's not an evaluation that tells you anything so what I do instead is I work through the whole sequence of workshops, and I do a formal evaluation at the end. I want them to specifically identify for me what changes occurred for them, not whether or not they enjoyed what we did. So we will ask them questions like: Which of these concepts can you handle? It might say, I can teach this with help, I can teach this now but with considerable help, I can manage, I don't need any help. Now we ask them to mark if this is a change or not. If they do that when they come into us then of course there's nothing to change but it gives us insight into the...changes that have occurred in them. Which of our lesson plans have been most helpful, which of our practices have you used most...what do you consider the weakness of the program to be" (Inter 1, 10–11)?

Summarizing, Ruth's practical "knowledge of curriculum implementation" is quite substantive and obviously acquired during her experience as a supervisor, rather than as a teacher. She does have an understanding of curriculum development, particularly as she has served on local and provincial curriculum development writing committees. However, she has a broad knowledge of practical strategies for encouraging educational change while recognizing she also has an administrative role in implementation. Finally, her practical knowledge also includes a knowledge of the milieu.

Knowledge of the Milieu: Images of the "Cactus Club" and "Dance Partners"

Ruth's knowledge of the milieu grows out of her association with staff in the schools, the Fine Arts Centre, the school system, the community, the department of education, the university, and commercial resource suppliers.

Schools. Ruth's knowledge of the schools within her school system is framed by her constant interaction with teachers, students, and principals within their own schools. During this study alone, I accompanied Ruth on thirty-seven school visits though she did a few more without me. She said to me on one occasion that since she knows all the principals quite well, she doesn't always stop in to see them. They know her views and feelings (FD 2 17). However, she may schedule visitations with the principals from time to time but she also works from a rule that "I never visit principals before the middle of October because there are so many variables for them to deal with at the beginning of the school year" (FD 6, 47). Ruth respects their responsibility towards the school and they in turn respect her authority of expertise. On one visit, a teacher was very concerned about the amount of art supplies available to the school. Ruth relayed this concern to the principal honestly. He in turn said he would check with the vice-principal who was responsible for ordering of supplies. In the discussion which ensued, he also commented to me that five years ago there was no art in the school, but now he has several teachers who are workshop leaders thanks to Ruth's client program. He was obviously grateful and showed a certain level of caring and respect for Ruth (FD 6, 39).

Ruth has maintained her interaction with principals as if she were a peer consultant in their school improvement efforts. A senior high principal commented:

> "I would have the opportunity to see teachers and talk with Ruth about some of the things I have seen or observed and she would be able to make comments...so I think in helping veteran teachers improve or change their style or whatever, she has been able to sit down with us for hours sometimes and talk about the kinds of strategies to use with this teacher and the kinds of strategies to use with that teacher. And I think from a principal's point of view, that's a major input for improving instruction" (Inter 13, 3).

In one particular senior high school, the principal and Ruth agreed upon the value of the fine arts and "over a slow process gradually brought in better facilities and better arts teachers" (FD 15, 85). Ruth was consulted regarding the designing of an art room and a drama theatre. She used the National Art Education Association specifications for art facilities and acted as a facilitator between the designer and the school. She also acted as a facilitator for the theatre which presently seats one hundred people and has a full stage with all the necessary equipment. These were obviously the best facilities in the school system, but it was a united effort brought about by the principal and Ruth during a recent building improvement project by the school board. Unfortunately, not all principals felt the same way, nor have they sought her advice during facility renovation. Another school for instance, relied upon the art teacher's advice, and even though the room is new, Ruth felt it was poorly planned.

Every two months, Ruth and her Fine Arts Centre team write and produce a newsletter for each of art, drama, and music, which is then distributed to all the schools. In the case of the September 1987 Art Newsletter, for instance, notices were given about upcoming in-service activities, university courses, city art exhibits, community childrens' art programs, and the Arts Council meeting. The one to two page documents for each of the three arts, were often hung on staff room bulletin boards and if Ruth noticed on her school visitations that they were not, she would check to make sure the principal had received them (Document 3, 1–2).

Ruth has an intense respect and appreciation for the classroom teacher and has acquired some beliefs about veteran as well as young teachers.

"And for all that many years, that thirty years, they have been in the classroom. Very rarely have they seen another teacher teach, very rarely have they had collegual exchange, you know with two people sharing something. Teaching is a very isolated activity from one viewpoint and a very public activity from another, in that everybody makes decisions about education…the challenge of teaching is tapping into the resources that you already have, not just giving people information. It is a high skill to be able to do that, but once you do it, once you awaken a mind, then you have a tremendous responsibility to keep it going. Now I say to teachers, you want to set a fire in the mind. Once you ignite that, you have an incredible complex task of orchestrating that for all the kids that are sitting in front of you. Teachers, good teachers suffer more, because they see what might be and they're trying to do that, but everything is so standardized that it's very difficult for them to achieve any flexibility at all. So they're caught between the real world and the shadow world. You know, it's an interesting profession and I would have none other for myself. But I can see that it is changing. When I started, older teachers helped you out. It was much more relaxed and now it's so tense, but, that's the way it's going to be" (Inter 1, 17).

From this text, the practical principle emerges that "once you awaken a mind, then you have a tremendous responsibility to keep it going" which then leads to the image of wanting to "set a fire in the mind." Images are quite different for Ruth when she speaks of administration. From this text, we see her image of "being caught between the real world and the shadow world" of bureaucracy.

In talking with her music consultant, who was concerned about the reaction of some young new teachers on staff, Ruth told her to ignore them and to proceed with confidence and assurance as often, young teachers assume they know so much and display the "arrogance of inexperience" (FD 30, 168).

Ruth had trouble accepting the trends in the schools to offer specific groups, such as the gifted and talented, class sizes of five for instance, while the regular classroom teacher maintains thirty or more students (FD 16, 90). Or in schools with two strands, such as the IB program (International Baccalaureate) and a regular program. The IB teachers "have lower class sizes, more preparation time, so there's tension on staff...having two strands in one school is difficult" (IO 9, 10). Again it is the regular classroom teacher for whom Ruth is concerned and whenever she can, she suggests that her staff spend time in the schools getting to know what teachers are up against (FD 14, 87).

The Fine Arts Centre and its staff.   Ruth has a different relationship with the staff of the Centre. She realizes the precarious nature of advocating the arts while receiving little support. This is an image aptly illustrated in a poem about a cactus which she wrote to her staff: the cactus club.

> At the end of the last school year, Ruth gave everyone a cactus plant and a little framed drawing and poem of a cactus plant, which symbolized a growing plant, surviving on little nourishment, care, and support. And yet it continues to contribute to its environment and to grow itself (FD 5, 36–37).

Cactus
Precarious, rooted, surviving—
Strange beauty,
Inward strength,
Survivor.
Protected, nourished, sharing—
Exotic grower,
Inward strength,
Survivor.
Elegant, independent, thriving—
Mysterious presence,
Inward strength,
Survivor.
Cactus—
And we
Survive.

Also guiding her relationship with her staff is her principle "to empower other people is the more powerful way to act."

> When Ruth works with people, she does not calculate outcomes or processes, it just happens. Ruth believes she holds the lifeline to her staff. She will take responsibility for any failures and she won't leave them defenseless. She

believes that "to empower other people is the more powerful way to act." "You give the people freedom to act," she said, regarding the four people on her staff, "by monitoring them, and touching base with some regularity." She is multiplying her power by four. No matter who, Ruth also felt that they had to value the organization, as well as being valuable in their own right. She feels everyone deserves dignity as human beings. All people have strengths and she believes everyone should operate from their strengths rather than their weaknesses. She feels people seldom go from weakness to strength...she believes we should celebrate excellence and does not agree with those who sneer at those who succeed. She believes everyone advances when one advances (FD 54, 299–301).

The practical principle of "to empower other people is the more powerful way to go" is furthered by her image of "everyone advances when one advances."

Ruth's closest circle of professional friends revolves around the Fine Arts Centre staff. "She believes her staff are driven by passion to improve the arts in the schools" (FD 28, 154). As individuals and as a group, they regularly visit one another outside of school time. Ruth has a unique relationship with each. Ann, her art specialist, has been with her the longest, and is outwardly the most devoted. They share common professional interests in art history, studio production, and professional and community involvement. Ruth admires Ann's ability as a mother and wife, though Ruth outwardly doesn't regret having been either one.

Ruth's relationship with Sharon was close-knit and perhaps motherly, particularly this year, as Sharon was going through marriage difficulties. Many personal conversations were held behind closed doors, over the telephone, and on weekends. Every time, Ruth offered an objective viewpoint couched in a firm love. And every time, Sharon's spirits improved. There was a different bonding here than between Ann and Ruth. If one extended this to Sharon's little children, the extension became manifold, for Ruth adored Sharon's children and visited them regularly, showering them with attention and love.

Ruth's relationship with Barbara was different again. Perhaps much of this was a result of Barbara's position as music consultant, which in itself, caused them to share a different set of understandings and roles than those of the specialist teachers. But perhaps, too, it was a result of Ruth's acquired passion for the school district choir Barbara was conducting. Ruth admired Barbara's ability in a field she was only now coming to know and since Barbara returned that admiration to Ruth for her talents, the two independent, ambitious, and visionary women were drawn together.

Ruth believes she has been "blessed with good people in her department" (IO 11, 4). Through experience, she has learned "I will never hire prima donnas again," a rule of practice acquired over time and experience. No one in the Centre now needs their ego boosted (FD 28, 154) and, therefore, the group works well together.

Ruth takes care of her staff in many managerial ways. With the change of staffing at the Centre, particularly with no secretary, the working conditions of the group became a prime concern. Ruth set up weekly staff meetings to air concerns, tried several alternatives for handling incoming phone calls, and through an intense lobbying effort at the Central Office managed to hire a halftime aide for December to June, minimally to handle what a full-time secretary did in previous years. The entry of such an outsider into the Centre was fascinating to watch for Ruth recognized the young aide's need to align herself with the pace of the Centre. Until she did, Ruth would not invite her to any of their social functions. Besides, it would be hard to be friends with someone who was not your equal (FD 54, 301).

Ruth also looks after her staff in many personal ways. The following practical principle illustrates this. "Change for sake of change is irrational." She says to her staff, "your career is yours to manage. Do not think of me, think of you" (FD 7, 48). In more managerial ways, at the beginning of the school year, she purchased personal daytimers or calendars and a blue binder for everyone to organize their meetings and activities for the year (FD 1 18). Anyone who has worked for Ruth can also be reassured that when they leave the Centre, she will look out for their well-being. During the study, one of her previous art specialist teachers was recommended by Ruth to give some rural workshops on the new curriculum. The woman was presently practising her own art and taking in whatever work she could find on the side. Ruth never forgets the strengths and needs of those who have entered her circle, her community (FD 35, 203), (Inter 5, 18).

Ruth's interest in her staff can also be extended into her concern for their own professional development, for example, she dedicated one weekly staff meeting a month to the review of video tapes on peer coaching. It was her hope that this would not only open opportunities for the design of model lessons for the implementation of new curricula and how her team could be more effective in their interactions with teachers, but also that it would bridge them with some of the present concerns in school improvement efforts. In so doing, if she were to lose any more of her team through budget cutbacks, they might be better prepared for reentry into the field (IO 2, 1–6).

The school system: The supervisor as the interface between teachers and administrators. Ruth has an image of herself or other consultants and supervisors working with teachers as "dance partners." It is an image defined by those dancing in unison and responding to one another.

"The consultant at work with the teacher is a dance, not a contest. It is two people engaged in the dance of learning, not a contest of learning. If you think of those two images, you see, it's not a consultant in an adversary position or a competitive position or in a position of imposing or forcing activity. It's not a game. It's more like a dance where two people commit themselves and then they move in concert together sensing each others rhythm. That's how it works. I am different, as you've probably observed, with different teachers. I do different things with different ones…that's heuristic ability. You have to find out where they are, where their strengths are, and what they might do. My team here, for example, I know what they do best and I get out of their way… empower them and eventually you can move on to another partner when they begin to take the lead" (Inter 2, 8–9; Irwin 1992, p.113).

The "dance partners" image is reinforced through the practical principle "giving is what makes people powerful, not taking," which in turn produces another image, "giving and receiving is a very powerful cycle."

"…empowering other people means giving them a chance to make their special contribution. It's very simple. That's all I mean by that. Your contribution may be a particular insight, a particular talent, a particular energy, a particular loving way to be with people. Part of my job is to see to it that I can create the conditions so that you can give. And giving is what makes people powerful, not taking…one needs to be able to receive what another offers so that there isn't any violence in giving and receiving. Giving and receiving is a very powerful cycle. Taking and refusing has a sense of force in it. And force and violence draws you inward upon yourself and so who you really are can't get out. It's a matter of energy flowing" (Inter 14, 2–3).

One of Ruth's main images, guiding her practice, is her view of herself as a "teacher of teachers." She does not view herself as an administrator first, though she recognizes that is the difference between her role and a teacher's role. The administrative aspect of her role deals predominantly with control, though the areas for which she is responsible are limited. She has great concerns regarding the bureaucracy, and portrays it as producing its own "shadow world along side the real world." As an administrator, she has the practical principle of "making sure the teachers have the conditions right so that they can give what they are capable of giving."

"As an administrator of a program, I pay attention to such things as department of education goals, the provision of resources, the design and following of a budget, setting a scale of issue, providing materials for the kids, keeping administrators informed of textbook changes, all of the things that deal with the administration of the program. I could very profitably spend every day sitting there at my desk. There would be tons to do and I could do it and, in fact, in actual practice, I let a lot of this stuff go as you have perhaps observed. I do not worry about all of those things because there's a strange phenomenon taking place right now in education and I dare say in society at large and it is this: It seems that nothing happens unless it is recorded. It's a kind of mental set that says that teaching is not taking place unless we have a teacher's long-range plans, we have a teacher's short-range plans, we have a teacher's evaluation, we have *all* those reports. It's written up so that we are creating a shadow world alongside the real world and the shadow world is one of reports, documents, video tapes, computer analysis, an entire structure of information. Now, you see, the fact of the matter is that every single teacher goes into a classroom every morning and teaches all day whether or not I exist or whether an administrator comes. No matter what, teaching goes on. But, you see, there is this really bizarre notion that none of this is happening unless it's written somewhere and someone has it on file....So, my job is to make sure that they have the conditions right, so that they can give what they are capable of giving. As a result, I do a fair amount of troubleshooting for them and I visit them a lot, you know, to praise theme. It's very intricate. You know, it's not a tidy operation, nor can it ever be" (Inter 1, 12–13; Irwin 1992, p. 116).

Ruth has a belief and an image that "the school system has a life of its own." It will survive while individuals come and go. Its function is to provide an orderly environment for the well-being of the student, and therefore all those involved in teaching students. But too much order neglects the attention of unique opportunities and abilities for the growth of the child, and it is with this balancing of oppositions that Ruth is most concerned.

"I think the people who are chosen to be supervisors in this district are people who have a passion for their particular subject area so they, like me, do everything possible to make it exciting, to make it attractive, to make it go. It is the next level of administration that is most concerned with administration, but then that is their job. But of course you see a school system is a system by definition designed to keep order and that is valued more than those who introduce disorder into a system. I'm a person who introduces disorder. The order-keepers are more valued in the system, which does have a life of its own, because they are paid more, have better working conditions, more value is placed on what they [do]....a school system has a life of its own. Now, people like me, as I said introduce disorder into the system, because teaching is not tidy. A teacher deals with the greatest variables that can be had, groups of kids. I mean there is no greater variable to deal with. They are like the wind. Their minds are changing, their lives are changing, their environments are all different, change is the variable. There's no way you can capture that on a piece of paper. So a teacher must have the ability to work with that change and all that unpredictableness of children, however, she must hang onto a vision. Now, I try to work in that arena to keep all that going. And the reason the order-keepers keep order is so the teacher can teach, but that is often lost sight of. The people who become the order-keepers keep interfering with the process, not to make it better for the teacher but to give them more data, which is the shadow world we talked about" (Inter 1, 14–15; Irwin 1992, p. 115–116).

This dialogue prompted me to note in my field diary that Ruth is very concerned about the current need for standardization. She believes creative vision is necessary though it is not valued in her district. Creative vision is usually disorderly until it gets settled. But one must take risks even though that presents a possibility for failure. Teachers cannot become so ordered that they cannot experiment. The school system itself will not take risks and with that, Ruth refers to her image of the "Administrative Council as a Byzantine place" (FD 14, 77).

The role of supervisors and consultants in the school district is not well-defined though the differences between pure line authority and staff expertise is often used to ignore supervisory influence. Nevertheless, Ruth views herself as the interface between the school and the school system, an image of being caught between the two.

In her role as supervisor, so much concern is given toward nurturing the teacher toward change that it becomes a very difficult role. The rule of practice, "you can change the circumstances, but you can't change the behavior" is illustrated below.

> "But it becomes very difficult and time consuming and unlike administrators in the schools who had their will accomplished by making rules upon command, the superintendent, the associate superintendents, all those people who have line authority, the principal can say, it shall be this way, and then walk away....Whereas a consultant or supervisor sits between those two groups. The group of teachers who are largely autonomous in their classrooms, and the group of administrators who are largely autonomous in their administration duties. A supervisor or consultant has to rely on the good will of both of those parties. You have to have an administration that will support your endeavors and give you the time and resources to carry out what you need to do...it's a long slow process, you can't order change. Change cannot happen by mandate, ever. You can change the circumstances, but you can't change the behavior" (Inter 2, 9–10).

Ruth feels that her power in her role lies with the image of the "power of knowledge" and says that "teachers recognize that I know what I'm talking about...they know that when I share with them ways of teaching, they know I have tried them out...they know they are authentic behaviors, they know I won't lead them astray. So I have authority of knowledge in fine arts in our district" (Inter 2, 10).

In reviewing the feeling of the supervisory group in regard to recently established teacher evaluation procedures, Ruth says:

> "In our district, our senior administration is the supreme authority. They make the educational decisions. Now, two years ago they went off for a retreat and established the system priorities. They returned and these priorities were shared with various groups. But the line authority people, principals, and senior administration often meet. They meet in the fall and they meet in the spring.

They have a two-day retreat. Their roles in the implementation of these priorities are very sharply defined. Principals know what they're supposed to do. Senior administrators know what they're supposed to do, and it's almost a closed loop. It just goes around and around. Now there's a reason for that because they are all line people and their concern is primarily administration, but what they are trying to implement can only be implemented through classroom practice, because that's the heart of the system. They can say communication is one of their priorities for evaluation, but unless the teacher does something about that, it's not going to happen. And, of course, the teacher who might try to implement evaluation cannot evaluate in a vacuum. She will evaluate inside some program, inside some subject. So that program supervisors are the linking agents, to use the terminology from all those articles you've loaned me, are the linking agents between the implementation of any program, even if it's one defined by your senior administration, and classroom practice. So that we see ourselves as a very critical component in this entire operation. But I think that our group has some concerns about the identity of their role in that loop because so far their evaluation has dealt with the evaluation of teachers by principals, and the evaluation of principals by zone superintendents. Which you see is a different component of evaluation from program evaluation so that possibly in the first few years of the application of those priorities that is necessary to do. But the context for their development is always in the instructional program. So we're staff and they're line. We're neither teachers in the schools nor are we administration, in the strict sense. So we're in this limbo in between at the moment. Now we all have job descriptions but our role, vis-à-vis those two groups is not sharply defined by the present administration. It's giving people some apprehension....I think this is the part that people find makes them uneasy, in the sense that the ownership for the program by the supervisors and consultants is at the moment, only implied...it's not that anyone has set out to ignore us, it's just that we are not taken into consideration and when they go off for two days and devise strategies for evaluating teachers, and they don't involve the program specialists, it puts us in an awkward spot, because if they're going to use certain instruments to evaluate teachers and we only learn about that second hand and we are working with the teachers to improve the instructional program, it causes us sometimes to give teachers advice, which, if they use it, will give them a bad evaluation" (Inter 3, 15–16).

On another occasion, Ruth reinforced the above viewpoint except from the orientation of changing teacher behavior.

"It's really difficult and time consuming and unlike administrators in the schools who had their will accomplished by making rules upon command, the superintendent, the associate superintendents, the principal, all those people who have line authority can say, it shall be this way, and then walk away from it....They can set policy, rules, and regulations for the operation of the district, for the good order of the system without consultation...whereas a consultant or supervisor sits between these two groups. The group of teachers who are largely autonomous in their own classroom, and the group of administrators who are largely autonomous in their administration duties. A supervisor or consultant has to rely on the goodwill of both   parties. You have to have an administration that will support your endeavors and give you the time and resources to carry out what you need to do. When I say time, they have to make a time commitment to people…it's a long slow process. You can't order change. You can change the circumstances, but you can't change the behavior" (Inter 2, 9–10).

Ruth talks about the importance of recognizing the circumstances of the teacher as the context for improvement before defining lofty educational standards. As a consultant or supervisor, "I have to make time to maintain research and reading in my area," a rule of practice for Ruth in her role.

"As a consultant or supervisor, you have to have the time to maintain research and reading in your area because you must be up-to-date. You are the spokesperson for that subject, and anybody in the district: administrators, teachers, parents, even students must be able to come to you as the source of accurate and timely information in that particular area. You see, they can't get it anywhere else. And so you have to be on the lookout for bad practice, people using ditto-sheets and coloring them in and things like that. So you have to constantly be working on people to make changes for the better as you have to find things that are better. But you see the trick is that.…I have to define what constitutes the most excellent art program that we can obtain within the circumstances in which we find ourselves and that includes having a whole bunch of generalist teachers" (Inter 2, 11).

Ruth has one responsibility which she handles singularly and that is finances. She carefully allocates all the money within her budget to the purchase of resource materials and equipment, the payment of clinicians fees, substitute teachers, or teacher dinners in lieu of in-services or workshops, and finally, necessary expenses to run the Centre, such as staff salaries and physical plant necessities (FD 5, 27), (IO 5, 2), (IO 4, 6), (FD 44, 245). This is the one place she feels she has power of control.

One critical place Ruth and her fellow supervisors have no authority is in the hiring of new staff, though Ruth lobbied throughout the study for the hiring of specialists particularly in the secondary schools. On several occasions however, principals did ask her for advice.

Ruth views the senior administration as having a different set of guiding images for their practice than those she has, but each has a "landscape of images."

They have different landscapes of images to guide them than Ruth which results in a conflict of images. She feels she is a member of a large (school district) community of which she forms several sub-communities and so treats her superiors as if they were in her community. From her perspective, the administrative council looks at the school district from authority of power where they sit in a linear fashion to one another in a hierarchy. Ruth also explained that in some ways this could be portrayed as a pyramid in which the top authority distributed power below, except that the power would be unequal. In her colleagual model, in a circle of community, everyone had equal power. Though she would be central, her only absolute control would be with finances, but everything else would be collaborative (FD 23, 133–134).

The community.   Much of Ruth's knowledge of the community in which her school district is situated grows out of her understanding of how the community influences her programs, or how she can influence the community regarding her programs. For instance, she was involved with the city Arts Council for which she attended one meeting during the study. The emphasis of that meeting was the upcoming spring childrens' arts festival.

Another cooperative situation exists between the two schools boards and several businesses who share a computer facility. In this case, Ruth's Fine Arts Centre team does demonstration lessons on using the computer in the arts for teachers and their students as a form of field trip (FD 43, 234). As well, she is aware that many students take private lessons beyond their school instruction (IO 9, 6) and the extension of adult programs into the local college of art (FD 47, 263).

On the other hand, Ruth takes some of her programs into the community. A very good example was a christmas concert given by the school district teachers' choir. Approximately 600 people attended this event which was also enhanced by the performances of a baritone soloist and a string quintet from the community (FD 51, 287), (FD 52, 288–289).

Beyond her immediate community, Ruth is also aware of a larger picture to some degree. She realizes that some rural school districts are shelving the new arts curriculums because they cannot implement them, and are essentially returning to their old ways (FD 10, 54). She believes that the Los Angeles move to a year long school year will have an impact upon every one in the next few years (IO 9, 5). Ruth also recognizes the limitations of the community in terms of advocacy.

"We don't have a powerful lobby of people and politicians out in the community saying that every child must be literate in music, because they themselves haven't got the experience....They don't know anything about it, so to them it's not terribly important. It's not a possibility for them, so they don't see it as a desired possibility for the whole population" (Inter 2, 15–16).

The Department of Education.   Ruth's knowledge of the Department of Education is limited to her direct involvement on curriculum ad hoc committees.

In the past, she has been instrumental in the development of secondary art curricula, and is presently sitting on a committee to review fine arts curriculum resources (FD 7, 42).

She has an image "keep a back door open to the Department of Education...so that we have often piloted provincial programs beyond the required pilots guided by the Department" (IO 9, 3). In this way she has kept abreast of the innovations before official adoption of curricula. This is currently the case as she will be unofficially piloting a series of music and art student achievement tests being field tested elsewhere in the province (IO 10, 1–2).

In her role as supervisor, Ruth is confronted with many of the regulations laid on by the Department of Education, for which she must become accountable. For instance, the department has recently recognized the abundance of suggested concepts in the secondary curriculum guides and has asked local school boards to define 70 percent of the concepts as mandatory and 30 percent as optional. Writing these curriculum specifications would be a necessary task of all curriculum personnel across the province (FD 47, 262), (FD 48, 268).

On occasion, one of the Department of Education Fine Arts Consultants has suggested that she consider taking on a position with the Department of Education. Ruth adamantly refuses. She doesn't want to be a part of furthering regulations. If anything, she tries to keep the rule of "the fewer the regulations, the better" (FD 14, 82).

University liaison.   Ruth has maintained her contact with the university art education and fine arts departments, even though she no longer holds any sessional appointments. With the art education staff, she keeps very close contact. One of the professors comments:

> "It was a delightful discovery, you know, to realize Ruth was working here because, as I am sure everyone else says, one comes quickly to value her input, you know, her ability to think clearly and to articulate the ideas that consume us. So, in that sense, I had instant camaraderie and you know, appreciation" (Inter 9, 2).

In the fall, Ruth was team teaching a continuing education course for teachers regarding the art curriculum as a way of extending the implementation of the new curriculum (FD 25, 142). Other than that, her only other involvement with the university became political as she realized that as professorial staff were retiring, hiring would be frozen. She wrote letters explaining the devastating effect this would have on the future of the art and drama education courses in particular at the university, not to mention, the ripple effect this would cause for the school systems as they hired new teachers (FD 29 158).

Commercial resource suppliers.   As mentioned under the Department of Education, Ruth must have some background knowledge of all the available resources currently on the market that may be applicable to her subject areas.

Sometimes, this may even mean that eager publishers will wish to approach her in order to review their current publications, or to suggest the possibility of providing her teachers with a workshop of a new series or material (FD 5, 29). However, more specifically in her role, she is often in contact with suppliers of media and equipment necessary for her fine arts programs (IO 3, 1). For special events, this may even mean, rushing posters to a local print shop (FD 36, 209).

In summary, Ruth's "knowledge of the milieu" is guided primarily by recognizing herself at the interface between teachers and administration. Much of her knowledge of the milieu reflects her strong ties with the schools, the Fine Arts Centre, the university, and commercial resource suppliers, but it also includes her managerial ties with the Department of Education.

SUMMARY

To Ruth, "it is knowledge that makes me effective in my work" (FD 43, 240), particularly knowledge of subject matter, but also knowledge of herself, instruction, curriculum implementation, and the milieu. But what makes her unique in her role, is the kind of knowledge or the particular content of her knowledge that is different from teachers' practical knowledge. As mentioned earlier, the literature on practical knowledge (Elbaz 1981) uses Schwab's five commonplaces: knowledge of self, subject matter, instruction, curriculum development, and milieu. In answer to the first research question addressing the content areas of Ruth's practical knowledge, several themes were uncovered inductively for each commonplace. This included the change of the curriculum development category to curriculum implementation.

Ruth's practical knowledge is structured differently from a teacher's practical knowledge in that she is concerned with "curriculum implementation" to a greater degree than curriculum development. She does have an understanding of curriculum development, particularly as she has served on local and provincial curriculum development writing committees. However, her experience as a supervisor has led her to acquire a broad knowledge of curriculum implementation. For instance, Ruth recognizes she has an administrative role in implementation. What she cannot change she does not bother with even though she is guided by a principle of "giving more to a few rather than a little to a lot." Particularly, she uses the "powers of participation, motivation, and persuasion."

In using her "knowledge of the milieu," Ruth recognized principals' authority. She also recognized the needs of teachers within schools, especially their need for colleagual sharing and empowerment. The images of "wanting to set a fire in the mind" penetrates this notion of empowerment. However, she is critical of her administration in many ways, which is illustrated in her image of "being caught between the real world and the shadow world of bureaucracy." Another association is her own Fine Arts Centre. She perceives the role of her staff through a self-written poem about a cactus, from which she refers to her group as the "cactus club." It is an image of advocating the arts while receiving little attention and support. It symbolizes strength and survival in adversity, and a strange exotic beauty mysteriously surviving outside forces. Again, her notions of empowerment of other people is the more powerful way to act becomes obvious, particularly in the image "everyone advances when one advances." Ruth is close to each of her staff members in a unique way and encourages each to shine wherever possible, However, she also believes "change for the sake of change is irrational." One of the major associations with the milieu is her own practical knowledge of her role as supervisor as the interface between teachers and administration. Personally she is guided by the image of "dancing partners," an image suggesting supervisors and teachers dancing in unison yet responding to one another. It is an image extended by another image of "giving and receiving as a powerful cycle." Another image, that of herself as a "teacher of teachers" portrays her affinity with teachers rather than administrators. This is furthered by another image portraying bureaucracy as a "shadow world along-side the real world." The image of "the school system has a life of its own" speaks of the inhuman nature of organizations and bureaucracy. Another image of the "Administrative Council as a Byzantine place" reinforces her antagonism toward the character of administration. Ruth believes she can change the circumstances in which teachers work, but she cannot change the behavior. She influences people through her power of knowledge. To this end, she believes she must always maintain research and reading in her areas. The fundamental difference between her practical knowledge and the practical knowledge she associates with senior administration, she believes, may be cast in a different "landscape of images."

The next chapter will address the various contexts from which Ruth's practical knowledge is situated, and in this way, our understanding of the differences between a teacher's and a supervisor's practical knowledge may be further examined.

Chapter 4

The Contexts of Ruth's Practical Knowledge as Fine Arts Supervisor

INTRODUCTION

To acknowledge Ruth's practical knowledge at the content level helps us to determine some basic areas of her understanding and to lay the foundation from which much of her work progresses, but it neglects to portray how it is dynamic, changing, and adaptable in problem solving. To render her content knowledge and nothing else would reduce Ruth's knowledge to static areas or divisions. But it is not that. It is situated within various orientations or sources, and thus Ruth herself wanted to talk to me about her reasons for doing certain things right at the time they were happening, because she said; "It is hard to talk about knowledge out of context" (FD 20, 115). What may be talked about on an intellectual level may be demonstrated in her practical efforts with teachers, students, and administrators. Given the contexts of her knowledge use, her practical knowledge may in fact take on varying shapes and contours rather than assuming a static shape. Freema Elbaz (1981) made the assumption that the teacher's practical knowledge included theoretical, situational, social, personal, and experiential orientations. These categories are considered here as knowledge contexts and extended by one category as inductively discovered: the political knowledge context. This is a significant difference from the practical knowledge of a teacher.

The significance of a political knowledge context is further witnessed in Walter Werner's (1987) concern with issues of power within educational change and implementation. It is true that teachers are often given opportunities to interact with one another, to share beliefs, and to help one another. It is also true that outside assistance contributes to individualized support toward teacher growth. Werner argues that little attention is paid to "issues of teacher power and involvement in their own training" (p.43). It is in this political dimension that Werner questions who controls the training of teachers and for what purposes.

Werner (1987) goes on to describe two metaphors that may be used to guide or question current thinking on educational change or reform. The first as defined by Aoki (1984), is the producer-consumer metaphor borrowed from industry. Producers are experts who market a product based upon their knowledge and experience. Consumers are mere recipients who receive the product as marketed. For school boards who may align themselves with this orientation, supervisors and consultants are considered "change agents" who act as salespersons for the innovation. In turn, teachers have little power to influence the innovation.

Werner's second metaphor is a colleagual[1] metaphor where "everyone is viewed as having different kinds of expertise and being involved at different times in the development of innovations" (p.44). School boards, which are aligned with this orientation, employ supervisors or consultants who will work with teachers to interpret, adapt, or extend innovations in the field of education. Provincial or state adopted innovations would necessarily be broad in order for school boards to work through colleagual networking for improved educational practice.

To many supervisors or consultants, these metaphors are often used simul-taneously within their roles. The producer-consumer metaphor is concerned with serving administration, that is, in bringing about greater system-wide control and accountability. The colleagual metaphor is concerned with meeting the professional development needs of teachers within specific situational contexts and experiences. Teachers and district personnel can come together to discuss critical issues. In so doing, teachers are granted "the power to define practice" (Werner 1987, p. 46). Through this scenario, the professional development of each teacher is increased.

Although Werner suggests there are strengths and limitations to both meta-phors, he asserts that the colleagual metaphor allows for interpretive accounts set within unique contexts. In this way, the participants may view educational change or implementation as a reflective activity individually and collectively.

Aoki (1984) calls this reflective activity "situational praxis." Three basic assumptions guide his ideas. "Humanization is a basic vocation...people are capable of transforming their realities...education is never neutral" (p. 14). These assumptions assert that teachers and supervisors would be interested in each others *becoming* within their roles, that everyone has a personal power to determine one's own reality, and that curriculum implementation is a political act concerned with issues of power and control. Ideally, teachers and supervisors would need to be critically reflective of what they see as well as of themselves. Through this reflective practice exists the potential for the transformation of self and the curriculum. Therefore, praxis continues through praxis. Implementation as situational praxis would be more interested in the liberation and fulfillment of the individual, than in demonstrating bureaucratic power and control.

The above literature points to two opposing viewpoints found within imple-mentation issues. To the supervisor, the need to resolve the implicit contradictions forms a dialectical relationship, thus illuminating a synthesizing perspective. Ernest House (1981), on the other hand, considers three perspectives on innovation: technological, political, and cultural. Implicitly, each portrays a different underlying image of what knowledge is important and how educational practice can or should be improved. The technological perspective is guided by an image of production. Through mechanistic processes (like flow diagrams showing the input and output of essential features), innovations become defined by economics and efficiency. The political perspective is guided by an image of negotiation. Through voluntary social relationships, power, authority, and competition become negotiated for the collective good. Therefore, educational innovations would be concerned with authorizing an acceptable distribution system of resources (Berman and McLaughlin 1978). The cultural perspective is guided by the image of community. Shared cultural values and beliefs would be critical to unification of the community (Sarason 1981).

If each of these perspectives were adopted individually, selective forms of knowledge could only be advanced in certain ways. Therefore, it is important to recognize how each perspective influences educational change. Although the technological perspective has been dominant for several decades, it is being challenged by political and cultural perspectives.

Supervisors are situated between teachers and administrators during the educational change process. From a cultural perspective, teachers need individualized assistance in learning about new pedagogical and programmatic innovations. Senior administrators and government officials, assume a technological perspective as they seek efficiency and accountability. The supervisor, at the interface between teachers and administrators, is confronted with reconciling conflicting orientations to change. The political perspective offers some hope for resolving such conflicts.

Aoki (1984), Carson (1984), Berman (1984), and Favaro (1984) regard implementation through in-service training and consulting from a perspective in which concern is for the individual, and more particularly, the individual within certain settings or situations, provides the context for dialogue. To this end, consultant-teacher relationships are not a matter of bureaucratic power and control, but rather "relationships involving touching, helping, freeing, and reaching. Mutuality, collaborative efforts, in-depth dialogue replace competency lists, so frequently the heart of inservice or supervisory programs" (Berman 1984, p. 58). Through dialogue, teachers are viewed with dignity and recognize their worth as individuals with credible ideas. Indeed, in a teacher-consultant relationship, a unique reality is realized rather than a predetermined reality by a consultant.

Michael Fullan with Suzanne Stieglebauer (1991) supports this by saying that the degree to which teachers interact with one another and facilitators of change will determine the degree to which change is successful. They assert:

"Understand the subjective world—the phenomenology—of the role of the incumbents as a necessary precondition for engaging in any change effort with them" (p. 131). Personal conduct is absolutely essential, although it is dangerous to assume that joint work always leads to deeper forms of interaction (Little 1990). Andy Hargreaves and Ruth Dawe (1991) go on to distinguish between contrived collegiality and collaborative cultures. Contrived collegiality would be indicative of formal, bureaucratic systems such as peer coaching, formally scheduled meetings, and job descriptions for consultants. Collaborative cultures are not designed around specific projects or events but are rather indicative of personal and enduring daily practices. Consultants working within these collaborative cultures would be concerned with long-term involvement and change rather than short-term goals and one-shot inservice sessions characteristically found in contrived collegiality.

Alternate Views of Consulting

In 1984, Favaro created a framework which outlined three ideal types of consultants. The ideal type of consultant-as-expert characterizes an objectivist orientation. A consultant working from this orientation would offer expertise in practical problem-solving situations, and is so doing, also decide what was significant in order to interpret and diagnose deficiencies in teacher skills and behaviors.

The ideal type of consultant-as-colleague may be aligned with the interpretive orientation. According to this orientation, consultants and teachers would come together in a collegial community. This community would dialogue about personal meanings given to the events and situations they experience.

The ideal type of consultant-as-coparticipant characterizes the consultant as one who not only interprets and questions the teacher's actions, but who is also self-reflective. Therefore, there is "mutual engagement in critical reflection as both consultant and teacher coparticipate in open dialogue and mutual questioning of the bases of the curriculum content of inservice acts" (Favaro 1984, p. 53). Favaro suggests that "to elevate the quality of inservice consultative relationships requires a change in emphasis from technical, cognitive knowledge to a focus on meaningful experiences" (p. 53). If this is the case, then the latter two forms of consulting offer the most potential for increased awareness and change in the lifeworld experiences of consultants and teachers.

For the research field, this delineation raises many questions, one of which is addressed in discussion of the need for descriptive studies of consultants who primarily fall into the latter two categories. It is from this viewpoint that a description of Ruth is offered, to provide for the research community a look into the lifeworld of a supervisor who contributes to the staff development of teachers in a meaningful way. In so doing, the field may come to understand what the practical knowledge of such an individual may look like, and in turn, cause others to reflect upon their own experiences with supervisors, or as supervisors. Though Ruth represents art, music, and drama in her role as fine arts supervisor, her primary area of expertise and interest is in art education. Very little descriptive research exists regarding the role of art supervisor (Hart 1984; Hurwitz 1967; Irwin 1989, 1992; LaTour 1985). What will be realized in the portrayal of Ruth's practical knowledge is the wealth of knowledge beyond content expertise. In this respect, this study offers all those interested in educational change a view toward the role of supervisor, regardless of subject matter content.

Given that these persons assume their positions with subject matter and pedagogical expertise and little or no other training for the role of supervisor, it becomes important to understand what personal practical knowledge individuals in these positions may hold, initially, and over time. Characterizing this knowledge may illuminate how one educator constructs meaning associated with change and how she proceeds independently and collectively with change efforts. This rendering should provide insights into the lifeworld of supervisors and in so doing, offer some understanding of the issues confronting curriculum change efforts.

THE SIX KNOWLEDGE CONTEXTS
FOUND IN RUTH'S PRACTICAL KNOWLEDGE

Theoretical knowledge will be portrayed first as it provides one pole against which all other kinds of knowledge are held in dialectical relationship.

Theoretical Knowledge Context: An Articulation of Voice and Vision

Ruth's theoretical knowledge context may be found in her understanding of the relationship between theory and practice, her use of literature to support articulation, and her ability to translate theory into practice.

The relationship between theory and practice.   Ruth's understanding of the relationship between theory and practice sets up a dialectic that constantly conditions all other contexts. It became a topic of discussion, during an informal interview, in which she shared with me some major assumptions of her role during the music supervisors' course she taught.

> Ruth: ...Teaching, as an intellectual and social act, is amenable to intellectual analysis. That's an assumption that we can make. Now many times teachers accept it as a social act—many times they don't think about it. But it is an intellectual act. As I said in my talk on Kodaly, "experience is a mental event, teaching is a conscious activity, and you get to the point where you're operating off intuition but that still means it has to be rooted in some understanding of what it is you're doing, so you can always

analyze it." The act can always be analyzed. Now you see, teachers have to do this themselves, but that's one of the roles of a consultant and supervisor. A consultant has to be able to analyze what's happening in order to give support where it is required.

Interviewer: This might be a deviation but I think that this might have some relationship with your understanding between theory and practice. Am I reading you right when you say that practice is, in a dialectic, let's say with theory, that it's happening...

Ruth: It certainly ought to be....You ought to have a reason for our practice.

Interviewer: Do you think that it is that way?

Ruth: On no, I don't think it is that way at all. I think that teachers, God bless them, have no time to consider theory. I think that once you're out in the classroom you begin teaching and the stress of dealing with the numbers and the unrelenting pace of teaching prevents you from the luxury of theorizing, because you see, to consider theory, you have to step back from practice. Theory is always abstract to practice. So you must step back from your practice to consider it from a different point, from an objective, scientific, and analytical viewpoint. And, you see, teachers are so pressed both for preparation and for teaching, they depend on others to generate theories. They would just as soon you never came near them with the theories. Just tell me what to do and I will do it, but you see those operations that are not rooted in theory, and theory is just a fancy name for having a reason, a reasoned strategy. Practice that's not rooted in reason becomes activity for the sake of activity. You just do it for reasons other than education of the young.

Interviewer: So you don't think that some theories could have become a part of their intuitions?

Ruth: Oh I do. I do, but then you are assuming that they are keeping up with the theoretical knowledge. Theories that, established teachers who have internalized theories, are operating from that assumption....Now teachers who do not match theory with practice, will not change their practice because they are not aware that the theory is analyzed. Nor do teachers have the time to analyze the theory. One should say when teaching I'll try something, then I'll consider the theory. Then, I'd say this flies in the face of common sense and experience. My practice tells me that this theory doesn't really fit what happens. So either the theory is incorrect or my practice is incorrect. If I adjust my practice and I still don't find anything, then I should go back and look at that theory again and see if I can learn anything. But that kind of intellectual activity has

> to have time, a person needs time and opportunity to do that. You
> see, this is one of our difficulties (Inter 3, 7–9).

Professional practice is action guided by implicit or tacit theories—intuitions—and by explicit or scientific theories supported by research. This is what professional practice in action is. Professional practice has to have a strong foundation of theory. You can't just hit and miss. In other words, you have to know what you're doing (Inter 3, 9).

Ruth has a personal understanding of how she can use theory in her own practice as a supervisor but she does not expect or assume teachers will be able to do the same in their own practice. Abstract theory, for her, is a necessary basis from which to work, to test new ideas, and to make consistent relationships between existing common sense theories-in-action. However, it is never assumed as truth and it is only acceptable if it is indeed consistent with practice or improved student achievement. For teachers to try new theories, they need someone like Ruth to decipher which theories are most likely to succeed and why they are better than other theories. In so doing, there is some assurance as to the validity of the theory.

Ruth feels she is able to distill her academic knowledge into practically-oriented statements and applicable strategies for teachers. "We had some in-services last winter where we had fifty-five teachers come out. Because you see they recognize that what they are going to get from us will translate into more enjoyable classroom work for them" (Inter 1, 11).

Much of this likely stems from her constant interaction with teachers while addressing the theoretical context. Ruth is able to take the theoretical knowledge found in educational literature and explain to teachers how it might be understood in practice.

> We must remember that all experience is thought. Every conscious transaction
> is made visible through symbols. And my point is that thought is always
> symbol specific. That is, they are framed by and expressed through any one of
> five ways: word, number, gesture, image, and sound. That's all we have. We
> have no thought external to those symbol systems. Right now, there's a great
> push on for teaching children thinking skills. I'm very uneasy about that,
> because I see people teaching thinking skills apart from these symbol systems
> that we have expecting that if you teach children in word and number there will
> be an automatic transfer. I think this is not so. I think there is not an automatic
> transfer, especially when dealing with the symbol systems of gesture, image,
> and sound with which we deal in the arts. They have their own discipline. I
> don't think that skills are remote from those systems of communication.
> Because those are the five major ways of knowing the world and of knowing
> ourselves (FO, 4, 4).

A university art education professor verified this as well.

"I think she has very successfully capsulized an idea I had been working on here with my students for a period of time, but she very clearly put this idea into simple terms. That was taking the discipline of the visual arts by putting them into place with other modalities and coming up with this little acronym, W I N G S (word, image, number, gesture, sound)" (Inter 9, 4).

There were other instances that Ruth integrated the theoretical with practical situations. Often in meetings, when questions arose for instance, regarding subject offerings, philosophy statements, or department of education regulations, Ruth would cite appropriate recent literature defending the arts, teachers' sense of efficacy, or the schools within certain socio-cultural communities within the city, to name a few. So when she would remind people that the Fine Arts Alternative School was founded upon "eleven years of collective research done through fine arts people" (IO 10, 6), it was not unusual and quite expected by her peers.

As a final example, Ruth encourages teachers to read professional articles for themselves, and during an Arts Council meeting focusing on evaluation in the arts, she took the opportunity to set the tone for the year by including three articles with the agenda.

The three articles are "The Art of Assessment," by Janet Waanders, in *Arts In Education* (September/October 1986); "The Kind of Schools we Need," by Elliot W. Eisner, in *Educational Leadership* (October 1983); and "Creativity: Concept to Measurement to Educational Goal," by Lawrence V. Castiglione, in *Arts In Education* (September/October 1986) (IO 6, 2).

Her drama specialist summed it up this way:

"For teachers, I think, she has a vision. She has a good overall vision of where the arts are going, what they should be doing in schools, and academically. Ah, her academic background is her biggest strength, because she can always support the practical with the theoretical. And, I think, that makes teachers feel justified that, you know where they're coming from. You know that they're coming from something that is valid, because the problem in the arts is that it's so 'airy fairy,' or considered to be or is perceived by the administration to be. So that if you have somebody who is in Ruth's position, at the level of administration, who is that solid in terms of her philosophy and theoretical underpinnings, then it gives everybody hopefulness as to where the whole program is headed…then by the way she talks to teachers, she talks about theory, she talks about philosophy, she talks about the underlying reasons for things…why the art curriculum, for instance, is structured the way it is. So that's really useful I think for teachers, because so often it is difficult to see the forest for the trees. You know you're dealing with so many curriculums, you're so worried about the practical all the time, it's good to have somebody take you back and say now this is' where it's all coming from. Then you start to have a clear perspective of what you're doing" (Inter 5, 9–10).

Ruth becomes the embodiment of theory. In supporting her, teachers are supporting what she stands for. In Biblical terms, support for the prophet implies support for the gospel.

Use of literature to support articulation.   Educational literature is a main source of gaining theoretical knowledge for Ruth and it is treated as a necessary part of her role. She planned to spend a half day a week reading at the university in order to keep up with current thinking and research, but it happened sporadically (FD 2, 13). Instead, she would read articles from journals as they crossed her desk, and if they seemed appropriate for future reference, retained copies, or if they applied to someone else, she would forward them to that individual (FD 35, 200). Her own personal library in her office reflected her arts and curriculum interests, while her home library also included history, mathematics, music, and literature. She also subscribed to *The Atlantic*, *New Yorker*, and *Scientific American* (FD 62, 344). In this way, she brings many perspectives to everything (FD 55, 312).

> "I continued to read extensively in the field of psychology, brain research, cognitive science, arts education, art generally, so I was trying to analyze this mysterious power that I felt made the arts and music certainly a unique curriculum offering" (FO 4, 2).

But it was educational reading that formed much of her foundational thoughts, and, though she did not always quote authors names and titles of references, she would if her audience was receptive.

> "While it is undeniably true that different powers reside in each hemisphere, it is also undeniably true that the mind operates as a unit. You have many, many minds. Robert Ornstein has written a book called *Multiple Minds* where he deals with this phenomenon. We have many minds. I am not the same person talking to you here this morning say when I am painting, or out walking. Something different is operating but it's always one thing. There's always that single identity of a single mind. So we have to look instead into the insights of the work of the cognitive scientists. Into the work of the people who are doing psychological research on creativity. Harvard's *Project Zero* is a case in point. The work of Howard Gardner, who has written *Frames of Mind*, deals with the different forms of intelligence. Evelyn Mayer, who writes on the psychology of the arts, deals with the very complex phenomenon that people can do many different things in many different ways, and not everybody is gifted at every single thing" (FO 4, 9).

Her art specialist, for instance, became very interested in art history as a result of Ruth. When asked how Ruth had encouraged her to grow, that is, what strengths Ruth had brought out in her, Ann said:

"I would say her background in art history has influenced my reading which has only been positive because now the art history is coming in very, very strongly in the secondary curriculum....So Ruth's interest and love for art history books,...she would say, have you read this? I wanted to stay on the conversational level with her and really couldn't at times concerning the works of Botticelli, Goya or works in the Louvre or pre-Raphaelites. I went back to university and finished up a B.A. in art history, which has led to working with the galleries and the education officers there, which is art history based. I don't think I would have. I might not have looked at that discipline that much without Ruth's encouragement because it's very academic" (Inter 6, 5–6).

To summarize, Ruth's use of theoretical knowledge was found in three contexts. To begin, she perceived the relationship between theory and practice for teachers as essentially dialectical (McKeon 1952). She accepted that educators are guided by implicit and explicit theories that are inseparable. But she also realized that often educators are under too many constraints to reflect upon explicit or scientific theories. From this she assumed that theory is applied to practice. This was referred to earlier in the document as the operational method and may be aligned with the notion of "change agent" as one applying theory to action.

To keep abreast of the new theories in the field, Ruth read extensively in several disciplines. Having this background, she was able to present this information to teachers and administrators in a way that could help them translate the theory into practice. Ruth's theoretical knowledge permeates much of what she does, whether it is consciously abstract or more intuitive, yielding to tacit theories. Much of her knowledge of the theoretical was shared with teachers and administrators in another context: the situational knowledge context.

Situational Knowledge Context: Building Community Through a Colleagual Model

Ruth's situational knowledge context may be illustrated in her colleagual model, in her relationship with subordinates, her physical presence, taking advantage of situations, problem-solving, decision-making, and her use of humor.

Colleagual model.   Ruth works from a "colleagual model." It is an image closely aligned with her image of "community."

Ruth told me she works from a colleagual model. She gets people to tell her how they would proceed, even though she has an overall idea or a universal goal. How the goal was achieved was flexible but she kept the universal always in mind. If she had to she would be deliberate in her delegation of duties. However, her colleagual model would lead itself to tighter ownership by those involved (FD 1, 2–3).

"So I want them to feel that they make a contribution and the contribution they make will be valuable. But they are not under pressure or coercion to produce something because classroom teachers are just swamped. I think that what I have tried to do in the job...with all those teachers is to make them feel that they are indeed my colleagues and that I am working with them to better their lot and not add to their burdens. I do that by making them feel welcome, not by judging where they are, particularly where they are at the moment" (Inter 1, 6).

Ruth believes in the colleagual model because it allows her to view others as experts in their own right, and in so doing, she gets ten times the work and commitment out of them (FD 2, 18).

"Each one has something that...she knows more or something different and it can be shared with other people. Like nobody has all the answers and not for one minute will I pretend that *I* do. I think though that I know who knows" (Inter 1, 19).

Ruth did not come to her role as supervisor knowing she would proceed with this model, but rather it was something that she came to know over the years as an administrator (FD 12, 62). Ruth told me how she might be different from other administrators because she does not need to have her ego fed like many administrators and so she doesn't want to be in the limelight. This is the basis of her colleagual model (FD 12, 62). Ruth feels it is critical that she be a part of her team and is quick to say they, too, have had an impact upon her practice.

"Oh I have changed the way I operate because of watching Ann. I have certainly changed a lot because of Barbara. As you know music is not my speciality, but I do enjoy it. In the choir she has taught me a tremendous amount. So in my daily life with my team, sometimes, I'm a leader, sometimes, I'm a follower, sometimes, I'm an instructor, sometimes, I'm a learner and, I think, that gives us a cohesiveness that we are all working together" (Inter 1, 9).

"I have been blessed that the people I have always had to work with, have been truly expert, devoted, dedicated, and generous; they're not prima donnas. They just do what they see needs to be done. As I said to you, 'I just get out of their way.' Once I recognize that they're proceeding, I get out of their way, and I get behind them then, getting them resources, making it possible, getting them the money, arranging them time, doing all those things. Now if I observe that they're flagging, or that I'm flagging, then I get back in front of them again. To prevent them, from burnout or whatever, I'll adjust their programs or I'll do something else, for example, have a breakfast or lunch meeting or I'll do something to take the pressure off if I can. It's tricky, because supervisors need to do two things and one is, to work on the program and the other is to deal with people. You must develop interpersonal skills; you cannot be self-conscious. You can't be involved for your own self-advancement, you just go for it" (Inter 2, 11–12).

The text above portrays her rule that "once I recognize that they're going, I get out of their way. Now if I observe that they're flagging, or that I'm flagging, then I get back in front of them again."

In conversation, Ruth talks about colleaguality in reference to many groups and relationships. For instance, her secondary art teachers resisted coming to workshops or meetings for a number of years. They participated, however, since she could offer them substitute teachers to take over their classes during some school days. Up until two years ago, Ruth did all the talking, but last year she ran each session so that she only did about half the talking and they were responsible for the other half. This year that would continue with even more of a seminar feeling so that the teachers would be encouraged to talk more about their individual programs. Reflecting upon this group alone, Ruth said they had grown in terms of colleaguality (FD 10, 54).

Other examples may include her Fine Arts Centre team and how they contribute to the functioning of the Center and to their unified role in the district. First of all, Ruth had the group review some videotapes on effective teaching in order to offer them some professional development, and also to have them begin questioning whether or not it would be feasible for them as a group to create their own videotapes of model fine arts lessons for teachers in their system to use. Ruth wanted a colleagual action towards the making of the tapes. To provide a receptive environment for the sharing of these ideas, Ruth and her team decided to set aside one Monday morning staff meeting per month for just this activity. Each time, they would visit someone else's home to begin the day with a breakfast meeting (FD 4, 22).

Second, Ruth had drawn a diagram to conceptualize the placement of her team relative to her and to the teachers within the system. This model is circular, with Ruth in the center inner circle. Her three team members representing art, drama, and music, equally divided the next concentric circle into thirds. The Arts Council would become the next outer circle, demonstrating the intersection again of all the arts. Finally, the outer circle was divided into thirds according to the original three sections. Within each of these there were twelve to fourteen divisions illustrating the activities and involvement of her team and the fine arts teachers within the district. For instance, within the art section, these categories were listed:

> elementary art implementation in twenty-one schools; senior high art planning; junior high art teachers; elementary art network; provincial curriculum committee; city-wide arts festival; C.S.E.A. (Canadian Society for Education Through Art) committee; school system arts festival; secondary art exhibits; open workshops; research; university liaison; university quarter course (Document 10).

When addressing her first Arts Council meeting, she also spoke about the importance of colleagues working together:

> "The purpose of this group is to...maintain the level of enthusiasm, motivation, and interest throughout the district....We need at least ten people....it does not mean more work for you to do...only the opportunity to brainstorm and dialogue with colleagues" (IO 6, 1).

Those members of her staff who have gone back into the classroom remain a part of her circle: her circle of empowerment. She does this through the rule of "you want them to still feel some ownership."

> "The chairperson from each of those groups be put together with the remnant from the Fine Arts Centre, plus the teachers from the Centre who are now out in the field. I didn't want them to just disappear. They worked for us all those years and are now assigned to a school. They have all that extra knowledge and gave that yeomen service during those years. You don't want people like that to just go over the hill and say thanks it was nice knowing you. Like, you want them to still feel some ownership and you want them to have opportunities to contribute" (Inter 1, 6).

Ruth also recognizes the closeness of her team in a different way. Inasmuch as possible, she treats them equally. If she is away for any reason, she makes a point of phoning each one to find out what happened while she was gone and to offer whatever immediate advice she can. In doing this, no one would feel left out, and no one would feel more powerful because they were singled out. Ruth knows and assumes they will discuss what she talked to them about. If there are any exceptions to this rule it may be the music consultant, because of her role designation (FD 8, 49).

Watching Ruth implement her notions of colleaguality may be found in many of her one-on-one meetings with her team. The excerpt below, taken from my field diary, is an example of a weekly meeting with her art specialist:

> From 9:00 A.M. to 10:30 A.M., Ruth met with Ann regarding the art program. They discussed which twenty schools Ann would be responsible for, when Ann would meet with the key liaison person at each school, and how she would in-service them. Materials were also addressed. "Art in Action" was approved and will be purchased by the board for those schools in the implementation cycle. During this meeting, it seemed as though Ruth was interested in how Ann wanted to proceed. As Ann talked about her ideas, Ruth reaffirmed them or made suggestions. Ruth did take the lead, however, in formulating letters. It seemed that Ruth wanted to complete as much as possible while Ann was present and could add her thoughts. By the end of the meeting, Ruth was recapping what they had completed, what she would have to follow up on, and what Ann's tasks were to be (FD 1, 1).

While interviewing a senior high principal, I mentioned that Ruth said she uses a collegial model and asked him if he had any sense of what that might mean to her:

"I think so. A collegual model is number one a recognition of who you are talking to; I think Ruth recognizes her peers as people of worth who require a considerable amount of dignity. She approaches them from a very positive viewpoint. If they have something good to offer, and they will offer provided that certain circumstances can be made available to them. I think that the collegual model she operates by is simply creating the opportunity to draw the best out of people and it doesn't matter whether the ideas are her own or their own. However, the parameters are drawn and then the professionals have the ability to make certain kinds of decisions as it impacts upon them at that level. Her model can be contrasted by the type of administrator that says 'this is the way we're going to do it. Now, people, go ahead and do it.' Under their model, there's no room for creativity or for the individual input or anything else. I think that the model that Ruth follows and anyone else is successful....Successful completion of the job must always mean that the people who really have to do it must have some input....I think if Ruth can launch a one-hundred year celebration and have people at the very bottom, say 'boy, I'm sure glad I was able to do this,' that's very significant" (Inter 13, 7–8).

In relation to subordinates.   Subordinates such as secretaries are viewed by Ruth as powerful in a very different way from the power demonstrated by senior administration. Ruth applied a practical principle:

"You have to be careful when working with service people like caretakers, secretaries, aides, etc. because they have tremendous power over you or who they work for. You cannot alienate them but rather keep them on your side. You must guard them from too much stress, as they begin to complain or fail to accomplish things if under too much stress" (FD 29, 156).

Ruth's presence.

So far the interactions I've seen Ruth in have been filled with respect and a genuine caring for her as a person. At one point today she told me she went in with the attitude that they (everyone) would be delighted to see her. So far this appears to work for her. Everyone is delighted to see her (FD 2, 12).

Ruth's interpersonal skills are held together by her image that "everyone will always be delighted to see me." Her love for teachers as people trying to do their best in their roles is manifested in her respect, trust, and compassion for them. To support this view, I will quote a teacher, the associate superintendent of curriculum, and her drama specialist, respectively.

Teacher: She just encouraged and loved us through it all. All our pain and our hopes and, I think, art teachers, and you would know this, are at the mercy of everyone, and especially the administration, who can throw a football into left field and they tell you to go get it way out there. Especially with all those implementations (Inter 8, 6).

Assoc. Super.: First of all, Ruth establishes a trust relationship. She has strong interpersonal relations or human skills, and she understands where the person is coming from; she's able to talk right from there onwards. She's a non-threatening person, she's knowledgeable, and she's respected. Okay. She has a lot of compassion and empathy for teachers. She knows where they are and where they've been because she's experienced it herself. So, as a result, she's very effective with working with teachers, extremely effective (Inter 12, 2).

Specialist: She leaves so much up to you. Like she really treats you as a professional.

Interviewer: Oh.

Specialist: And there was no sense that, she may have been evaluating you but…you have the sense that Ruth respects what you do in your line of work. In other words, for me, in drama, she assumed that I could do their job. I mean that's obviously why she hired me but as the job wears on, there's no sense that she was checking up on me to see if I could actually do it. We would have periodic meetings where we would sit down and say, 'here, this is what I've done, this is what I've covered with these teachers, this is what I feel has been working really well, and these are the problems that I've had.' A rehashing of what was worked on. Then that gave her the chance to see where your program was going, but it wasn't in the sense that she was checking up on you or evaluating you. It was just an evaluation of how the program's going" (Inter 5, 1–2).

This presents a practical principle verified in Ruth's own words:

"You not only have to know your subject area, but you have to have some insight into what is possible for that teacher to do. And that teacher must see in you the trust, the support, and the desire that she sees in herself that by making the change it will indeed make her better in what she is already going to do" (Inter 2, 7).

Ruth's attitude of loving everyone perhaps stems from her religious background. She believes that the fundamental teaching of the Catholic church, "love your neighbour," is very difficult but it is the most fundamental virtue (FD 57, 323). Though she admits she loves and cares for everyone, she is also careful to keep her distance so that she herself feels in control of her emotions, behavior, and involvement with others (FD 50, 286). On this note, it is interesting to look at something Ruth wrote for a secondary drama teacher who has known her for a number of years, and who obviously trusted her. The teacher was under a lot of stress and had gone on a sick leave just before her drama group was to go to performance. Ruth gave her some suggestions on how to stay in control of her own life.

LEARNING TO CHILL OUT

1. Learn to recognize when you are in a stress situation.

2. Determine if you have control over the situation.

3. If you have control, do something about it. Act on it!

4. If you don't have control (and you have been stewing for three days anyway), relax and let go.

5. Live in the present—the now. Enjoy the sunset, take a long bath.

6. Find hobbies that make you relax and feel happy. (Read a good book, go to the movies, feed the birds.)

7. Exercise.

8. Make time for yourself. Don't get so caught up in work or family that you don't have time for you.

9. Avoid self-pity. Avoid those who feed the negative side of yourself.

10. PRACTICE DETACHMENT! (FD 50, 286).

Ruth always seemed to be perceptive to the stress level or the amount of pressure the teacher was under, and if it could hinder growth, she would provide simple guides for the teacher to follow (FD 6, 45).

Ruth was called upon at different times to offer advice, sympathy, or caring to teachers who needed someone whom they could trust and also understood their situations. The example below illustrates Ruth's firmness during tough times.

Ruth broke into talking about change again.

She said "You cannot change others, you can only change your reaction. You are only deceiving yourself if you do. People do not want gratuitous advice. Instead they must trust you first before they will listen."

Ruth then showed me a thank you note she received from a teacher who had been depressed at work. Ruth had told her straight that she was feeding herself negative thoughts, and would have to change her attitude. By continually looking at things negatively, she would be burying herself deeper and deeper, and she must not expect others to give to her. One must look after oneself first. The note expressed how the teacher was feeling—disappointed at first that she didn't get sympathy from Ruth after she had unloaded all her troubles, but now that she'd thought about it, she was glad Ruth said what she did, because it was changing her life. She was seeing things more positively (FD 54, 297–298).

Ruth is quite sympathetic toward teachers (Inter 5, 10). It was obvious that as she works with teachers, she thinks only of them, not herself (FD 6, 40). As a principle, she believed "they must trust you first before they will listen." During one school visitation, Ruth went out of her way to introduce herself to a first year teacher who was going to start an extracurricular choir, telling her how pleased she was that she had joined the staff especially since she had a music background. Noticing the teacher's enthusiasm, Ruth spoke to her about the school district teachers' Centennial Choir and how they were always recruiting new members if she was interested. The next teacher she visited was the school's choral band teacher, who was in a very different situation.

> She said she did not mention the choir to this last teacher because she was just surviving in this position (replaced a tough program). She said she tries to be sensitive to where the teachers are at. She will give those who are ready, more, and those who are overwhelmed, ideas on how to do less (FD 15, 86–88).

For another first year teacher who was hired midyear to replace an art teacher out on sick leave, Ruth stopped in to see how things were going.

> Ruth told her to phone her for two things: the first was to celebrate anything good the teacher was proud of and Ruth would come out and see, and the second was to phone for any kind of help she might need. The teacher was just so pleased to see Ruth at all, that these two things seemed to be extra. Ruth later told me she thought it was important to affirm the good things the teacher was doing and therefore included it as an important time for the teacher to call her (FD 60, 330–331).

Ruth is not interested in bureaucratic control. She wants people to be happy and able to fulfill their potential and so she follows the rule, "affirm the good things the teacher has done." She believes people need to play, so she guards against being overbooked, and tries to instill that with her staff as well. She also tries to build in fun times or celebrations (FD 5, 35–36). Her presence has a certain energy and determination that can also be noticed in her physical presence. Often I noticed her giving eye-to-eye contact (FO 1, 2) or sitting side by side with a teacher (IO 4, 1), (IO 1, 1), (FD 5, 34). If she seemed to know the teacher very well, there were times I saw her walk off with the person arm in arm, talking quietly between themselves (FD 16, 96). All of these were perhaps ways of bridging the gap, a way of saying "trust me."

The music consultant reflected upon what Ruth does particularly well with teachers in regards to influencing change.

> "I think she understands them. She understands the work load they have. All the demands that are put on by central administration and what she tries to do with the demands she's putting on them is to simplify it and make it in workable terms for them and in workable situations. And I think they know...they believe it's good, they try it, they found out it is good and she's there for support, too, all the time" (Inter 4, 3).

Taking advantage of situations.   During her weekly visits to the schools, Ruth would often take advantage of the moment or the situation in order to bring to someone else's attention something that was not originally intended in that particular situation. For instance, one day a central office administrator dropped into her office to talk about his concern for continuing in the school district choir given his limited abilities. Ruth encouraged him saying it would take a while before he'd be truly comfortable but that it would happen and he'd feel really good about it, since he genuinely wanted to be in the choir. Ruth took advantage of the situation to tell him this was Barbara's last year of her three year contract, and it had already been renewed once. According to school board policy, she could not have it renewed again. He said he was really impressed with her teaching abilities and that it would be a shame to lose her. Afterwards I asked Ruth if she thought he would share this idea with others and she said emphatically, yes! (FD 13, 68). Ruth was desperately trying to keep Barbara as her music consultant. I later learned Barbara's position was advertised and filled, leaving her to return to another role in the district.

Another example of Ruth taking advantage of a situation was noticed when she went to visit a substitute secondary art teacher whom her art specialist was helping.

> Ruth was coming out to see for herself what the situation was. It turned out that the principal was not happy with the situation and felt that the regular teacher would not be returning from sick leave. He wanted to hire an art major. So Ruth pitched in and told him some things to look for when hiring (the kinds of courses in art, other background, etc.). The principal accepted this, wrote down Ruth's suggestions, and told her several names he had been given several months or so before when he first enquired. Ruth knew two of the three names and gave detailed descriptions of those two and their strengths for the role. Ironically, while we were there, he received a call from personnel, with another list which essentially included the first three with two more. The director of personnel leaned toward the one that was a physical education major with an art minor, but Ruth tried to say an art minor might not really know enough yet.

So the principal should ask key questions aligned to the curriculum, that is, on drawing, composition, and encounters, to verify what the candidates knew and how much. Ruth really gave a plug for a teacher who had been on her staff last year. The principal said he appreciated hearing all this from Ruth even though she was not technically supposed to be involved. Ruth said later this was a very different principal visit, but she took advantage of the situation to push for a fully qualified individual in the program, thus strengthening the program system-wide (FD 60, 331–333).

There are numerous other examples of how Ruth, by seeing as many teachers as possible on a school visit, took advantage of situations in order to cause people to look at what they were doing or to use the time wisely (FD 26, 148). Often, she was "on the lookout for bad practice, people using ditto sheets and coloring them in and things like that" (Inter 2, 11). And often, she was well aware that she had to do a lot of politicking, or applying a form of diplomacy where long conversations would need to ensue in order to talk someone into something. For instance Ruth said "it would be nice if you could just say something, but people don't act on reason alone" (FD 53, 293). Thought or reason was always tied to emotion or feelings. One could not happen without the other, and so any kind of problem solving would have to account for both.

Problem-solving in situations. "I always have a plan for what I will do but those plans are always open to change after discussion" (Inter 1, 16) is the key practical principle in Ruth's problem-solving capacities.

Problem solving is a critical area for Ruth and she always keeps in mind that one viewpoint does not reflect every viewpoint, and in fact, she makes a rule of practice "to view a problem from all viewpoints before making a decision." This was demonstrated many times among several constituents such as teachers and principals, secretaries and consultants. One example is provided below. During her visit to a school, the fine arts teachers raised some concerns which Ruth agreed were problems. However, she only noted them and said she would discuss them with the principal.

> Ruth talked about her visit with the principal. She went in and told him what she liked was happening first and asked about some concerns she had. She discovered, as usual, that the principal had good reasons for what he did. Most of his reasons rested with the management of the school, for instance, keeping the junior high separate from the elementary. There also seemed to be some discrepancies between what the teachers said and what the principal said. Ruth said teachers assume that administrators do not understand them (FD 16, 99).

Ruth feels that problem solving is a major area requiring attention by a supervisor. This is reflected in the attention it received in her music supervisor's course, as noted below in a reproduction of one role-modeling situation.

Teacher: Outline a problem/concern you are having in your music class. Tell the supervisor what you wish her to observe. Work with the supervisor to define the problem and work out a trial solution.

Supervisor: Listen to the teacher's concern. Write objectives for the teacher and for the students. Work with the teacher to define the problem and work out a trial solution (Document 5).

Problem solving becomes an opportunity for both the teacher and the supervisor to work together, to define the problem, and to follow through with not one solution, but with trial solutions. As one principal said:

"I think she is one of the most diplomatic administrators. She never works in confrontation...instead of one way of solving she will have several. She definitely uses divergent thinking. If one way doesn't work, she suggests other ways which she generally has already thought out" (FO 6, 4).

A university professor remarked about Ruth in comparison to herself:

"Maybe she's more diplomatic....I think she probably has stronger capabilities to deal with problematic situations...she can deal with the here and now, the present contingencies and the improvements that are required" (Inter 9, 7).

Her associate superintendent of curriculum states: "It's interesting to see her relate to people. I've never seen her in a real confrontation mode. She may feel like that inside but she never lets it show" (Inter 12, 5). But some of her problem-solving capabilities may also be a result of her ability to define the problem, as implied by a fellow supervisor who notes: "By and large my only contact with her as a colleague is at our weekly supervisors meetings in which she is very vocal and I found her very much able to sift through all the crap, as we sometimes say, and get down to really what is or really should be" (Inter 10, 2).

Problem solving not only becomes an opportunity to define a problem differently from a wide perspective of alternative solutions, but it is also a process of approaching everything from a positive viewpoint, and in so doing, Ruth "rises above the situation."

The principal said that she admires Ruth's determination. Even though Ruth lost so much last year she made the best of it—she always comes up with a creative solution. Ruth told me later that she does not sulk; she approaches everything from a positive viewpoint and in that way she rises above the situation (FD 16, 100).

Decision-making in situations.   Though Ruth definitely has decision-making responsibilities, often she is limited within the context of the organizational structure. Once major decisions are made at the department of education level and subsequently at the school district level, she may either choose to enforce them blindly or to influence any further decisions. She customarily follows another practical principle of "trying to influence their decisions as much as I can so that when their decisions do come they will be favorable." When asked what she felt were the major changes she had to deal with due to the budget cutbacks, she said:

> "Right, I didn't bring about the change. It was a decision on the part of the department of education side to delete the special opportunities fund which meant that right off the top we lost $210,000. Now the school board cannot possibly replace that. As soon as I realized that was the way things were going, in order to salvage as much as I could, I prepared a chart of action and its results....It's a one page chart showing numbers, showing what we do now with this staff and what we would do then. Across the top I wrote: If we lose one teacher, if we lose two teachers, this is what the program will look like, and so on. So, rather than just sit back and wait, I gave them many, many alternatives for a reduced operation to be effective. I try to influence their decisions as much as I can so that when their decisions do come they will be favorable. Now when the decision finally came down on what they were going to do, they had salvaged $100,000, which was better than not having any money at all. So that when you ask what do I do, I try to influence the decisions, but I try to influence them with authentic data so that they have some notion of what they are dealing with. Often times you expect people in top administration to make decisions that will be favorable but they will make decisions for reasons other than the survival of your department. Therefore, you must be the one to make sure they have enough information so that what they will decide upon or at least have some basis in fact. I can't wait around. I don't wait for them to ask....I mean the senior administrative officers who form our administration council. These are the associate superintendents. They make all the decisions for the operation" (Inter 1, 1–2).

One situation illustrates Ruth's attitude toward decision making in her role very well. It is set in a situation in which Carol, a secondary drama teacher, was forced to take a sick leave ten days prior to the school's drama production of the year. She was very upset with what she had heard the substitute teacher was "doing to her production." The situation illustrates Ruth's rule of practice: "No decision will satisfy all parties—rather find one that everybody will be a little satisfied with." It is also set in the context of her image of the "parable of the sower of seeds."

> Due to a series of coincidences, Ruth ended up being a mediator at the school. Carol, the drama teacher, had phoned Ruth that morning after Ruth had phoned the principal to say she was coming over. Carol was very upset with the sub who apparently was moving in with a lot of arrogance. When Ruth arrived at

the school, she did not tell the principal she had spoken to Carol because that would have betrayed her. The principal welcomed Ruth and asked her to mediate the group into a decision (principal, vice-principal, department head, substitute teacher, and several other teachers who were involved in the production). Ruth said there were two easy decisions they could make. One was to have no play, that is, to cancel it altogether. However, that would cause a lot of suffering for those involved, especially for the students. They would feel betrayed. The other easy decision would be to have the play but to disregard Carol. This would satisfy the kids but it would professionally wound Carol. Arts people identify themselves and their programs with the products produced. Carol would lose this achievement. Ruth explained that it was not ego gratification so much as it was an expression of self on the line. Either solution would be easy, either would hurt someone a lot. A third alternative was to have the play continue, but have Carol appoint a neutral school-based coordinator to whom she would give one last set of instructions and then she would divorce herself from it, however, retaining the title of director. The department head complained that this was no decision but Ruth was tough and said on the contrary, all views had been weighed and the best possible for all concerned (though all will suffer some) had been resolved. The department head seemed to feel he should do the lighting because he always had. Carol refused because he never attended rehearsals. So, when he complained to Ruth, she asked him if he had attended rehearsals. When he said no, she told him he would have received plans if he had. Since he was not there, he chose not to participate. Ruth told me she then spoke to the substitute teacher. She had been told by the principal to take over and so she did. She was a young highly qualified drama teacher. Ruth told her she had the challenge of her career awaiting her this month. She would have to bring the play to successful completion in one week and then take no credit for it. If she could do that, it would immediately place her as an exceptional candidate for a job....After returning to the office, since he had to leave early, the principal phoned Ruth to hear how the meeting had ended. I overheard Ruth say: "Decisions are easy if you don't mind the fall out. After twenty years in this, you learn a lot of diplomacy. I know these people— their programs are visible." Ruth told me she would see Carol that night. If she had felt Carol would not agree to a coordinator, Ruth would have suggested backing out. She also told me no decision will satisfy all parties—rather find one that everybody will be a little satisfied with. Ruth said Carol is passionate for the play and has invested interest, therefore it is hard for her to let it go. I told Ruth I found it interesting that in a problem-solving situation she would give a little to a lot but in her implementation situations she would give a lot to a few. She said she saw the two as complementary because she worked from the parable, the sower of the seeds. At that point, she described the parable—a sower cast seeds on stony ground, then on desert ground, then on fertile ground. Ruth feels she gives everyone opportunities but she only responds to those who decide they want to change. Once they do then she will give as much as she can to them to support their growth (FD 46, 254–259).

Ruth freely admits she is not afraid to insult peers (FD 43, 240), nor afraid to make a decision right or wrong, for she is not in a popularity contest (FD 43, 238). A university professor reinforces this notion in regard to Ruth's ability to deal with other people's emotions during certain situations.

> "For one thing she doesn't get bogged down with trivia or the manipulation of other people; some people can make situations strongly emotional and, I think, Ruth can cut through those things. I think she can keep the work efficient and effective, you know, without getting bogged down with other people's problems or unexpected interferences" (Inter 9, 5).

The associate superintendent of curriculum says "Ruth gives you the impression she shrugs off any tension and goes on" (Inter 12, 5). Perhaps it is her need to remain in control of the situation while remaining realistic. Sharon, her drama specialist, said:

> "At one point, I got very exasperated with something that Ruth was saying because she sounded so bureaucratic, whatever, and I said, 'but that's not fair.' She looked me in the eye and said, 'but life is not fair!'" (Inter 5, 3).

Ruth realizes that most people make decisions more on an intuitive sense than on rationality.

> "People make decisions; they think they are based upon reason and rationality, when really they are based upon an intuitive sense. It shows you cannot program people; above all, they resist that. That's the thing they will resist more than anything in the world" (Inter 1, 16).

Use of humor in situations.   One thing that I noticed often with Ruth was her use of humor, so much so that it seemed she used it as a matter of course, particularly with humorous stories. Usually, it loosened people up and it always brought home the reality of living, teaching, and learning. Several examples given to a group of Kodaly music teachers attending a talk she gave are:

> "I talked with a principal the other day who said, 'Our school is going to organize itself around the arts, the academics, and the athletics.' I said, 'I have news for you. The arts are academics.' 'Oh well, you know we don't see them as that, we see them in the aesthetic domain.' We had a very heated discussion. I mean I was sitting there with a Ph.D. and there's nothing more academic in this God's world than that (laughter). And he's telling me I belong in a separate category. And I said I didn't get this by standing up and dancing and singing" (laughter) (FO 4, 8).

"The behaviorists are now not in great favor but for years, and probably we still do, write behavioral objectives. I remember writing "The children shall..." but a little voice was always saying in the back of my head, "Yes, but they may not" (laughter) (FO 4, 11).

Summarizing, Ruth's situational knowledge is a very substantial context from which she operates. Her "colleagual model" is an image closely aligned with another image: "community." Both acknowledge teachers with dignity and respect. The first views people as coming before the program. Both are extended by the principle, "you want them to still feel ownership" even though some may leave her circle of colleaguality. In relation to subordinates, Ruth is careful when working with service people because she recognizes they have a tremendous power over those they work for. To do so, she respects their role in the organization and their needs as people.

Ruth recognizes the power of her own presence and is guided by an image that "everyone will always be delighted to see her." Again her respect and compassion for others becomes obvious. Perhaps her image of "love your neighbor" reinforces these images. She does not wish to have bureaucratic control but does exude a great deal of personal control of her own actions, emotions, and behaviors.

Ruth often took advantage of situations to influence decision-makers, or to cause teachers to reflect upon their practice. She also used problem-solving skills in particular situations. For instance, she has a practical principle of "I always have a plan for what I will do but those plans are always open to change after discussion"; also, a rule of practice, "to view a problem from all points of view before making a decision." Problem solving becomes an opportunity to define a problem from a wide perspective of alternate solutions, a process of approaching everything and "rising above the situation." In so doing, Ruth also uses decision-making skills in situations by trying to influence other's decisions as much as she could toward a favorable end. Even so, she recognizes the rule of practice "no decision will satisfy all parties, rather find one that everybody will be a little satisfied with." This is consonant with her image of "the parable of the sower of seeds." Finally, Ruth often used humor in situations, either to loosen people up or to bring home the reality of living, teaching, and learning.

Ruth's situational knowledge context is also linked with her views found in her social knowledge context.

Social Knowledge Context: The Act of Raising Consciousness

Ruth's social knowledge context is portrayed through her social views and women's issues.

Social views.   Reflecting upon Ruth's apparent academic and intellectual bias in her personal biography might suggest a certain social class status. Though her closest friends and professional associates refer to her as Ruth, all of her memorandums and letters are referenced to Ruth Britten Ph.D. With strangers, or on formal occasions, she referred to herself as Dr. Britten. Each way was approached honestly and with political integrity toward the circumstance and the social setting. Yet her valuing of the academic did not suggest that only those who had acquired such knowledge were better. She viewed life as a series of opportunities from which everyone could learn.

Ruth was cognizant of the schools in her district as having varying socio-economic backgrounds, and of their apparent social class affiliations. During one school visit to an upper-middle class school, she contrasted it to the schools in an area of the city in which she lived for seventeen years "where it was multi-ethnic and thus, varied considerably in all aspects. The schools there were not like the ones here—the kids were not academically interested" (FD 16, 92). The latter was an area of the city in which she began her teaching career in Mountainview. When offered positions in either a high socioeconomic or a low socioeconomic area, she choose the latter by following her practical principle "because I could give more to them" (FD 48, 282). Learning to Ruth was not knowledge acquisition so much as it was a process available to everyone. However, she did have a rule of practice that "there are times you have to spoon feed them."

Ruth not only had insights into the social class structure within the city but she also was well aware of the authoritarianism attached to the school district bureaucracy. Nevertheless she upheld her own values. With the push from senior administration for principals and thus teachers to provide long range plans early in the school year, Ruth aligned herself with a teacher perspective, even though she provided the administration with what they wanted.

> "I have been in a classroom recently where a teacher could not teach art, but had to supply the principal with a long-range plan. I said, 'Relax! I will write one for you.' The teacher said, 'But I can't teach this....So I said, 'But don't worry about this, it's all they want....I'll help you throughout the year...there are times you have to spoon feed them....' I have sympathy for teachers...they teach eleven subjects..." (IO 7, 3).

Ruth has insights into the school system bureaucracy but these are tempered with her need to establish a particular environment. A setting in which teachers were viewed with dignity, and with an understanding of how people come to change. She would protect them if necessary and offer them hope for the future. Often this hope was manifested in the form of celebrations. For example, after a series of budget cutbacks and the devastating blow everyone at the Centre felt as a result, Ruth turned the situation around by looking at it in the most positive light possible; she created an appreciation night for all those who had contributed to the Centre over the years.

"So in June we chose to celebrate our accomplishments in our Centre rather than mourn. I find it difficult to work with people who have negative attitudes. I also find it difficult to work where the atmosphere is negative" (Inter 1, 3).

Women's issues.   Probably the greatest single social issue raised with Ruth was her view of women in society and especially as fulfilled professionals. This was captured in her form of leadership detailed in chapter 2. Prefacing this form of leadership was a deep affiliation with other women. Most of her contacts in the system were with other women, perhaps a result of more women in art(s) teaching roles (Inter 12, 15), or perhaps a result of her deep abiding interest in their well-being. The following excerpt illustrates her relationship with women during a period of just one morning.

> Our next stop was St. Catharines. When we arrived, the whole school was in the gym singing some songs lead by Marie who was at the Fine Arts Centre last year. Ruth went up to the principal (female) and spoke with her quietly while the children sang. Once the children were to go off to their rooms, Ruth sat down beside Marie at the piano and they hugged one another. Again, Ruth spoke quietly. Once most of the children had left the gym, Marie stopped playing the piano and they walked off together arm in arm. Marie took us to see the music room....I did not go in because...the two of them seemed so bonded....On our way out, Ruth said that the principal had been a strong public supporter of the arts. I recalled noticing that the principal had been very warm to Ruth. It was obvious that a strong relationship existed between them in the past. We immediately went to Catholic Central High School to see the fine arts department head. Ruth said she makes a point of seeing the department heads specifically in order to invite them to special events or meetings. She feels they are not department heads in name only, for they have status. This female teacher had been offered an assistant principalship last year but declined because it involved also teaching the entire music program. She didn't feel she could do both. Ruth was concerned she lost her chance. Ruth wanted more people in administration with an arts background. Ruth also felt women tend to look at positions not for what they can make them into but for what they are presently, whereas men take on positions and make them into what they want (FD 16, 98).

More fundamentally, it was her view of herself as a woman in management. Until several years ago, she was the only woman supervisor in the central office. She had applied for the position of superintendent of curriculum but was not selected. It was, from her viewpoint, decided ahead of time who would receive the promotion. Two other people I interviewed brought up the system's inability to recognize her talents and expertise through promotion. When they were asked to comment on what strengths Ruth had in dealing with senior administration, respectively, a principal and a fellow supervisor commented:

Principal: I would say she has tremendous ability and capacity to perhaps do a great deal more than she is doing in our central office structure....She's also a woman. I think that in our district we're not well known for promoting women into high positions which is unfortunate because Ruth Britten has had the paper qualifications for...a long, long time and there have been positions that have opened up over time that could have used the kinds of personal skills Ruth has (Inter 13, 4 - 5).

Supervisor: Well, I think they know her, they know her abilities very well. They respect her ability. And sometimes, and again this is just a perception; this is just a perception on my part. I sometimes think that the senior administrators do not take her as seriously as they should; it may have to do with her being a woman. Now, I'm just perceiving that. She's articulate and she's vocal and it may (pause) sometimes ruffle feathers, male feathers.

Researcher: Do you have any women in senior administration?

Supervisor: No, we don't. In fact that has been one of her criticisms, that there should be some women in senior administration. She's certainly very involved, and enough of a feminist but not in the sense that, there's all degrees of feminists, she's certainly not a fanatic feminist, but, I think, sometimes the male ego may be touched by that (Inter 10, 4).

Ruth's social knowledge, in summary, draws upon two categories. The first is her recognition of the differences between various socioeconomic backgrounds and the subsequent differences between schools having children from several social class affiliations. Though this knowledge was not obvious, it became more obvious as she recognized other's needs for social status. She herself did not seek such status.

Ruth was also concerned with women's issues. She held a deep affiliation with other women, and tried to raise their level of consciousness concerning women as professionals, their rights, circumstances, and special abilities. Much of this was a result of her own strengths and struggles as a woman in a man's world.

This leads us to the next section that describes the political knowledge context Ruth acquired as a supervisor. The data suggest this orientation is a major difference from a teacher's practical knowledge.

Political Knowledge Context: The Powers of Motivation, Persuasion, and Participation

The political knowledge context is categorized in two ways: her image of the system as having a life of its own, and how she is not interested in the power of authority. Though it will not be repeated here, other context areas of her practical knowledge, such as the situational knowledge context, have strong political overtones.

The system has a life of its own.   The political context is a reality which Ruth cannot ignore. She is bound by it as a result of her position. She neither has the power associated with line authority, nor does she possess the power of autonomy associated with teachers in the classroom. She believes her power is derived through expertise of subject matter and pedagogy led by powers of persuasion, motivation, and participation (FD 6, 48). But this power is precarious when compared to the power and control of administration. In order for her to exercise the unique power granted her within her role as supervisor, she must first of all be aware of the cultural and political reality surrounding and influencing her (FD 6, 46). After all, the image of "the school system has a life of its own" provides stability. Through a political orientation, Ruth works within that structure (FD 2, 12).

> "If you come on the job as a consultant or supervisor, you must be very aware of what the system environment is. You must know who are the people to whom you report, what is their position, how much flexibility you have, how much of your job is rigid, how do they treat people, what are the ways you can deliver, what are the ways you can deliver your power and so on" (Inter 3, 2–3).

Lack of interest in bureaucratic power.   When, in one interview, Ruth was asked what she felt were some attributes of politicians and whether or not she ever felt like a politician, she answered:

> "... politician simply means, you know, it comes from, polis, the people. Now a politician is someone who is skillful in organizing and representing people. Now when we use the word now, we usually use it in the pejorative sense...we have a sense that it is insincere, that they are acting for popularity or reasons other than truth or passion or relief or conviction. They are responding to the will of the people more than they are responding to their own conviction about the way things should be. If I had a leader who said, 'I voted even though I didn't believe it, or I voted so I could vote with the majority,' I'd think that's a political decision. What motivated that action was not an intense belief in the object under consideration. What motivated it was an intense desire to stay in power. So I think what we call a lot of political decisions are selfish. And I think that at many times, that's what marks the politician, it is a love affair with the self. It's unfortunate because it's a perfectly good word. But it has come to mean that. The reason it has come to mean that is that some politicians make empty promises to people. They play upon people's baser instincts and their emotions so that they can stay in power. Therefore, it has a lot to do with their own needs, and that's what I mean about energy going inward is then nonproductive...I hope, in the good sense, I am a politician since I take the

people—the people being the teachers, the clients—I take them into consideration so in that sense I am a politician. I am a politician also in the sense I will try to work within the system to accomplish what I need to accomplish, not for my own power but for the needs of the programs and the programs I serve. It would be fool hardy on my part, I would accomplish nothing were I to take a stand, the white lady on the white horse charging through the district and telling everybody off. Because, you see, of course, this would be bizarre. I don't have any corner on knowledge, power, or anything any more than anybody else. I am no better or worse than any other of my colleagues. What I have is a very clear vision of what I want our programs to be, and I also have a somewhat clear vision of how I can accomplish that. It's in the how I accomplish that, that I am a politician. I am sure that I follow the rules, the protocol. I make sure I don't undercut my colleagues. I make sure that I don't run around Ron and go higher. I don't lobby the school board. I play it straight. So everybody has to be political in that sense…but that just means the arena of the people" (Inter 14, 5–7).

Ruth's rule of practice to follow protocol was mentioned on many occasions throughout the study (FD 2, 12), and even though this was essentially the case, there were instances of lobbying if it would mean accomplishing her goal (FD 53, 293).

"I will do intense lobbying, subversive and every other kind, legitimate, of course, I won't go outside the structures, but I will certainly do anything I possibly can to influence their decisions about Barbara" (Inter 14, 14).

During a conversation with an ex-central office associate superintendent, Ruth said that she would continue her subversive activity in order to keep the Centre and her staff (FD 54, 297). Ruth's art specialist referred to Ruth as being diplomatic, and perhaps she was, but to Ruth, it was more a matter of realizing that people do not act on reason alone and so she would have to be cognizant of any variables that might affect their decisions (FD 53, 293). And even though she believed in following protocol, if the opportunity arose, Ruth would take advantage of the situation. A good example of this was her lobbying for a teachers' aide to assist at the Centre since they had lost all secretarial staff during the budget cutbacks. She inquired through her associate superintendent of curriculum to no avail. By chance, one day, she met the superintendent of personnel and asked to talk with him about a staffing concern. She returned afterwards and told her associate superintendent what she had done and what he said. Essentially, she had been told there simply wasn't any money available and was encouraged to make use of volunteers. Ruth was disappointed in the outcome but was determined to correct the situation at the Centre and said she would follow through with securing volunteers (FD 33, 183). Within a matter of a few days, she received a memorandum saying funding had in fact been found for a halftime teacher's aide. Ruth surmised that the fact that she had gone to the superintendent of personnel bothered her immediate supervisor or associate superintendent of curriculum and so he worked harder to find her the money (FD 34, 186).

Much of Ruth's knowledge that is held in a political context is integrated with her situational knowledge. For instance, Ruth said she would supply extra materials on the "black market" for the Fine Arts School, since they needed so many consumable supplies and had so little funding (FD 7, 43).

> On another occasion, Ruth personally referred to inviting principals to have their schools participate in a project rather than sending around a memo and hoping they would participate. In doing so, she was using her rule of practice of "do not leave anything to chance" (FD 56, 320).

In many other instances it was obvious that Ruth lacked interest in bureaucratic control (FD 5, 35). She wanted fewer regulations (FD 14, 82), and would even advise teachers to ignore some rules if she felt they were unnecessary (IO 3, 1). The system's need for control was highlighted one day when she metaphorically related the mandated report writing from the administrative council to an image of a "procrustean bed":

> She explained to me that Procrustes was a king in the ancient world who had a daughter to be married. Because he had a bed, all the suitors had to fit the bed or their limbs were cut down. This was a metaphor for situations when someone tries to fit everything into a model (FD 54, 301).

Ruth was uninterested in bureaucratic control herself, but she recognized the need to have people in administrative positions who were sympathetic to the arts.

> Ruth said, "What you don't know, you don't see." Therefore, principals without a background would not understand the significance of arts programs. Ruth suggested that the others (her team) should seek administration if they were interested. She wanted arts people in administration (FD 1, 6–7).

A junior high art teacher summarizes Ruth's political inclinations and leads us into her personal knowledge context.

> "She's a politician and a poet. And she's an artist all the way. So, she can sell you on even something you don't know how to do or can't do; she will sell you motivationally, and give you the best PR job; she makes you feel that you can do it. That's a real talent" (Inter 8, 8).

Perhaps this is a summary of her powers of motivation, powers of persuasion, and powers of participation. Her way of having a vision, yet knowing how to bring people around to take ownership for their own change in that direction.

In review, Ruth views the political context through an image of "the system has a life of its own." She realizes her power in the system is neither associated with line authority, nor the power of autonomy associated with teachers in classrooms. Rather, she possesses a power of expertise in subject matter and pedagogy led by the powers of persuasion, motivation, and participation. To work within the system, she also recognizes her lack of interest in the power of authority, that power associated with bureaucratic control. She has strong ethical beliefs and will follow protocol as much as possible, except, of course, when subversive lobbying for causes is necessary. For the most part, Ruth wanted fewer regulations and even counseled teachers to ignore some rules if she felt they were unnecessary. Her image associated with the administrative council who needed to fit rules into models, was that of the "procrustean bed."

If Ruth held characteristics of a politician, she also held characteristics of a poet and an artist, which may be aligned with a personal knowledge context.

Personal Knowledge Context: The Courage of One's Convictions.

Ruth's personal knowledge context is illustrated in terms of how she views reason and passion, the courage of her convictions, and the need for heuristic ability which comes from experience.

Reason and passion. Ruth uses her practical knowledge to give meaning to her work as supervisor. Much of this meaning is derived from her understanding of the dialectical relationship between thought and feeling, or reason and passion. An image of "knowledge feeds passion" links the relationship between these two and summarizes Ruth's words and actions:

> "I think that given our biological structures we can never divorce reason from feeling or passion if you wish to call it that. Indeed, it's passion that activates reason. You want to find reasons for doing what you're doing. You see, reason will lead you but so will passion so those two things are not separate. If you had a passion for music, the passion would draw your knowledge. Way back in the thirteenth century Thomas Aquinas said, 'knowledge is perfected by will,' meaning that if you do not love what you want, knowledge doesn't go anywhere. You don't do anything with what you know. So I have come to believe that you don't even know something if you don't have the will for it....I think that knowledge feeds passion. All I'm talking about is intense interest that causes you to put your energies out in a self-forgetful way....Now more times than not that is engaged by someone else we have touched. I came across that university professor my first year of university and she had a passion for learning. She was a philosophy professor and in her class, I came to life. She empowered me to be a seeker of truth and a seeker of knowledge and to have a thirst for knowing" (Inter 14, 3–5; Irwin, 1992, p. 114).

Ruth goes on to say, "anything you do with passion is powerful. The power of science, the power of learning. Anything that claims you passionately" (Inter 14, 1). To her, the principle of "passion is powerful," is a will to create, an energy causing one to be moved, to believe, and to learn. It is consistent with purpose. I overheard Ruth talking with the principal of the Fine Arts Alternative School when the principal was complaining about her so-called passionate staff that week. Ruth was quick to point out that she was passionate but not emotional and that was a distinct difference (IO 9, 5). To be emotional was to place more emphasis on feeling than on thought, though the two were always together (FD 47, 266), (FO 4, 7).

Courage of convictions.   Ruth stands by her beliefs and is not afraid to make decisions, even if it means she may make a mistake. She has an image of herself, namely, "I have great courage about my convictions...I'm not afraid to make decisions...I'd rather make a few mistakes than be too cautious and never do anything" (FD 5, 30). This courage of her convictions is implicit in her belief in the human being. In talking about her Fine Arts Centre team, she spoke about her trust in them, and in so doing, she made it possible for them to demonstrate their interest in their work, their dedication to the profession, their loyalty to her as a leader, and their support of one another. They, in turn, would trust her as she demonstrated her interest in her work, her dedication to the profession, her loyalty to her team, and her support of their programs. Loyalty to each other was not overtly demonstrated but implicit in everything they would do (FD 43, 241).

> If you give people power to make decisions, you have to support those decisions. In other words, take risks with people, but you know and trust people. A supervisor has to establish a climate of mutual trust—you have to trust your clients—they have to trust you (FD 43, 238).

As a rule of practice, she believed one should "take risks with people." Ruth's beliefs were grounded in positive thinking (IO 5, 1). She doesn't want to waste any energy on dislike, hatred or bitterness. "Instead of thinking negatively, think pink" (FD 5, 35). Mutual trust and positive thinking was confirmed many times as I spoke to others and they shared with me their relationship with Ruth (FD 43, 239), (Inter 6, 2), (Inter 4, 13).

Heuristic ability comes from experience.   Ruth believes that the need for heuristic abilities sets her role as supervisor aside from other roles. To her, it means an accumulated amount of experiential knowledge, the ability to take risks, and to try different things. It is also an ability to have accurate hunches.

> "Success in jobs like this can be attributed to heuristic ability. I've got a lot of that. Heuristic ability comes from experience and learning on the job....That's why I don't believe in change for the sake of change. I would change people (in positions) if I observed they were not developing such abilities and if they

were bogged down in detail and couldn't handle new things and just kept repeating the same patterns of operations over, and over, and over again. Heuristic ability enables one to take a risk, to do something different, to have accurate hunches, to have an intuitive sense of what can work....one of the things about a job like mine or any job, consultant or supervisor in a school district, is the fact that these people have no specific training for the job. Usually they're picked because they've been good classroom teachers. Doesn't always hold that they will become good as consultants or supervisors. It's quite a different operation entirely, but the best you can guess is that if the person has been a good classroom teacher they have some sense of the dynamics of the teaching act and so they should get a chance. But there's no training for it; there's no university courses that I know of that prepare people for jobs like this. It's just get in there and through your own native intelligence and the seat of your pants, get going and try some" (Inter 2, 5).

In summary, much of Ruth's personal knowledge context is grounded in her understanding of the dialectical relationship between thought and feeling, or reason and passion. She believes "knowledge feeds passion," and passion empowers learning. To her, "passion is powerful." These images and principles express an energy, a will to create, to believe, to learn. Passion would, therefore, also make the difference between a successful and an unsuccessful supervisor or consultant.

Ruth also has great courage of her convictions, an image that allows her not to be afraid to make decisions. In so doing, she empowered others to demonstrate interest in their work, dedication to their profession, and loyalty to leader. She was not afraid to take risks with people, because she knew and trusted people. Mutual trust penetrated much of what she did.

Ruth also believed that heuristic abilities were of great importance to consultants and supervisors. To her, heuristic abilities came from experience on the job combined with the ability to take risks and to try different things. It is an ability to have accurate hunches.

All of the contexts considered so far are linked to Ruth's experiential knowledge context.

Experiential Knowledge Context: The Rhythms of Life.

Much of Ruth's practical knowledge is dominated by dichotomies. In regard to her role as a supervisor between teachers and administrators, she wrestles between order and disorder. Neither of them is ever singularly dealt with: each remains in a tension of consciousness as she works through the dynamics of her role. This tension is manifested in two qualities of her lived experience: temporal and spatial. Both have aesthetic qualities for Ruth while at the same time serving instrumental functions.

Temporal perspective.   First of all, Ruth is led by an image of "time is the greatest gift of all." Ruth spoke of a close friend who once worked at the center.

She did some kind things for her and her mother. To this Ruth said, "time is the greatest gift of all" (FD 61, 336).

Ruth uses a temporal perspective ion many areas of her knowledge. It is a way of defining her experience, confining it to the here and now, or viewing it more intuitively, plus placing faith in the nature of time itself. The first significant conception of time within the temporal perspective deals with the nature of working within a bureaucracy which forces certain time constraints and thus, a time management orientation. Ruth was aware of using her time efficiently, as could be noticed, for she clustered her school visits around the city (FD 16, 92), wrote memorandums while talking or waiting on the phone (FD 22, 122), and dedicated early morning office time to returning and making phone calls (FD 15, 83). She was careful to remind her staff about using their time efficiently, regarding work related tasks appropriate to their roles rather than to secretarial duties (FD 1, 2). She was obviously aware of this whole notion, with the amount of attention it was given in the course she taught for music supervisors (Document 6). Time management there was treated as it reflected three levels of tasks within her role. The first dealt with those tasks and functions central to her role, such as school visits, staff development activities, budget preparation and administration, personal professional development, and developing curriculum materials. The second level dealt with any other tasks she would need to perform such as, attending administrative meetings, report writing, collecting information, and writing proposals to secure funding. The third level would include anything that would get in the way of the other two. For instance, meetings she was expected to attend of which she had no real part, last minute requests from administrators, too many useless reports, correspondence, or memos, interruptions from staff, phone calls, or clerical chores, and finally, no time to plan for the first two sections previously listed. Consciously choosing the best use of one's time given certain circumstances, was significant.

Ruth recognizes her own limitations and is conscious of her own time management. An apt example emerged during a situation in which the associate superintendent and Ruth were working on writing a proposal for the Fine Arts School extension into Junior High, and with only a week left before the due date, he backed out and gave her the task. Ruth said she would do it instead of...rather than in addition to....She is very concerned about controlling the situation; she does not want to burn out. She is conscious of teachers flagging, and so she is very conscious of her own time management (FD 45, 252).

Ruth compares her time frame in her role as supervisor to that of teachers, saying:

> "One immense advantage about working in this program is by and large the control of time. The fact that we work from 7:00 A.M. in the morning to 10:00 P.M. at night is our own foolishness in some ways. We do it ourselves. Nobody

is demanding we do it. However, there is no let up at all for the classroom teacher" (Inter 2, 14).

Ruth's knowledge of time management was also shared with her staff, not only in her giving them a day organizer at the beginning of the year (FD 1, 8), but also in her recommendations towards taking personal time and intellectual time during their busy schedules.

> Ruth talks about getting her group to slow down, or to take some personal time to read...."You must realize teachers get professional time...take some time to bring energy in...so it's time management...you need to take intellectual time to grow...book some time for yourself like Monday morning or Tuesday afternoon (IO 5, 1).

Ruth does not mind and follows the rule of "working from dawn to dusk Monday to Thursday, but Friday night, Saturday and Sunday are my own" (IO 5, 4). Though this appeared to be a rule of practice, it was in fact not always followed as choir performances, Christmas concerts, writing speeches, and other tasks and functions of her role stole her personal time.

A second conception of time centered upon the rhythms of her role and teachers' roles, for each day, month, and year, and on occasion, even longer periods of time. Ruth is careful not to overbook each day, allowing time to reflect before and after each meeting (FD 2, 13). This might be considered a small rhythm within other larger counter rhythms. After three weeks into the school term, Ruth told me this was the end of the first cycle. When she finished with those teachers who requested her assistance the first week of school (FD 12, 59), she allowed herself to remain on call and later, as these lessened, schedule visitations to the schools (FD 2, 13). Other cycles were borne out of more specific interactions with the schools such as newsletters going out every two months (FD 5, 27) or a practical principle that she "never visited principals before the middle of October, because they had too many variables to deal with" (FD 6, 47), or that new schools need a year to get on their feet (FD 14, 78). The imagery of "cycles in the school year" were evident.

She also recognized and encouraged recognition of cycles with her team. Overall, she felt Ann's "implementation of the new art program in twenty-one schools was a wonderful model of time management" (Inter 3, 14). However, in looking at Ann's logbook, Ruth commented, "my opinion will be that in November and December you gear down and try to complete one cycle by October, November...sometime in these cycles I will start joining up with you. I want to give principals an implementation statement" (FD 5, 32). Though it was not in the scope of this study to reflect upon the implementation of the new curriculums over time, Ruth talked about the months ahead in regard to her services to the schools. Usually, they were a reflection of the rhythms of the school year, although some would be made toward the upcoming school year (FD 46, 261). One particular yearly cycle was the evaluation of the implementation schedule by participating teachers at the end of the year (Inter 11, 1). On an even larger scale, Ruth was aware of a twenty year cycle: things have returned to the way they were twenty years ago when she began as supervisor (FD 2, 13).

Other conceptions might not be considered so much as cycles as they were an acceptance of the necessity of allowing time for human change and growth. Educational change is a slow process (FD 15, 85) yet Ruth had definite notions about how long it would take to change people's behavior, whether it be as a new consultant, or for a generalist teacher, to feel competent teaching a subject. For each it would take three years (Inter 2, 5), (IO 1, 3), (Inter 1, 8), (FD 2, 15). She was particularly frustrated with the dilemma most consultants were in and it is compounded by her belief and experiential knowledge that educational change requires considerable time and effort (Inter 3, 3). The image of "tending a garden" was used to describe the time needed to change people. When asked about the difficulties neophyte consultants experience, she said:

"They usually have ambitions to see change in a short time. It takes a long, long time. It's more like tending a garden than anything....It's a slow growth process, which also presents a problem for these jobs [which are] short term contracts. Short terms contracts in consultant jobs have so much frustration built into them. The first year on the job, because you don't usually have prior training...you don't have any internship, and you don't have any practice, you just have to get in there and start working it out. It usually takes you an entire year to find out how you're going to begin to operate. Then the second year you begin to become effective and you're working for change and then you're gone. A lot of school districts are trying to put consultants on two year terms. My reaction to that would be, don't bother, don't bother at all. Because in two years you cannot do anything except frustrate the consultant and the people with whom the consultant might be working" (Inter 3, 3–4; Irwin, 1992, p. 113–114).

"On the other hand, it takes at least, at least three years for the person to begin to hit her stride" (Inter 2, 6). Unfortunately, with budget cutbacks, this experiential knowledge was ignored, and Ruth had to put a three year implementation cycle in place which meant every school was given special attention for only one year during the cycle (FD 4, 22). She was desperately fighting to keep her music consultant whose contract was expiring after a renewed three-year term.

In regard to the creation of art, she again refers to a temporal perspective when she said:

"Nobody whips off a painting. One person asked an artist once how long his very expensive painting took him to paint. He said two hours but it also took thirty years of preparation. Sometimes I will paint ten or twenty sketches for a painting. Sometimes I will paint for a long time and only save a few..." (FO 2, 4).

Ruth has another understanding of time. One which speaks to an image of "the rhythms of life," to understanding what it means to be human.

The rhythms of life you see, mark time for us. And time itself is a structure of duration and pattern. Consequently, natural events, while they are not thought, they are the foundation of thought. We can't escape them. Our minds play over and against them. Now music is the essential art of time. Music creates for us, using very complex rhythmic patterns, both the illusion of movement and the shape of time (FO 4, 6).

"Rhythm is a felt phenomenon. It's part of our existence, the tide, the seasons, the changes from light to dark, heartbeats, waves, all testify to the commonness of recurring events. The intuitive person structures his events according to rhythms that are meant not only to be felt as a natural occurrence, but also to be understood as mental rhythms in life. We must always remember that music is heard by the intelligence. We realize that biological rhythms are significant to us only when we introduce elements of order, causality....To illustrate, consider the heartbeat. We can't do much intellectually about that. Its constant beat, its ebb and flow, its constant interval that sustains life goes on without knowing. But its beats are the background against which our lives are played out....Consider then the rhythms of the natural world, for example, take a breaking wave. Each wave is a new event that is predicted by the previous one. The rise and fall are expected. But what of energy and the subsequent release that marks the essence of rhythmic pattern. That gathering of energy and that release, tension and release, expectation and fulfillment. That's what constitutes a rhythmic pattern. Now if we want to make experience significant, we try to capture the essential element of tension, release, and recurrence, to make a structure that mirrors these internal events and so allows us to participate intellectually in a phenomenon that marks our very existence, and indeed the existence of all that surrounds us" (FO 4, 5).

Perhaps it is in this rhythm that Ruth is most sensitive to other people and to the events surrounding her role as a supervisor. She is aware of another image:

Everyone has rhythms. Some of her people like Barbara keep getting better every year, because that's her rhythm. Some others on the other hand have lasted at the Centre only two to four years because their rhythm was that they had done all they could or wanted to in that role for that time period. They needed a change and so they moved on (FD 16,101).

Ruth was also sensitive to the notion of celebration, and includes on a yearly rhythm, several celebrations that her team looks forward to (FD 62, 344), as if to admit to another form of tension, release, and recurrence.

Spatial perspective.   Perhaps the best way to begin this section is to refer to a story Ruth shared with a group of curators at a local gallery. It addresses the idea that we all have a landscape of images directing us and they are derived from their context in our personal and cultural history.

"In the 1940s, four boys went on a treasure hunt...preparation included taking ropes, lunches...they came upon a hole of an uprooted tree. One boy dropped a stone in the hole...and discovered the bottom was not far away...here was an accessible instance...the twentieth century minds landed in the Great Hall of Lascaux. Hundreds of painting of horses and other animals in all positions... dying, young, old...art historians view that experience as significant. There was a creative explosion...that cave provided for the young boys of that society a landscape of images. The culture depended upon an ability to hunt, a ritual...in the flickering light of the cave the boys could see images moving... impacting the survival of the culture. We all have landscapes of images...these images are energizing...if they are art, then your energizing is a contemplation or making of art...since we all have landscapes of images, then we do not have an innocent eye...if we understand the cultural context then we can enter the power of the work...the power of art resides in the image...image connected to a mental event...as educators we deal with not just the image but the mental event" (FO 3, 1 - 4).

It is in this notion of a "landscape of images" that Ruth's practical knowledge takes on a spatial perspective. She assumes she has many images from which she operates, believes, and appreciates. Much of her language is couched with concrete images, analogies, or metaphors illustrating abstract concepts (FD 11, 57). The role of supervisor itself is experienced through several images. "The parable of the sower of seeds" portrays someone constantly giving, encouraging, faithfully attending to the unseen and seen alike. The image of "the cactus club," however, portrays a solitary, lonely existence, surviving precarious situations and little nourishment. Yet both images demonstrate growth or implied growth. Another set of images portrays a similar dichotomy. The image of "community" suggests a circle of people all dynamically contributing to the well-being of each other, but the shadow world of the bureaucracy portrays a nonhuman, unreal existence that nags at reality. It is in her need to resolve these different forces that Ruth integrates her experiences and arrives at a certain tension of consciousness.

Tension of consciousness.   Tension of consciousness (Schutz and Luckmann 1973) is that level of attentiveness Ruth brings to her experience, and is demonstrated in the variety and quantity of considerations given attention in certain situations. Examples of this may be found throughout the data, where a variety of viewpoints needed to be coordinated. A critical example is her concern for bureaucratic order and her role as an individual encouraging disorder. Given certain situations, she would provide one or the other, or a compromise of both. At other times, her experience as a practising artist helped her identify with classroom art experiences or the artist-teacher in a school setting. This would provide an outlet for her concern for the integrity of the artistic process and might cause concern for the value of the school art activity, or the value of teacher developed programs over the art curriculum. Ruth's attention to the individual needs of teachers before the program, accounts for much of her imagery of community, mentoring, and following passion. Yet, her desired goal is the eventual implementation of the curriculum.

In summary, Ruth's experiential knowledge context is constructed according to a tension of consciousness manifested in two qualities of her lived experience: temporal and spatial. Both have aesthetic and instrumental qualities.

Ruth views the temporal perspective, or time, as "the greatest gift of all." She realizes the importance of time. Of significance, is the importance she places on time management in her role. It is a conception that needs to be balanced with her personal and intellectual time.

Ruth also views the temporal perspective from an aesthetic viewpoint. She perceives rhythms and cycles for her role and individual teachers, as well as for certain months and seasons. The image of "cycles in the school year" guides some of the interactions with teachers and principals. But she also recognized that educational change is a slow process, as if "tending a garden." Coupled with the image of "the rhythms of life," Ruth understood human needs and patterns during educational change.

Ruth's spatial perspective acknowledged the notion that everyone has a "landscape of images" and for her, this meant a distinct difference from those held by administrators. Her imagery is based upon many spatial metaphors. For instance, the "parable of the sower of seeds" portrays a supervisor constantly giving, encouraging, faithfully casting seeds to the unseen and seen alike. The image of "community" suggests a circle of people all contributing. Her tension of consciousness between the temporal and spatial perspectives is that level of attentiveness Ruth creates from these perspectives. Ruth's experiential knowledge context was the last of six context categories explored relative to her practical knowledge.

SUMMARY

Ruth's practical knowledge is influenced by or held in the context of six different conceptions: theoretical, situational, social, personal, political, and experiential. Although the notion of a political orientation or knowledge context was only briefly considered in light of the political implications of a teacher's personal practical knowledge (Elbaz 1981), it is included here as it emerged from the data as a significant context in which Ruth operates. It not only addresses the issue of bureaucratic power and control, but the cycle of colleagual power and empowerment. Much of Ruth's role as supervisor forces her to resolve the conflicts embedded in these opposing views.

Ruth's practical knowledge comes alive as the content is brought to bear upon a variety of contexts simultaneously. Through a repertoire of experiences, Ruth has located rules of practice, practical principles, and images, that illustrate at a point in time, the evolution of her practical knowledge.

Chapter 5
Ruth in Educational Change

To discuss the findings of the case study of Ruth, it is important to answer the guiding research questions but it is also important to relate the findings to current literature in an attempt to further understand Ruth in her role. In this way, one may appreciate Ruth's practice and the contradictions inherent in her role. Such an analysis will more completely provide an overview of her practical knowledge, how it was constructed, and how her style as a supervisor may be portrayed relative to Favaro's model (1984). I will relate the findings through a review of descriptive literature conceptualizing power in two ways: power over others versus sharing power with others. This will be followed by a brief review of research in curriculum implementation. These areas of analysis represent theoretical dimensions most appropriate to the data collected. This will be followed by a section dealing with a discussion of Ruth's practical knowledge, illuminating the two opposing "landscapes of images," namely, teacher power and empowerment in educational change, and bureaucratic control and educational stability. The final section will interpret Ruth's style as a supervisor and explain how it may be a result of her personal biography or narrative unity. The conclusion will provide an overview of the answers to the research questions.

A DISCUSSION OF THE FINDINGS

Ruth's Practice: Power over Others versus Sharing Power with Others.

Many have criticized bureaucratic settings for their dehumanizing structures (Freire 1970 and 1973; Schon 1983; Kreisberg 1992; etc.) and have advocated personal and institutional transformation through liberation, distribution of power, and participatory practices which are committed to a mutual process of action and reflection. The predominant conception of power found in society may be viewed as power over others. This form of power is often conceived as influence or coercion. It is a causal relationship between the desires of one person being imposed upon another person.

Adrienne Rich (1976) is concerned with this notion of power over others as it perpetuates domination and control over the submissive and powerless in society. The powerful become separate entities from the powerless other, and in so doing, become free to ignore the other's feelings, experiences, and voices. As dialogue among people is dismissed, domination takes on even more control.

This dominant conception of power not only exists in society in general but also in educational practice. Donald Oliver and Kathleen Waldron Gershman (1989) detail how contemporary educational practice relies upon this form of power. Teachers typically control information, activities, and settings in such a way that causal relationships are prescribed. Students who have learned what the teacher has taught are rewarded through promotion. The influence of one person over another becomes predictable and controlled.

It is interesting to note that power has only recently become a concern of educators, particularly those concerned with critical and feminist pedagogy (Nyberg 1981; Luke and Gore 1992). They are concerned with an alternate form of power, that is, sharing power with others. They believe that the narrow conception of power over others is incomplete. Sharing power with others offers an alternate and perhaps more complete understanding of the concept of power. Seth Kreisberg (1992) suggests that in order to conceptualize sharing power with others we need to reexamine our taken-for-granted assumptions of existing dominant theories of power. For instance, power over others is filled with concepts such as compliance, fear, and conflict, while sharing power with others is often characterized through collaboration, community, and mutuality.

Jean Baker Miller (1976) discusses the concept of power in this way: "Power has generally meant the ability to advance oneself and simultaneously to control, limit and if possible destroy the power of others. Power so far has at least two components: power for oneself and power over others" (116). Miller is critical of this predominant notion of power and argues that there are ways of enhancing one's own personal power while increasing the power of others. Rather than beginning from a competitive arena where someone will win and another will lose, power is conceived as a renewable resource that is shared through cooperation, dialogue, and reflection. Miller is convinced that the conception of power over others is based upon male patterns of development that celebrate individual advancement and autonomy. She asserts that this conception of power should be replaced with the notion of having agency within a community. People within such a community would support the advancement of self but also the advancement of others. Her definition of power is highly appropriate to this study: power is "the capacity to produce change" (1982, p. 2). She goes on to suggest that women need the power to develop themselves rather than the power to limit or diminish the power of others to develop themselves.

Janet L. Surrey (1987) argues that sharing power with others is essentially empowering because people take response/ability within relationships. Individuals relate in a mutually empathetic way: through increased awareness of self and others each person is changed. The enthusiasm which ensues helps to create an environment which celebrates making connections through collaboration. Response/ability requires individuals to consider not only one's own interests but also the interests of others. Therefore, the concept of sharing power with others becomes guided by an openness to and with others which is manifested in principles of giving and receiving, caring for self and others, inclusion, nurturance, and creating community.

Implicit within this conception of sharing power with others is dialogue among individuals. Dialogue requires faith in people and in their power to create and recreate. It is therefore founded upon love, humility, and faith, in the midst of a relationship of mutual trust. Dialogue also, in the truest sense, cannot exist without critical thinking, that is, thinking which does not divide the world from people, which perceives reality as a process of transformation, and which does not separate itself from action. It is in this sense that people are in a constant search, "a search which can be carried out only in communion with other men" [*sic*] (Freire 1970, p.80). Leaders would not bring salvation, but would come to know through dialogue with others both their objective situation and their awareness of the situation. In essence, communion elicits cooperation. In almost evangelical style and language, communion brings cooperation through humility, empathy, love, and communication in order to be liberating.

Ruth's images of "love your neighbour," "community," "parable of the sower of the seeds," and "giving and receiving is a powerful cycle," all suggest communion with others in order to encourage response. They are further developed if one considers Ruth's numerous references to the "power of...," for instance, the power of participation or the power of art. More specifically, they are in unison with the teachings of the Catholic Church (Wojtyla 1981). Each speaks of the necessity of personal meaning within the closeness of a human community and each seeks the common good. Perhaps Ruth's charismatic nature is deeply and personally responsive to her Catholic ties. Nevertheless, she demonstrates an active relationship while in dialogue with everyone she meets in her role as supervisor.

The notion of dialogue is antithetical, however, to power structures which seek to control people's actions and thoughts. It is with this opposing power that Ruth, as a supervisor participating in educational change, finds herself face-to-face.

RUTH'S PRACTICE AS INTERPRETED THROUGH RESEARCH ON CURRICULUM IMPLEMENTATION

Paulo Freire (1970) describes the relationship between oppressors and the oppressed in ways that may be related to the bureaucratic power and control demonstrated over teachers and Ruth in her school district. One of the basic elements Freire suggests is that of prescription: imposing one's views upon another. As bureaucracy defines more and more prescriptions, fewer choices are made by teachers. Feelings of alienation and silent acceptance can contribute to a sense of powerless ability to transform one's reality. If concrete situations are to be transformed, a radical change of consciousness needs to occur in both parties.

This is compounded and understood through the metaphor referred to earlier as the producer-consumer metaphor that Werner (1987) used to explain two opposing views toward implementation. From a technological perspective, consumers are viewed as passive receivers, and it is the product, marketing, finances, or time which would be at fault if the implementation were not successful. This viewpoint serves administrative interest through greater control of implementation activities. In the case of curriculum implementation, people are taught how to carry out someone else's decisions on the assumption that the decisions are best for all concerned. It is an instrumentalist curriculum orientation, suggesting an ends-means rationality. Supervisors would be delivery agents, transmitting knowledge as if they were experts managing the production of a product for a consumer. Theory would be treated as factual and law-like.

In chapter 3, four types of theory and practice methods were examined. In this case study, there were occasions when senior administration employed the "logistical method" toward theory and practice, evaluating teachers according to the "effective schools" research. There were also times when Ruth was forced to apply the "problematic method" as she needed to act as a "curriculum manager" in problem solving and decision making, and occasionally applied the "operational method" as she tried to assess the needs of teachers. But overall, her concern was with accounting for theory and practice as theory-in-action and if theory and practice seemed incompatible, it was the theory rather than the practice that was deficient. In this way, the "dialectical method" is viewed as most appropriate in discussing the practical knowledge of Ruth.

As a consequence of this, Ruth sought to raise the consciousness of teachers in ways that brought them to realize they could transform their own realities. Learning was the responsibility of the learner. Commitment to change was the responsibility of the teacher. Ruth opened the window onto liberation through her evangelical character: one which emphasized the powers of participation, motivation, and persuasion; one which was also enveloped in trust, love, humility, and communication. In this way, Ruth was demonstrating the second type of metaphor Werner talks about: the colleagual metaphor. Implementation would not automatically occur because of someone else's prescription, nor in the way developer's necessarily intended. Through her "colleagual model" teacher interpretations would instead be a result of dialogue between teachers and supervisors, as their combined knowledge and experience were critically shared. In this way, teachers were given the power to define their own practice within particular classroom contexts: implementation as situational praxis (Aoki 1984).

Ruth's characteristics were not a result of her designated position in the hierarchy of central office. She considered the bureaucracy to be a "shadow world to the real world." Perhaps a metaphor for the dehumanizing, inauthentic character of a system of control. Ruth wanted to protect teachers from bureaucratic control, and sought through dialogue with senior administration to bridge their prescriptions through reference to the realities of the classroom. Nearly always this was met with resistance, and often, she was left with frustration. This did not stop her, however, from turning upon bureaucracy again and again. Through reflection upon her actions and the actions of those in bureaucratic power, she sought to transform others' consciousness of classroom realities. In effect, in many ways she felt like a victim of the bureaucracy, and so could legitimately offer teachers a model from which to operate as they could chose to liberate their own consciousness. Her conviction for change could not be packaged and sold. To be authentic would mean a totality of reflection and action occurring in her own involvement in reality, within a historical situation, which in turn would lead her to criticize reality and desire it to be changed.

Ruth continually questioned the bureaucracy and its endless policies toward regulatory power and control. She sought to empower the powerless but not at the expense of her "expertise" or ability to manage implementation efforts when necessary. In so doing, she maintained a precarious blending or a dialectical orientation to colleaguality and negotiation, and theory and practice in her efforts toward educational change.

Praxis, or the dialectical unity of theory and practice, is reflection and action upon the world in order to transform it. "In action oriented language, praxis is action done reflectively, and reflection on what is being done" (Aoki 1984, p.13). Reflection makes conscious the unconscious through the disclosure of underlying assumptions and intentions, it also seeks to determine the implications for action as a result of the newly gained critical knowing. Implementation then, should be interested in liberation of the teacher from hidden assumptions and intentions.

Although some authors may argue that teachers and administrators should align themselves with one paradigm, what the two studies presented here have uncovered is the need for supervisors to resolve dialectically the oppositions between the two extremes of bureaucratic power and control versus teacher power and empowerment, or, power over others versus sharing power with others. Therefore, root activities may include both colleaguality and control: a political context for negotiating between the roles of teacher and manager, the authority found within staff and line positions, and the power derived from teacher power and empowerment and bureaucratic power and control. Or as

Wayne K. Hoy and Cecil G. Miskel (1978) suggest, the conflict between "professional expertise and autonomy and bureaucratic discipline and control" (p. 113). If this is so, then using the operational, logistical, or problematic methods for studying theory and practice may be viewed as inadequate. The dialectical method would be considered more appropriate, more functional, and more encompassing of the parameters found within the role of Ruth as supervisor.

It is true that as one reads through the description of Ruth's practical knowledge one may come to apply the "linking roles" of resource finder, process helper, and solution giver as previously outlined in this document (Butler and Paisley 1978). One may also see signs of Ruth as a "curriculum manager" (Leithwood 1982) as she plans, organizes, coordinates, and controls certain aspects of implementation. But again, this form of delineation limits what we know as a result of this portrayal. Her knowledge contains more than fragments of management roles, functions, and skills.

Ruth's practical knowledge of curriculum implementation and educational change employs a knowledge of working with teachers and working with managers or administration. Ruth applied different strategies toward the two groups, for she recognized the strengths and weaknesses of both. For instance, her expertise was important from an administrative standpoint in that it gave her the responsibility of determining the "quality" of educational experiences for students. If in fact, teachers were unable to reflect upon their practice or had chosen inappropriate methods, her "expert" judgment and evaluation was brought into practice. It was her way, given her role, to control the quality of art education practices in her district. However, the primary emphasis from senior administration was for so much control that Ruth found it necessary to counteract these forces with more attention to the liberation of individual teachers. What this scenario may teach us is that "implementation as situational praxis," for instance, may be an ideal state while working with teachers, but it may not always be realistic. The supervisor needs to be able to do whatever it takes to bring about quality education for the students. One may conclude from this that a supervisor's practical knowledge will be founded upon numerous dialectical relationships, all essentially based upon order and disorder, control and facilitation, power and empowerment.

Recent research in the area of educational change supports this dialectical viewpoint. Fullan (1993) points out that "we have learned that neither central-ization (federal or state or district) nor decentralization (school) by itself works. We also see that reform strategies struggle between *overcontrol* and *chaos* (Pascale 1990)....Evidently, change is more complex than we realized" (p. 123–124). What is needed is the establishment of change cultures. All people become change agents who through the acts of collaboration and continuous improvement of practice work toward restructuring education. Insights into the strategies Ruth used during educational change efforts and which account for dialectical relationships between bureaucratic power and control, and teacher empowerment will now be portrayed.

Teachers in Implementation

If teachers are to be liberated from their hidden intentions and assumptions in order to determine action according to an acquired critical knowing, certain understandings about the way adults learn need to be addressed. To this end, three key concepts have been outlined by Susan Loucks and Ann Lieberman (1982): developmentalism, participation, and support. Aware of the developmental needs of the adult learner, Ruth developed the client program. It contained four levels of knowledge and process acquisition over four or more years. Each level attended to different needs. Strategies embedded within the program encouraged (1) active involvement, (2) mutual trust, (3) affirmation of teacher strengths, and (4) making learning more autonomous. Though there were similarities in the approach to the "levels of innovation use" literature (Hall, Loucks, Rutherford, et al., 1975), Ruth's practice was to go beyond, to look at what teachers were doing, and to question teacher attitudes, reasons, and concerns during in-service and consulting activities.

Active participation by teachers in their own professional development was viewed as essential by Ruth and permitted her to recognize the idiosyncratic nature of each teacher's style, skill, and commitment. Through mutual trust, she was able to provide mentoring or the networking of teachers between schools. The significance of participation rested with the handling of implementation activities rather than the content of the new curricula.

Support was granted by Ruth in three ways. Material support was found through the acquisition of new materials and equipment. Human support was given not only to the teachers implementing the curricula, but also to principals, in an effort to encourage their support of the new curriculum as a school priority. Probably one of the most critical factors in support was Ruth's ability to attend to the individual needs of teachers, intentionally delaying the full implementation of the curricula until teachers could be gradually guided through the necessary changes. Time, therefore, became an important commodity for successful implementation.

Leadership During Educational Change

Ruth also acknowledged the importance of the principal in the adoption and implementation of the fine arts programs in the schools. Because principals were viewed as plant managers and instructional leaders, Ruth set out to inform them of changes in all of the fine arts curricula. In this way, she was recognizing the pivotal role of the principal in influencing school-based change (Bowes, Chomas, Illaszewicz, et. al., 1983), and especially in art education curriculum change (Eisner 1988; Manuel 1988).

Edward Pajak (1993) draws from the work of Peter M. Senge (1990a, 1990b) and Henry A. Giroux (1989, 1991) to support the idea of the leader as teacher. In fact, James M. Burns (1978) suggested that great leaders may come very close to being considered great teachers. He referred to this type of leadership as transformational leadership. Giroux combined the roles of teacher and transformational leader in order to define transformative intellectuals who would reflect and act upon powerful ideas. Senge (1990a) believed that the leadership role of teaching should be the central process of a learning organization. Pajak (1993) detailed four common dimensions for educational leaders to encourage learning: "(1) an empowerment of self and others through cooperative effort, (2) an intellectual activity that helps group members transcend superficial understanding, (3) the collective application of knowledge to practical problems, and (4) a commitment to making the future somehow better than the present" (p. 175). Embedded within these dimensions are a commitment to taking the time necessary to produce change, working in a holistic and integrated manner among groups of people and varying interests, promoting reflective practice among teachers and administrators, while all the while being concerned with our ethical responsibilities toward others. Ruth's practice was an apt example of a leader as teacher who worked to empower teachers through reflection, cooperation, collaboration, and commitment while working together to establish a collective vision for the future.

Unsuccessful curriculum implementation efforts do not either account for or minimize the practical knowledge of teachers. It appears in this broad portrayal that Ruth respects, nurtures, contributes to, and empowers the teacher's autonomy as an active holder of practical knowledge. In this way, educational change may be more "mutually adaptive" than "faithful" to outside developers' intentions.

Another viewpoint that is important to consider is Ruth's relationship with other women and as a woman in a man's world. Carol Gilligan (1982) suggests that women view themselves in a web of relationships, that it is important for them to care for others within all relationships, and that there is a certain morality attached to women's moral development. "The standard of moral judgement that informs their assessment of self is a standard of relationship, and ethic of nurturance, responsibility and care" (p. 159). Ruth exemplified these notions through images of community, people before the program, and giving and receiving as a powerful cycle.

Ruth's practical knowledge of educational change and bureaucratic stability is best handled through a deliberate overview of her personal practical knowledge and will be examined in the next section, followed by a description of her "landscapes of images" and her style as a supervisor.

RUTH'S PRACTICAL KNOWLEDGE

Introduction

Educators hold a unique, complex, practically oriented set of understandings which they actively use to guide and provide form for their work in the profession. Through the description of Ruth's practical knowledge, we can come to understand what one supervisor in her work believes, values, and knows as a result of her biography, expertise, and experience.

In the work of Elbaz (1981, 1983), assumptions were made that practical knowledge was knowledge of something, and therefore it had content. To characterize this content she relied upon the five commonplaces laid out by Joseph J. Schwab (1969): self, subject matter, instruction, curriculum development, and teaching. For this present study, curriculum implementation subsumed and extended Elbaz's category of curriculum development since the mandate of the supervisor was the implementation of currently viable theoretical and practical innovations in fine arts education, and more particularly, in art education. This is the first important difference between a teacher's and a supervisor's practical knowledge. Each commonplace spoke of the knowledge used or considered for use.

Elbaz (1983) went on to portray five orientations which reflected the way practical knowledge was held and used. I considered the use of "context" as a better descriptor especially since Ruth referred to the difficulty of talking about her knowledge outside of the "context" from which it was derived. Practical knowledge orientations used by Elbaz were situational, personal, social, experiential, and theoretical. Upon replacing the term context for orientation, I also needed to add the political knowledge context as it emerged from the data. Elbaz chose to address the notion of political awareness within a description of the milieu. One might consider this as an critical difference between a teacher's practical knowledge and a supervisor's practical knowledge. Ruth certainly had content knowledge of the political milieu, but her political knowledge went deeper. Within the political milieu, political is assumed to mean negotiation or the effect of power and control between two parties. However, Ruth was caught between the notion of bureaucratic power and control and another, that being the cycle of power and empowerment. Political in this sense, takes on a different meaning of power. Rather than having a status orientation, people contribute equally. Rather than controlling others, nurturing, affirming, and loving become essential acts in the empowerment of others. One might ask, if a teacher were considered an active participant in a cycle of power and empowerment, how might this alter his or her practical knowledge? In respect to this, Ernest House (1981) refers to a political perspective on innovation as involving such concepts as power, authority, and competition with social relationships viewed as voluntary contractual agreements. For Ruth, the political context is a critical component of her practical knowledge as she seeks to influence change in her school district. Her colleagual model with its four stages of staff development, was an apt practical example of identifying the need for voluntary contractual agreements during educational change. The addition of the political context is the second significant difference between a teacher's and a supervisor's practical knowledge.

While the contexts of Ruth's practical knowledge serve to order the content of her knowledge, the internal structure of that knowledge guides her practice. In this way, Ruth's practice has some consistency, though there would be flexibility and adaptability as the structure was applied to particular situations. Elbaz devised a hierarchial organization of levels, varying in generality, that were used and reflected upon as guides to everyday practice. These cannot be assumed to be linked in progressive order. Principles are generated through experience and reasoning derived from reflection on experience. In this way, complex situations or inexperience within situational contexts may prevent the formulation of explicit rules of practice. Images are the most all-encompassing, yet the least explicit. All of Ruth's feelings, beliefs, values, and goals merge as she forms images of how her interactions with teachers or administrators should be, and through experience, give substance to each image.

Each of the three terms reflects different ways of mediating thought and action. A rule of practice is a guideline on or from which the teacher acts; it exists and she follows its dictates. She formulated it herself, in many cases, but for just this purpose of eliminating the need for thought. An image, conversely, is something one responds to rather than acting from. A practical principle mediates between thought and action. Elbaz (1983) pointed out that the outward appearance or statement of each of the rules, principles, or images was not as important as the way in which these statements sought to organize or give structure to practical knowledge. In fact, in appearance a statement may describe a rule, yet function as a rule, principle, or an image, or in any combination simultaneously.

Ruth believed consultants needed to have heuristic abilities. Michael Polanyi (1958) describes heuristic acts as applications of knowledge that may look routine but are acts of invention and discovery. A heuristic act is the "adaptation of an interpretive framework to comprise the lessons of a new experience" (p. 105). Ruth's ability to combine, adapt, and/or create different rules, principles, and images, within and across contexts is an apt example of heuristic ability. The fundamentally "tacit" nature of Ruth's practical knowledge prompts another investigation: What is the best way to teach another consultant? Ruth believed the best way for her to teach another consultant was through mentorship. Consequently, tacit knowledge might be acquired through tacit instruction. Robert J. Sternberg and David R. Caruso (1985) suggest that "one's ability to acquire tacit knowledge on the job will be a key factor in one's success or failure as a teacher" (p. 148).

If the above is true, we may conclude that Ruth's exemplary status is a result of her wealth of practical knowledge in her role as fine arts supervisor. One may also speculate that she has more practical knowledge than others. It would be advantageous for neophyte consultants or supervisors to be mentored by a role model. This is critical if we accept the unique form of practical knowledge found in the role of supervisor. Through reflection school district personnel should reconsider short term contracts for consultants which fail to recognize the need to acquire a new epistemology of practice implicit within the change of roles.

What is central to this study is the description and interpretation of what an exemplary fine arts supervisor's personal practical knowledge may look like regarding educational change and stability. To approach the significance or value of this element requires a thematic look at Ruth's choice of imagery, rules, and principles.

Landscape of Images

Power and empowerment in teacher change.[1] Ruth's notion of empowerment is built upon "a powerful cycle of giving and receiving." It is an image that is furthered by another image of the teacher and consultant dancing; as "dance partners." They are images of a rhythmic leading and responding in unison, of acceptance and assurance. The artistic nature embedded within the dance brings to our attention the flow of giving and receiving, of the uniqueness of individual couples dancing a pattern of steps. Principles of "when any two people come together, both should grow," "give more to a few rather than a little to a lot," and to "make sure the conditions are right so they are capable of giving" suggests further attention to individual teachers, their particular needs, desires, values, and biographies. There is an emotional coloring, of caring, believing, trusting, and nurturing. It is brought together in the principle, "to empower other people is the more powerful way to act."

It is in this sense of personal and interpersonal empowerment that power takes on new meaning. The image of "knowledge feeds passion" and the principle of "anything you do with passion is powerful" rings of intensity and enthusiasm. They reach beyond limiting forces and bring forth meaning-making, creation, and love. Allison M. Jaggar (1989) asserts that "just as appropriate emotions may contribute to the development of knowledge, so the growth of knowledge may contribute to the development of appropriate emotions" (p. 163). Knowledge and passion are not mutually exclusive but rather reciprocal and responsive. This union attracts people that are, or encourages people to be "compassionate yet thoughtful; loving yet just" (Swoboda and Vanderbosch 1983, p. 6). To Ruth, individuals are be granted the autonomy to express themselves freely. The image of "love your neighbour" reinforces passion, perhaps more quietly, but with the same conviction, for "people follow passion." That image suggests the inner need of everyone to participate in living to the fullest possible degree, and in consequence, if given the right conditions, they will be empowered through passion to learn more and more. "We can never divorce reason from feeling" is a rule that guides these notions, for rational thought is never without feeling, and feeling is always tempered by reason. To assume otherwise would disregard the constant dialectic found in experiential knowledge.

Ruth extends passion and love to include these principles: "you can only draw what you love" and "you can only teach what you feel passion for." Both have a personal dimension, and both have a relationship with a subject. Again it is an intensity for life, learning, and teaching. One senses an immersion in a subject, a letting go, a freedom to explore and experience personal horizons.

Although it seems that many of Ruth's images focus upon the individual, one should remember to consider her sense of "the community." It is in that image of colleaguality, that her "colleagual model" is reinforced. The principle, "we come together for a certain time so we should all grow" engenders a notion of people joining together in community. Power becomes real through parti-cipation and in so doing, "an enlarging circle of professionally developed people in fine arts instruction" also becomes a reality. It is a form of bonding, of uniting, of linking people's strengths within community. Ruth's principle that "supervisors demonstrate leadership most effectively as a participant in the process of educational growth" suggests that Ruth is willing to grow along with her colleagues. Growth implies positive change or improvement in one's professional efforts and outcomes.

Encouraging educational growth in teachers takes on a nurturing quality. "People come before the program" is a principle that speaks of humanism before consumerism. If anything were to be treated as being secondary, it would be the curriculum document, for the teacher is the person creating meaning. It is the teacher who brings to the act of teaching, all of his or her human needs, desires, fears, inhibitions, and so on. Before any significant treatment can occur in program change, the individual must be treated with dignity and respect. This is extended by the principle, "you must have some insight into what is possible for that person to do, and that person has to see in herself that making the change will indeed make her better in what she is already going to do."

Rules of practice that suggest how Ruth might go about encouraging this kind of change are, "take risks with people," "don't be afraid of failure," and "affirm the good things the teacher is doing." The principle of "people must trust you before they will listen" suggests that Ruth must speak first, perhaps showing a level of vulnerability, humility, or compassion before teachers will take the uncertain first step in her direction. But there is a certain comfort born in another principle: "celebrate excellence because everyone advances when one ad-vances." There is no competition, no seeking of status, no inequality. Unless of course, the circumstances call forth a type of leadership either by Ruth, or by those advancing. "Once I recognize that they're going, I get out of their way…if I observe they're flagging or that I'm flagging, then I get back in front of them." This principle is reflective of Ruth's personal strength to allow others moments to shine, while realizing that in a moment's notice, she may have to recover her own or another's fallen ground. It is at once nurturing and leading.

The image of "the parable of the sower of seeds" reflects Ruth's image of herself casting seeds of curriculum change everywhere, in the hope that someday, somehow, teachers will desire professional growth. There are inherent qualities of commitment, determination, patience, and human understanding. But it is also consistent with the images of "the art of making people want to learn what I have to offer them" or "wooing knowledge," and Ruth's view of herself as a "teacher of teachers." "The art of teaching" becomes an enticing yet intuitive interaction between Ruth and her teachers. It is through the "powers of participation, persuasion, and motivation" that her teaching activates and empowers teachers to learn, and furthermore, to take responsibility for their own learning. It is through this empowerment that I suspect Ruth's image of everyone being "delighted to see me" is built. Throughout the school system, a definite warmth, love, and respect abounded in every visit Ruth made to people she already knew. To those newcomers, her passion for the arts and the child, soon connected with her "people follow passion" image and the newcomers, too, were becoming delighted to see her.

Teaching and learning are linked in many ways, and though Ruth has many rules and principles guiding her practice, there is a central image: you want to "set a fire in the mind." It is an image passionate with intensity, vigor, force, and commitment. It is a rigorous image for personal fulfillment, especially with the extension of the principle "once you awaken a mind, you have a tremendous responsibility to keep it going." Curiously, Ruth must balance oppositions on occasion. The rules of "there are times you have to spoon feed them (teachers)" and "don't ever take anything for granted with teachers," directs our attention to experiential knowledge and deliberate reflection on action. They are not necessarily negative comments inasmuch as they are acceptance of ignorance, a place to begin constructive change. If she needed to provide specific directives to teachers, she would do so. Though "the teacher has to be the coach so that the student can master the curriculum" is an important principle, Ruth also believes "it is the learner who learns." Everyone in the teaching and learning process is responsible for his or her own actions. This notion is refined as one realizes that "you only notice what you know" is a rule that is extended to a principle by the phrase "and your tastes change as you come to know more." It was particularly evident in her concern for principals' limited knowledge of the fine arts. She had observed that if they do not know anything about the arts then they would not know what to look for. To guard against this, Ruth maintained the rule that "you have to have time to maintain research and reading in your area in order to stay up-to-date."

A strong temporal quality is reflected in many of Ruth's images. "Change is a slow process" may seem taken-for-granted, but it is given more character through the image of "change takes a long time: it's like tending a garden." Again, strong characteristics of patience, caring, and faith in people, permeate the image. More specifically for art education, the rule of "just do a little at a time when implementing a discipline-based program" reinforces the above stated qualities. Without escaping the time management functions of her role, Ruth had a rule that said she "will work from dawn to dusk Monday to Thursday, but Friday night, Saturday, and Sunday are my own" was often, but not always, followed. Time was a true commodity.

Ruth also spoke of the "rhythms of life" and observed that "everyone has a rhythm." Each suggests cycles, the first on a large scale, and the second, on a small scale. Recognizing the inherent strengths and weaknesses within the notion of rhythm, Ruth might be better able to guide her teachers.

Finally, teacher power and empowerment are guided by Ruth herself. She recognizes that she is "well-suited to the role of supervisor." She knows her strengths and weaknesses. She steps out confidently as a result of her "courage of convictions." These are images of herself personally and professionally. Ruth has a strong sense of personal efficacy: she believes she makes a difference. She is determined, persistent, idealistic yet realistic. Yet she does not assume any superiority. Her view that, "I don't take myself seriously," is perhaps a reinforcement to the principle "we go as far as we can but on the way we're going to have a good time."

As a final image for the section on teacher power and empowerment, I have kept aside "the cactus club." It is an image of a growing plant surviving on little nourishment, care, and attention. It is not an image totally consistent with what has been briefly described and interpreted. It is rather, an image that links survival with determination, passion, and belief in one's direction. It is an image given by Ruth to her Fine Arts Centre team as they worked in the field. It causes one to realize that beyond Ruth's circle, her community, her colleagual model, lies a different world.

Bureaucratic control and educational stability.   To begin, Ruth spoke of the senior administration in her school district as having a different "landscape of imagery" from hers. Where she sought a circle of colleaguality, she felt they visualized a hierarchial pyramid. Where she envisioned equality, she felt they envisioned superiority. Her personal images, regarding the bureaucratic need for power and control and thus stability within the school system, raises an interesting collection of rules, principles, and images, that are quite different from those just presented.

"The school system has a life of its own" brings to our attention the inanimate life of an organization that perpetuates itself. It will go on regardless of individual successes or failures; it will go on regardless of the employment or retirement of staff. It does not give nor does it receive, for it simply is: it is a fact of life. Ruth chose to "work within the system, not for my own power but for the needs of the program I serve." Perhaps this describes a rational acceptance of the structures in which she works. This is furthered by, "Keep a back door open to the Department of Education." These are political images recognizing her placement in the hierarchy.

Ruth denies the need for personal status, something that she associates with the administrative council, for she said "I do not need to have my ego fed like many administrators: I don't want to be in the limelight." This is further characterized by the image of the "Administrative Council is a Byzantine place."

Ruth resists rules and resolutely states: "I won't use those blue cards because workshop leaders who work long and hard and put in many hours of preparation are in fact many times graded on performance." She resisted this system rule, replacing it with a rule of practice "change for the sake of change is irrational." This in turn, follows the rule "I never just form a group for the sake of just getting together." Change must be purposeful, personally meaningful, and attentive to the needs of the population. "The fewer the regulations the better." The guiding image to these rules and principles was the "procrustean bed": resisting the idea of fitting people, ideas, or things into a model that was foolishly applied.

Though Ruth had these few conflicts or concerns with bureaucracy, she too encouraged some educational stability. She said, "I do not leave anything to chance," and "I always have a plan for what I will do but those plans are always open to change after discussion." These rules and principles suggest her directional nature as a leader, with an interfaced form of teacher participation.

Ruth also recognized the stability of the "cycles within a school year" and how that influenced her practice. For instance, she believed: "never visit principals before the middle of October because there are so many variables for them to deal with at the beginning of the school year."

Her decision-making capacity exhibited characteristics of control. "View a problem from all points of view before making a decision" and "no decision will satisfy all parties, rather find one that everybody will be a little satisfied with." In regard to influencing those above her, Ruth said "I try to influence their decisions as much as I can so that when their decisions do come they will be favorable."

Ruth recognizes what she cannot change. For teachers, "you can change the circumstances but you can't change the behavior." For resources or other factors in educational change, "what I cannot change, I don't bother with."

What is curious about the notion of power, is Ruth's acknowledgement of powerful subordinates. They, too, could control one's experience. Power, interests, and control, though dominant in bureaucracy, were also found in other relationships.

The interface between teachers and administration.   At the interface of Ruth's role between teachers and administration, come two important ideas. First of all, Ruth was "loyal to my leaders," even though they did not have the same landscape of imagery as she possessed. Even so, she followed the rule "always follow protocol." These have strong moral and ethical overtones. The second idea, remaining at the interface in her role between teachers and administrators, is Ruth's image of being "caught between the real world and the shadow world." Both are reminiscent of the imagery supplied in the preceding section, yet strongly indicative of the opposition facing Ruth in her practice.

As a final image I have kept aside "the cactus club." It is an image of a growing plant surviving on little nourishment, care, and attention. It is not an image totally consistent with what has been briefly described and interpreted in either of the preceding sections. It is rather an image that links survival with determination, passion, and belief in one's direction. It is an image given by Ruth to her Fine Arts Centre team as they worked in the field. It causes one to realize that beyond Ruth's circle, her community, her colleagual model, lies a different world.

"Image" as a conceptual tool.   Connelly and Clandinin (n.d.) suggest that an image acts as a glue that brings together a person's various life experiences to form a narrative unity for one's life. If one reviews the various images followed by Ruth and applies these to the biographical sketch provided earlier in the document, it may be conjectured that her life as a nun, artist, scholar, and single woman, has greatly influenced her choice of imagery and the narrative unity from which she is personally and professionally guided.

Gareth Morgan (1986) has written about popular images of organizations, and though he carefully defines the ideal states of many, he is quick to point out that several images of organizations may be found working simultaneously. Ruth's practice illustrates that different metaphors or images lead to different ways of organizing, managing, or acting in practice.

In recognizing how taken-for-granted images or metaphors shape understanding and action, we are recognizing the role of theory. Our images or metaphors are theories or conceptual frameworks. Practice is never theory-free, for it is always guided by an image of what one is trying to do. The real issue is whether or not we are aware of the theory guiding our action (p. 336). Ruth's images act as theories-in-action that guide her practice.

Morgan coins the word "imaginization" purposefully to break free from the common instrumental restraints of the concept of organization "by symbolizing the close link between images and action" (p. 343). Rather than just interpreting the way organizations are, one may realize that through a creative process, new images and ideas can create new actions.

> People can change organizations and society, even though the perception and actuality or power relations passed down through history may at times make

change difficult. Prescriptively, I would thus like us all to recognize that reality is made, not given; to recognize that our seeing and understanding of the world is always seeing as, rather than a seeing as is; and to take an ethical and moral responsibility for the personal and collective consequences of the way we see and act in everyday life, difficult though this may be (Morgan 1986, p. 382).

It is in this regard that Ruth moves toward breaking the hold of bureaucratic thinking in order to foster less exploitative, more equal modes of interaction in her organization. To her, there is a certain dominance given to what Morgan may consider a "cultural metaphor." The implications of this metaphor rest with her resistance to a more "machine-like" metaphor. The simultaneity of them is assumed between people, but it cannot show complete consistency in one person's personal practical knowledge. Often, she acts within the "political metaphor" in an effort to resolve the two. It is in this way that contradictions within practical knowledge force the owner either to find images that serve as an interface between the two forces or to bring about organizational change in the direction of a specified image or metaphor.

Consistency of practice is critical to the literature on practical knowledge. With that in mind, we turn now to the description and interpretation of Ruth's style as a supervisor.

RUTH'S CONSULTATIVE STYLE

Ruth's Style as a Fine Arts Supervisor During Implementation of Art Education Innovations

The final research question addresses the style Ruth exhibited in her role as fine arts supervisor. Elbaz (1983) chooses to describe the teacher's cognitive style in a way that may be better described as a personal style for the individual. This section will describe Ruth's personal style in a very general sense and then more specifically as it relates to Favaro's delineation (1984) of consulting styles.

Personal style. Ruth's personal style may be compared to that of an artist in several ways. Many of her images include a sense of time, of tension between rise and fall, of rhythmic patterns, cycles, and energy. Many reinforce her sense of space, of enlarging circles, rigid procrustean beds, fire, shadows, back doors, and people joining together. Others speak of balance between giving and receiving. There is an awareness of bringing these notions together through the art of teaching and the art of making people want to learn what she had to offer them.

Ruth's personal style is humanistic. She respects the human spirit, admires human abilities, and seeks to stimulate those notions in everyone she meets. Her evangelical character may be deeply spiritual, as words of trust, passion, empowerment, and awakening abound in her images, principles, and rules. But there is a profound knowledge of people and the human condition. People come before the program. There is a sense of protection from bureaucracy, of liberation and fulfillment. But when necessary, she was not afraid to demand excellence of those requesting her expertise.

Ruth's style may be compared at times to that of a storyteller or poet. Concrete stories were always presented with ideas, theoretical notions, or issues. It was her way to capitalize on the moment of metaphor and analogy. People could then presumably understand the abstract through the concrete.

Ruth's personal style also reflected the style of politicians. "Power" and its various meanings touched upon most areas of her practical knowledge. Anything done with intensity, rigor, dedication, and fullness of feeling provided the passion to mobilize an individual's power. Ruth's strengths all came back to this passion and power. But this was not the only form of power she knew. Bureaucratic power and control, though often forced upon her, were sometimes used by her to maintain certain standards of practice. Negotiating between these two forced a strong dialectical nature to her practical knowledge.

Ruth joins characteristic styles as an artist, evangelical leader, storyteller, and politician into a coherent unified cognitive style. Depending upon the needs of the individual or the situation, Ruth heuristically adapted to new experiences and maintained a sense of the ideal while having her feet firmly planted on the ground.

Consulting styles. It was obvious during the course of the study that Ruth was not only trying to implement a discipline-based curriculum guideline, but she also was trying to raise the consciousness of those teachers who were employing an outdated, stereotypic approach, or the controversial "school art" style. By recognizing the needs of the individual teachers, she would either give specific directives (often to first time teachers), enter into dialogue in order to share meaning, uncover hidden assumptions and intentions, or endeavored to raise the critical consciousness of teachers as they reflected upon their personal and professional conceptions of their education practices. Her practical knowledge thus needed to include several consulting styles. Favaro's alternative paradigmatic framework of consulting types was first described in chapter 4. Using this framework, Ruth may be described as a supervisor who draws upon the category of her view of social relations from the perspective of "consultant-as-colleague" but she also drew upon the other categories of "consultant-as-coparticipant" and "consultant-as-expert," if the situation or the ability level of the teacher warranted their inclusion. As consultant-as-colleague, Ruth assumed an interpretive orientation, where she sought to understand the practical world of the teacher. More particularly, she was able to bring teachers into dialogue, to talk about their situations, and to realize that their viewpoints were valid, justified, and worthy of sharing. Although less often, Ruth demonstrated her understanding of the everyday world of children as well, usually during her school visits, and in her personal relationships with children outside of school. All of this was accomplished in dialogue: the root activity of communication with teachers. She judged her own practice upon how relevant and meaningful her relationships were with teachers and administrators in her efforts toward personal and professional development.

As consultant-as-coparticipant, Ruth took greater interest in the lived experiences of teachers, that is, their historical and sociocultural backgrounds. She would invite teachers to begin critically questioning their underlying assumptions that could cause limiting personal and professional conceptions. In this way, she was raising the consciousness of teachers toward educational issues, not necessarily related to the curricula. This occurred if teachers were ready, almost as if she cast seeds of change everywhere, waiting for those to risk raising their own consciousness in order to obtain liberation from their assumed notions of practice. Ruth's personal understanding of her role may be found in the deeply responsive character of her guiding images. She is forever reflecting upon participants' needs, views, and commitments. Through dialogue and authentic involvement with a teacher, both come to reflect upon practice, raising each other's consciousness, and thereby changing practice.

Finally, Ruth acted as a consultant-as-expert whenever her judgment of the teaching situation suggested the need for her intervention. It was not her intention to dominate or control the teacher's world. Rather, she used her judgment as a guide to the ideal, and if teachers needed specific directives, or if administrators needed reassurance as to the standards of teacher conduct, Ruth would apply her knowledge and expertise. This was particularly noticeable when efficient problem-solving was necessary in certain situations. Ruth customarily gravitated to the role of consultant-as-colleague.

THE RESEARCH QUESTIONS REVISITED

In Answer to the Research Questions: The Findings

In summary, this chapter has sought theoretically to ground Ruth's practice and her practical knowledge in relevant literature based on practical knowledge, curriculum implementation, and supervision. It has also provided an overview of the answers to the research questions, namely:

> 1. What are the content areas of the fine arts supervisor's personal practical knowledge? Schwab's (1969) commonplaces proved to be useful in the interpretation of the content areas of the fine arts supervisor's practical knowledge. The content areas were: self, subject matter, instruction, curriculum implementation, and milieu.
> 2. In what contexts may these content areas be found? Elbaz's (1983) practical knowledge orientations proved to be useful starting points for the interpretation of the knowledge contexts of the fine arts supervisor. The

knowledge contexts in which the above content areas may be found are: theoretical, situational, social, political, personal, and experiential.

3. How is this practical knowledge constructed? The use of Elbaz's (1983) distinctions of rules of practice, practical principles, and images proved to be useful in ultimately uncovering a dialectical relationship between two themes or "landscapes of images": Teacher power and empowerment, and bureaucratic power and control. The resolution between these two opposing views was contained within a few rules, principles, and images that acted at the "interface."

4. What consulting style(s) appropriately describe the fine arts supervisor? Favaro's (1984) paradigmatic framework for interpreting consulting styles proved to be useful as a way understanding Ruth's overall style as a supervisor. The fine arts supervisor's consulting style may be interpreted to be primarily that of "colleague" in educational change. Given the amount of practical knowledge of teachers and administrators with whom she worked, and their desire, will, or passion toward educational change, Ruth on occasion acted as an "expert" or as a "coparticipant."

An all-encompassing finding to this study is that a teacher's practical knowledge is different from a supervisor's practical knowledge. It is different as a result of a shift in the fundamental conceptual framework primarily in the content and knowledge context areas.

In the next and last chapter, I will discuss how Ruth's rich practical knowledge may guide the field in considering a reconstruction of leadership. Concurrently, I also will reflect upon the research process and suggest implications for practice and further research.

Chapter 6
Reconstruction and Reflection

In previous chapters, we have explored the practical knowledge of one exceptional fine arts supervisor. We have also examined the influence of her practical knowledge upon those with whom she worked. Unfortunately, there are few case studies or biographies of women administrators compared to the work done with male administrators (see for instance, Martin and Willower 1981; Wolcott 1973). As such, the narrative provided here offers a critical case study for the field to consider. Ruth is just one of many, many women who need to have their voices heard. The field and research community need to collect more descriptions of leaders (Lincoln 1989) and particularly of female leaders (Lyons, Saltonstall, and Hanmer 1989).

With a lack of knowledge of the leadership experiences of women administrators comes a variety of other concerns and issues. For instance, it should not be a surprise that the supervisor portrayed here is a woman whose subject matter expertise is in the fine arts. Carol Shakeshaft (1987) states that women who succeed in getting into administration within their first few tries will typically either attain an elementary school principalship or a position as a subject matter specialist, usually in language arts or fine arts. Very few will be promoted to central office supervisory positions or secondary principalships. For women who choose to be specialists, there are increased opportunities for sharing expertise with colleagues, and for increased flexibility and visibility. As such, the position offers some valuable administrative experience which could lead to other promotions (Sagaria 1985).

Learning about the practical knowledge of Ruth calls us to reconsider and reconstruct the notion of leadership. Although Carolyn Desjardins warns us that there is no behavior that is gender-specific (1989), women are more apt to experience life and behave in ways that are different from men. If there is a difference between women's and men's experience, then it follows that men and women may experience leadership in different ways. Ruth's form of leadership is rooted in her own experience but also in her experience of women working together. Although men have worked with her in her milieu, during the time of the study the staff at the Fine Arts Centre were only women. It would have been very interesting to see how male specialists would have fit into the structure and dynamics of the group. If we reconsider leadership from Ruth's perspective, we may be able to offer the educational community an opportunity to rethink and reconstruct leadership, not just for women, but for men and women. Both genders need to understand the experiences of each other and in turn learn from each other. Hopefully, female and male leaders will come to appreciate their experiences more fully and with more critical awareness.

A RECONSTRUCTION OF LEADERSHIP

In recent years, educational administration has been criticized for its gender blindness toward leadership issues (Blackmore 1989b; Hearn and Parkin 1983; Martin 1984; Shakeshaft 1987). Starting from feminist theory, one would argue that women experience the world differently than men and therefore understand the world in different ways. In turn, women in leadership positions would perceive and conceive of leadership in different ways as well (Donovan 1990). Sandra Harding (1986) asserts that "gender is a fundamental category within which meaning and value are assigned to everything in the world, a way of organizing human social relations" (p. 57). Therefore, as a socially constructed phenomenon, leadership should be reconsidered according to the gender of the individual. In turn, these reconsiderations could enhance a reconstruction of leadership for both men and women.

From a feminist perspective, gender may influence leadership in three important ways (Bensimon 1993). First of all, women tend to define themselves in relation to others (Gilligan 1982; Gilligan, Lyons, and Hamner 1990) while men often define themselves independently of others. Second, women are inter-dependently governed by an ethics of care and responsibility toward others (Noddings 1984). Men on the other hand are more often governed by standards of independent achievement (Ferguson 1984). Third, women perceive the world as a concrete, unique, and dynamically related entity, which contains socially embodied ideas, events and things, directed by desires and needs. Men often perceive the world as a disembodied, rational entity governed by laws which can be understood and used by people (Ferguson 1984). Although not all women and all men will perceive the world through these distinctions, the majority do.

The assumption that guides most theory development and leadership practice is founded upon male experience. Recently, hierarchial models based in a bureaucratic rational organization, have been associated with masculinized thought (De Lyon and Migniuolo 1989). The assumptions embedded in these theories, experience, and models have been uncritically accepted. Jill Blackmore (1989a) outlines four assumptions that need to be re-examined.

One assumption is that formal authority is synonymous with leadership. A second assumption is that this authority is necessarily imparted through hierarchial relationships. A third assumption sees leadership as technique and expertise, and a fourth assumption puts forth the belief that leadership means making rational decisions based upon empirical evidence (p. 20).

Essentially, these assumptions may be credited to a positivistic view of the world which separates theory from practice, means from ends, process from product. Positivism also fails to contextualize decisions within a broad view of the organization, community, or culture. These assumptions logically lead to the conceptualization of leadership as gender-neutral, with identifiable personal attributes that focus upon specific behaviors and skills. With this criteria in mind it becomes easy to disregard the paucity of women in leadership as simply an issue of unsuitability of women in the role, rather than criticizing the conceptualization of the role (Blackmore 1989a, and 1989b). Therefore, women and their experience have been traditionally ignored in educational thought.

Another group of theorists in educational administration, interpret leadership from a humanistic orientation (for instance, Sergiovanni and Carver 1980). These theorists argue that leadership is essentially a political, moral, and sociocultural activity that requires decisions based upon complex and dynamic value judgments. Unfortunately, these theorists also neglect to consider the differing experiences held among women and men. Humanist interpretations are still premised upon perspectives that males, rather than females, are capable of making higher-level value judgments. The theory is based upon an assumption that there is one view of moral development: a male view (see Blackmore 1989a).

Neither of the above perspectives toward leadership take into account that women experience leadership differently than men (Blackmore 1989b). In order to accommodate women's experience, a reconstruction of leadership is needed. Leadership reconstructed from Ruth's perspective, may not be generalizable to all women but the findings of the studies presented here are consistent with much of the feminist material written over the last decade. Integrating what I have learned from working with Ruth and her colleagues, and the feminist work I have read, suggests to me that most women conceive of, and wish to experience, leadership as described in the following passages.

Leadership framed from a feminist (socialist) viewpoint would conceptualize power as a sharing of responsibility, decision-making, and action among participants in an activity in an effort to share power with others or nurture empowerment. Through leadership, people are empowered to improve practice. The process of leading would be changed to become communitarian in nature and would encourage a democratic process for all involved (Rosener 1990). The creation of community would provide for mutual needs and desires, in and through time. The ongoing process would continually connect and reconnect members of the community and how they define their particular community. Within the community and through a relational view of morality and judgment, the interdependence of all people becomes paramount (Tierney 1989). Concern and responsibility for self and others become situated within specific contexts. Carol Gilligan (1982) has argued that this relational morality should not be regarded as a deficit model but as a different model that reflects another kind of understanding. Set against the studies here, a relational model for leadership would demand a reconstruction of a masculinized construct (Blackmore 1989a).

Leadership conceptualized in the above way would break down the conventional dichotomy between leaders and followers (Smyth 1989, p. 191), and replace it with a conceptualization of leadership *through* others rather that leadership *over* others (Blackmore 1989a). William Foster (1989) believes that leadership is always situated within a context: the community of individuals is responsible for making the community viable rather than a few superior individuals. Foster also believes that leadership involves negotiation and shared leadership. To him "leadership cannot occur without followership, and many times the two are exchangeable: leaders become followers and followers become leaders" (p. 42). Leadership has a dialectical character. Visions and ideas are negotiated with followers who in turn become leaders. The assumption that leadership is a result of status or position is fallacious since the kind of leadership described here cannot be interpreted as managerial in nature. Leadership and management are two entirely different concepts and have too often been equated as one in the same. When visions and ideas are negotiated in a dialectical relationship, leadership becomes pedagogic. Colleagues who are committed to this dialectical view of leadership would in turn see leadership as transformative and therefore, pedagogic. Leadership as pedagogic would be concerned with continuity with the past while critically reflecting upon possible alternatives for the future. This act of teaching leadership is an act of creating other leaders and thus leadership becomes a shared process within the community. Perhaps Foster (1989) said it best in the following way:

> Leadership, in the final analysis, is the ability of humans to relate deeply to each other in the search for a more perfect union. Leadership is a consensual task, a sharing of ideas and a sharing of responsibilities, where a "leader" is a leader for a moment only, where the leadership exerted must be validated by the consent of followers, and where leadership lies in the struggles of a community to find meaning for itself (p. 61).

Foster's view of pedagogic leadership is similar to the ideas expressed in feminist pedagogy. Feminist pedagogy refers to "leading or instructing others in an unbiased, learner-empowering, diversity-respecting, women-affirming way" (Van Nostrand 1993, p. 143). The emphases in this approach is on the learner, process rather than product, and dialogue among participants. Cooperative learning becomes the key to empowerment and liberation. Foster's (1989) view of leadership as well as many in a feminist arena would agree with R. Barth's

(1990) description of transformation leadership as a "community of leaders" (p. 9), or as P. Schlecty (1990) suggests, a "leader of leaders" (p. 241). Both views place faith in individuals to be responsive toward the good of the community. As leaders teach leadership, the leader of leaders nurtures a community of leaders. It is an exciting form of leadership that builds upon commitment and enthusiasm, optimism and energy, vision and renewal (Roberts 1985). The collective action derived from this form of leadership is critically responsive toward a collective vision. Members of the community will work toward overcoming obstacles because they believe in and are committed to their vision (Brown 1993).

Although much of the literature on transformational leadership disregards women's experiences, many of the ideas within the conceptualization are congruent with feminism. We must be careful, therefore, not to forget that women's experiences must be honored through descriptions and interpretations of experiences for both men and women to appreciate and learn from one another. It is not enough to integrate the main ideas of a reconstruction of leadership. The reconstruction must be felt deeply and by the whole person. And one must remain critical to preconceived assumptions. A feminist view of leadership would always be concerned with the woman's view as a way of ensuring that the conventional male model is not taken-for-granted. Let me also say, I agree with Blackmore (1989b) that a women's perspective is not bio- logically predetermined or universal, nor is it morally superior to the perspec- tives of men. Rather, for a specific moment in history, roles, traditions, and societal expectations prescribe different attitudes, skills, and behaviors to males and females across varying ethnic groups, class ability and ages. Feminists who believe in this complex interrelationship among biology, environment, and society would not expect everyone to be treated exactly the same. Rather, responsibility within relationships would be grounded in historical and temporal contexts.

If educational leadership is going to attract women, then more recognition will need to be given significance within a specific context: for instance, parenting, community work, volunteer activities, and so forth. More recognition will also need to be given to an emphasis on community, collaboration, and caring rather than the autonomy and agency of the individual.

Sally Helgeson (1990) noted in her diary studies of women in leadership that they all saw themselves within a web-like or circular system. The women in her study spoke of circles in which expanding series of orbs radiate from a center point of leadership. The circle is not a static figure with rigid directional lines and specific configurations that connote a top-down hierarchy. Instead the circle expands and contracts as more or less connections are made. As the circle enlarges, more connections are made and interwoven (Van Nostrand, 1993). Leadership from the center point is conceived of as being in the middle of things, of being connected to those around them. No one position dominates another position. Learning taking place in this arrangement would be dependent upon the wishes and actions of each member of the group and the evolution of thought among the group members.

Within this form of leadership comes an implicit notion of community or group affiliation rather than individual achievement. Individuals are encouraged to grow and develop but not at the expense of others. Everyone grows when one grows. The process of leading from the center of the circle is very subtle and derives its strength from empowering those participating in the community (Aburdene and Naisbitt 1992).

Exemplary leadership may often be considered charismatic (Conger 1989) in that successful leadership is often courageous, passionate, and intense. In education, we are sometimes lucky to have supervisors and consultants who are committed to positive educational change and through the courage of their convictions, promote specific innovative projects. They are also often individuals who have a passion for people, learning, and loving. Coupled with expert and practical knowledge of the discipline and teaching, a powerful dynamic occurs. Eventually, through the act of empowerment, the power of a leader's experiential or practical knowledge will be used to influence the practical knowledge of the novice or colleague.

The characteristics of Ruth as a successful leader may be portrayed in four interconnecting dimensions: visionary qualities, communicating the vision, creating trust and commitment, and empowering others. Each of these blend together into one another yet may be seen to stand as separate entities. I prefer to interpret these dimensions in a circular format which places the supervisor as leader at the center of the circle. From this small inner circle radiates 4 sections, like pieces of a pie, which represent the 4 dimensions. These sections are not rigid but rather dynamic. The whole image of the circle is dynamic, enlarging with growth, contracting with resistance. Other consultants and supervisors, and particularly those who are women, may feel that their work resonates with the dimensions outlined in this circular image. Both male and female leaders would benefit from considering the benefits and limitations of these dimensions in their leadership context.

Visionary Qualities

Supervisors and consultants need to have a vision for their curriculum area or area of concern. The vision needs to be simply stated in order for teachers or other colleagues to recall the vision easily. Often leaders need to interpret their own practical knowledge in order to recognize how to provide opportunities for all teachers to become involved in educational change. Anyone involved in leadership should look at what they are doing to encourage commitment to change. For Ruth, it meant working with those people who wanted to change or take hold of the vision rather than those who were not interested in changing their professional practice.

Communicating a Vision

Having a vision is often not enough. Consultants or supervisors need to tailor their language to different audiences. Inevitably with any audience, one must remember to provide concrete examples and stories that reinforce the message. In this way, contextual information justifies the vision.

In the studies reported here, Ruth believed in the image of "the parable of the sower of seeds." Using this image one may readily see if you scatter grain, some fall on fertile soil while others do not. Those which fall on fertile ground grow and flourish. Supervisors who see themselves acting as the power of seeds, make themselves available to all teachers realizing that it is the teacher who decides if she can flourish with the idea. As teachers decide to take hold of ideas, consultants can become more involved.

Creating Trust and Commitment

It may be important to remember that supervisors often have to persuade their colleagues that they can transform an ideal or vision into reality, and in order to do this, also need to persuade others that they have the prerequisite skills necessary to achieve such a vision. If a supervisor has extraordinary commitment to a vision, and teachers are encouraged to participate in that vision, then they, too, will develop commitment for achieving the vision. The power of persuasion often encourages self-confidence in others. In so doing, mutual trust and commitment ensue. As teachers or colleagues begin to experiment with and develop their own practical knowledge set within their life experiences, teachers and consultants grow simultaneously. If supervisors express profound concern for the needs of teachers, their encouragement, concern, and devotion soon become interpreted as confidence in another's abilities. This reciprocity between two people forms mutual trust. Once this is established, teachers are more likely to reach for the high expectations set for themselves.

Empowering Others

As teachers and other colleagues begin to realize self-confidence so, too, will they become empowered. In order to encourage this, consultants or leaders require great and persistent energy within themselves and with those with whom they are working. Often, this means acting as a role model. By demonstrating confidence in one's abilities and achieving the tasks set out to be accomplished, leaders can actually model personal empowerment. Once this is modeled, others will likely wish to join in.

Supervisors are in a unique position to play a teaching role by setting up appropriate learning experiences for teachers. In this way, leaders are able to empower others to fulfill their own vision while fulfilling a collective vision for the school system.

The above four dimensions were interconnected for Ruth. She valued making connections, working cooperatively, allowing for intuitive insights, and playing with ideas. Setting this against a backdrop of professionalism that called for higher standards and greater expectations created a dynamic dialectic that often called for the support that was found within a mentoring relationship. Ruth recognized that she had been mentored and that she was now actively mentoring others in the profession.

Supervisors and Consultants as Mentors

Supervisors and consultants are named many things: specialists, change agents, change facilitators, supervisors, resource personnel, and so forth. To some they may also be mentors. In a study on change facilitators by Gene E. Hall, William L. Rutherford, Shirley H. Hord, and Leslie L. Huling (1983) it was found that the style of those facilitating change varied in many ways yet had a profound effect upon the success of change initiatives. That study found three styles of change facilitators: responders, managers, and initiators. This order also illustrated the least to most effective styles.

Leslie L. Huling-Austin (1990) went on to discuss how mentor-teachers may be considered change facilitators in their role with new and beginning teachers. In doing so, mentor teachers may fulfill one or more of three styles of mentors: responders, colleagues, and initiators. Although her description is set within the context of a teacher mentoring an inductee, it appears that these mentoring styles may also be used as a point of discussion for consultants who work with new teachers or more established teachers. Ruth and her colleagues followed the image of "the parable of the sower of seeds" which metaphorically relates to each of the following styles of mentoring. The accompanying circular image is consistent with Ruth's model for working with her staff and teachers. The three styles of mentoring are described below.

Responders. Supervisors may respond to teachers or other colleagues as the need arises, usually for immediate material resource assistance. However, supervisors may also make themselves available to teachers, therefore, encouraging them to ask for help or advice. Later, the necessary assistance can be provided.

Colleagues. Supervisors who make frequent informal visits to teachers invite consultation. Teachers are more likely to seek assistance from consultants who take an interest in their work. As concerns are raised by teachers, the supervisor offers the necessary assistance.

Initiators. At this level supervisors may believe it is their responsibility to facilitate the professional growth of the teacher. Therefore, in addition to providing the necessary assistance, initiators often make specific suggestions for the teachers.

For women supervisors, these three styles of mentorship may be informally connected with the ebb and flow of activities, time and energy, and move in and out of any of the styles. Supervisors and consultants naturally work with many teachers. Women supervisors may believe that working with a community of teachers (subject-based; school-based; project-based) is vitally important. Therefore, a supervisor who sees herself as a change facilitator and as a role model vis-à-vis mentor, may be involved with many teachers: some at the responder level, others as colleagues, and still others as initiators. This is particularly true given the dynamics of formal or informal arrangements between mentor and mentee. What is needed is an adaptation of Huling-Astin's (1990) ideas set within the consultant as leader and mentor notion.

If we take the same circular format described earlier in this chapter as a starting point, another format might be superimposed. The supervisor as leader is retained within a small inner circle. Radiating out in 3 concentric dotted (thus fluid) circles are the three levels of responder (outside ring), colleague, and initiator. The mentee(s) is represented beyond the outer ring. The image is another circular format which radiates outward from the inner circle of the consultant. This image should portray the enlarging circle of professionalism and the expanding nature of involvement between individuals. It also illustrates that consultants may have a number of mentees who may or may not be connected and learning together.

The two studies outlined in this book portray two interrelated functions of the supervisor's or consultant's role: leadership and mentorship. The circle of empowerment is a circle representing leadership *and* mentorship at once. In my mind this might be seen as two versions of the circle superimposed over each other thus portraying the dynamic complexity of the supervisory role.

Given that the participants in the studies were all women, we are left to consider if the findings are indicative of women, or of men and women. To my way of thinking there is no reason why men and women cannot both subscribe to the dimensions of leadership and mentorship provided here. However, there is an overarching recognition for the women participants in the studies detailed here as these ideas may be woman-centered. Ruth, for instance, subscribed to a circular format when illustrating how her Fine Arts Centre was organized and run. Using a circular format, the most desirable location for the leader is at the center of the circle therefore allowing one to draw others in closer, to strengthen the outer fabric with more interconnections and to honor feminine principles of inclusion and connection (Gilligan 1982).

If we superimpose the two figures representing leadership and mentorship one over the other, the complexity of the role of consultant becomes apparent. For those who are comfortable with a hierarchial model, this process may seem unfocused and too scattered. But to many women, this kind of format will seem highly appropriate.

Strategies that supervisors or consultants may use as a result of a circular format are often led by opportunity, intuition, and patience. The result is a growth-centered notion of success. With a vision, rather than goals, with a voice rather than rules, with trust and commitment rather than selfish competition, and with empowerment rather than power and control, women leaders can change the face of education. They can also mentor teachers at all levels of responsiveness to educational change (see Fisher 1988, for in-depth discussion).

Having considered a reconstruction of leadership, it is best now to reflect upon the research process undertaken in the studies reported here.

REFLECTIONS ON THE RESEARCH

Reflections on the Research Process

The two studies reported in this book have described and interpreted the practical knowledge and leadership of a fine arts supervisor. Ruth was portrayed as an exemplary case study through the triangulation of various data, collection techniques, and sources. Her exemplary nature and abilities were constantly recognized by myself and other professionals in the field. However, one cannot be so naive as to believe Ruth was a saint. Given the exemplary nature of her as a subject, there is a danger that the portrait may be two dimensional, too perfect. In some sense, that is true, and is a limitation of the studies.

Constantly during the data collection process, I looked for moments or events that would suggest weaknesses even though I knew the intent of the research was not to evaluate her practice. It was not an easy task, perhaps (in part) because of Ruth's ability to protect her status. She recognized her position in the field, her expertise, and the adoration given to her by many people. I suspect she found it worthwhile to protect this status. For instance, she assumed a definite distance from me until she was certain of my integrity.

On several occasions Ruth spoke of control. By controling her involvement in other people's lives and the involvement of others in her life, Ruth was exhibiting a type of personal control. This, in turn, influenced her personal actions within her role thereby allowing her to protect her professional status. Thus, my descriptions necessarily form an incomplete picture. Ruth controlled me, in excluding me from talks with superintendents. The extent to which she was in control, or not in control, in these situations remains a mystery. In an interview, her associate superintendent of curriculum suggested Ruth should become more politically active throughout the school system. The comment was made as a possible suggestion for improvement. From my viewpoint, it may have hinted at an area of limitation in Ruth's practical knowledge.

There were other occasions which Ruth controlled. I was not invited to informal gatherings with her staff until late in the first study. She did not share with me several personal family concerns until after many others already knew.

To that extent, she controlled my interpretation of her success story. She may have been motivated by a desire to keep to herself certain sensitive aspects reflecting the success of her career or of other people's opinions of her professional status.

One particular incident stands out for me. I had heard through the grapevine, so to speak, that Ruth had been a nun. Though I tried to draw this out of her throughout the study it was not until the last interview, when I asked her directly whether or not she had been a nun, that she actually talked about her experiences as a nun. Ironically, the subject came up around the Center's conference table with her staff the very next day. It was obvious they knew of her involvement, but not necessarily in any detail. She had protected herself from sharing certain incidents with most of her associates. She controlled what people knew of her personal life and certain portions of her professional life.

There were moments when Ruth displayed those more human frailties: irritation, frustration, anger. One incident (FD 15, 84) was directed toward my presence. After three weeks into the study, and having been at provincial curriculum meetings for two days, Ruth returned to a backlog of memorandums, tasks, and phone calls. My presence, I sensed, was the cause of further annoyance. She suggested I take the afternoon off to do some of my own work. I agreed and returned the following morning. She had barely started work when she called me to her desk and disciplined me. I had briefly filed a broken fingernail during a meeting the day before. She told me to watch this since it was different behavior and would be noticed. Though I agreed, I could not help but see it as a way for her to have some immediate control of the situation between the two of us. I did not let it bother me, though I made a greater effort to be aware of any nervous habits that might be distracting. During the first study, I paid attention to other factors that would allow me to blend into the woodwork. For instance, I chose a limited selection of clothing to wear. In this way, my usual bold colors were bypassed for more subdued colors, and my selected attire was not overstated. My intent was to minimize the interactive effect of two personalities engaged in discussion on an equal footing.

Personally speaking, the two studies had a greater influence on me than I had anticipated. I felt like Ruth had been my mentor. My consulting experience had prepared me, but watching Ruth in action offered me an opportunity to refine my knowledge, to think about my own practical knowledge, and to enjoy the whole process of field research. On the other hand, the shadowing aspect of the study forced me to put my "ego" on hold for those few months. Everything was directed to Ruth and the study. Nothing was directed toward me, and at times, that was difficult to handle. I learned a lot about myself in the process.

As I completed the first study, Ruth was much more comfortable with me. When we met again some time after the data was collected, she commented on missing my presence. Perhaps with more time, a greater understanding of her "humanness" might have been captured. One cannot know for sure. But in one important sense, Ruth remained an enigma. I never saw her when she was potentially most vulnerable, that is, in her dealings with others who were in positions of authority over her.

Reflections on the Research Study

This research was founded upon the assumption that the subject occupied exemplary status as a fine arts supervisor. One might ask in retrospect what it was about Ruth Britten's practical knowledge that perhaps made her more successful than her counterparts. Though it was not within the scope of either of these studies to compare Ruth's practical knowledge with that of other supervisors, Ruth herself believed that consultants and supervisors needed to have great "heuristic abilities." Perhaps Ruth's heuristic ability to handle the dialectical nature of her role and knowledge implicit within that role, was greater than that achieved by many of her counterparts. As mentioned earlier (Sternberg and Caruso 1985), success may be associated with having greater amounts of tacit or practical knowledge. If this is true, then the portrayal of Ruth provided in this document, is a description and interpretation of a wealth of practical knowledge. Moreover, there is an unmistakable character to Ruth's practical knowledge that may more fully develop its scope: that is, her conviction, her desire, her will to influence positive change. It is her "passion" for people, for the arts, for learning, and for loving. One cannot escape her intensity, her search for excellence, and the power of her personal practical knowledge. Not only the power associated with order, control, and stability, and the power of empowerment found in love, commitment, and mutual trust, but also the power of a supervisor's personal practical knowledge to influence the decision-making of others, to winning others over, and thus to influence teachers' or administrators' practical knowledge.

Implications for Theory

An important implication for theory exists: educational change or curriculum implementation is essentially a political act. Aoki (1984) suggested this, since he felt implementation was an activity involving power and control. His work, however, focused upon the power of individuals to transform their realities. The first study presented here extends our understanding of the dialectics found within power and control during curriculum implementation, and how that is reflected in one fine arts supervisor's practical knowledge. Future theoretical constructions regarding curriculum implementation or practical knowledge should account for this dialectical orientation. Conceptual analyses should also explore the notion of "power" more thoroughly, particularly as it applies to curriculum implementation.

Implications for Practice

Several important implications for practice should be considered. These studies contribute to existing knowledge in the area of practical knowledge through the identification of the adaptations a supervisor's practical knowledge must make from that of a teacher's practical knowledge and how a supervisor's practical knowledge and dimensions of leadership influence the practical knowledge of colleagues. Many implications result for practitioners in the field.

First of all, it is fallacious to assume "master" teacher knowledge is enough or even appropriate for a teacher who assumes the role of consultant or supervisor. Rather, supervisory practical knowledge is in some respects different from teacher practical knowledge: curriculum implementation is a major content change and the political knowledge context is a significant contextual change. If this is so, several implications arise. As the second study implies prospective consultants or supervisors should receive internship study through the guidance of "mentors," presumably people with significant practical knowledge as consultants or supervisors. In this way, tacit knowledge may be developed through tacit instruction.

Ruth's experiential knowledge told her "it took three years for a consultant to reach her stride." Assuming this means the acquisition of a satisfactory amount of practical knowledge to do the job, school district personnel officers who implement policies requiring consultants to be hired for short two or three year contracts are being unrealistic in their expectations. Instead, policy development should allow opportunities for consultants or supervisors to remain in their roles for longer periods of time. Practical knowledge is gained from on-the-job experience. Given the complexity of the role and the significant structural differences from a teacher's practical knowledge, time and experience are essential factors in the acquisition of supervisory practical knowledge. This is further verified if we accept that the more practical knowledge one has, the more successful one may be in the role (Sternberg and Caruso 1985).

If policy development remains unchanged, another implication should be considered. Once the fundamental structure of one's practical knowledge has changed, can the consultant return to the classroom and revert to teacher practical knowledge? Would one try to apply the structurally revised practical knowledge to the realm of teaching? It would seem logical that one would not simply "forget" or "deny" acquired knowledge. Perhaps then, the latter becomes the practice. If so, how might the ex-consultant or supervisor resolve the difference?

The research field has verified the necessity for the role of supervisor or consultant during educational change efforts with teachers. What these studies suggest is that supervisors act in dialectical relationship between teachers and administrators, and as such, fulfill a unique role in the organizational structure of the school district. Supervisors are a necessary interface between teachers and administrators. They may offer senior administration a continual refocusing of the student-teacher world of learning and teaching, rather than simply of management and enforcement of policies and regulations. At the same time, supervisors and consultants may remind teachers of the necessity of standards throughout the school system, rather than simply encouraging individual teacher efficacy. Without this political interface role, perhaps greater incongruity would exist between teacher commitment and administrative expectations. Without such a position, administrators and teachers would need to act in ways that would bring them closer to negotiating between the extremes found between having power over versus sharing power with others.

The dialectical orientation between teachers and administrators, found in Ruth's images of teacher power and empowerment and bureaucratic power and control, is a critical interface organizationally and humanistically. Supervisors and consultants need to recognize the political perspective of curriculum implementation and thus the dialectical notion of "power": its extremes, varying qualities, and differing strategies. Having done so, supervisors may then begin to reflect upon their personal conceptions of power in relation to teacher empowerment and administrative power. Through critical reflection, one may begin to recognize implicit theories-in-action regarding one's own understanding of power.

The original study illustrates the dialectical nature of rules, principles, and images apparent in supervisory practical knowledge and the subsequent need to act heuristically. Perhaps the success of a supervisor rests, at least partially, on the ability to manage the complexity of the role in an inventive and adaptive heuristic way. If so, not just any educator should or could become a successful supervisor.

It is wise to recall Ruth's "passion" for her role. It would seem that one's ability to mobilize one's practical knowledge becomes another form of power. In Ruth's case, her passion for the arts in education may have underscored her exemplary status. The implications of this suggest that the amount of accumulated practical knowledge may encourage one's ultimate success, but to ensure success, one must extend a personal power; that is, courage of conviction, dedication, will, belief, desire, personal passion, or a strong, profound personal sense of efficacy. "Knowledge feeds passion," "passion is powerful" and "people follow passion."

It would be beneficial for supervisors and consultants to engage in dialogue with one another, to begin to verbalize and uncover the consistencies and contradictions inherent within their practices, in order to reflect critically upon their ability to influence educational change. In so doing, practitioners will come to view their taken-for-granted practical knowledge in an explicit manner. Having done so, efforts may be made to alter, adjust, or reinforce practice and thus, implicit rules, principles, and images. Supervisory courses could be developed so that supervisors and consultants may come to a greater awareness of their own narrative unity, and thus strengthen their personal power.

It would be particularly beneficial for women consultants and supervisors to dialogue with one another in order to discuss their beliefs and values toward leadership and mentorship, and teaching leadership. This would lead to greater understanding of issues related to having power over versus sharing power with others. It would also lead to the sharing of strategies among women leaders who desire to see improved educational practices.

Implications for Research

As a result of these studies, there are several suggestions which other researchers may use in conceptualizing further research studies. The original single case study described and interpreted the personal practical knowledge of one fine arts supervisor in depth. This is valuable as a starting point to understanding the complexity of the role of supervisor but further research should seek to verify the adaptations made to the overall nature of supervisory practical knowledge through multiple-case study research projects with several supervisors. In this study, internal validity is strengthened with the researcher acting as the instrument, the device, and the measure. The degree to which this validity is sound lies in the correspondence between what is measured and what was intended to be measured. Validity can be claimed if the results are generalizable to other settings. Other supervisors or consultants reading this study may feel there are similarities between their practical knowledge and what is portrayed here. However, greater validity would be achieved through multiple-case study research.

Through the identification of several exemplary supervisors from varying subject-matter disciplines, researchers may study the nature of success in regard to practical knowledge. These studies explored power, empowerment, and passion. Perhaps power can be more fully conceptualized in a study of several exemplary figures' practical knowledge. Further integration with feminist literature and research would also offer more insights into an emerging trend towards women in educational leadership positions.

Further research should also be conducted within communities of women in educational circles in order to portray similar or different forms of practical knowledge of leaders and teachers and to learn about the influence of practical knowledge of individuals upon one another. Although literature in the area of women in education is growing, a great deal more work needs to be done. We simply do not know enough about the experiences of women in every educational role. This book tells the story of one individual's experience in an in-depth way. Further research should continue to tell the stories of other women in education.

Appendix

This section examines research methods used in the studies reported here. Field research methods are derived from such disciplines as anthropology and sociology. These disciplines will be outlined in the section providing an overview of field research and in the section presenting theoretical underpinnings. Following this, the pilot study and the justification for choosing single case study research will be reported. Subsequent to this, a description will be given of data collection concerns, techniques, and ongoing data analysis.

Overview to Field Research

The situational interpretive orientation to inquiry seeks to relate man [*sic*]-to-his-social-world (Aoki 1978). In order to understand this orientation, researchers endeavor to uncover whatever intersubjective meanings are held by the participants as part of their respective worlds. Situational knowledge portrays a structure of interpretive meanings people assign to their situations. Explaining then, is "striking a resonant chord by clarifying motives, common meanings and authentic experience" (p. 56).

Certain research methodologies are particularly conducive to this orientation. Each participant sees reality as a social construction; the social researcher in response, adopts an attitude of "respect" or "appreciation" (Hammersley and Atkinson 1983). The disciplines of anthropology and sociology have formed a strong linkage in field research, a term used by anthropologists and sociologists alike to denote the fact that their data are collected directly from the field as opposed to, for example, laboratories (Junker 1960; Becker 1970; Hammersley and Woods 1975). Qualitative research implies a similar approach, acting as an umbrella term for several research strategies that share certain characteristics (Bogdan and Biklen 1982). Still other terms are used interchangeably. Naturalistic inquiry, focusing on the natural setting, stems predominantly from the symbolic interactionists in sociology (Glaser and Strauss 1967; Blumer 1969, 1976), while anthropologists have sought to describe culture through ethnographic research (Spradley and McCurdy 1972; Spindler 1982).

This family of terms serves to denote a contrast to positivism, or the empirical analytical orientation modeled after the natural sciences, and the critical orientation deriving from some kinds of psychology. In positivistic research the logic of the experiment is used to establish through universal laws regular relationships between variables under certain conditions. Theories must be tested for confirmation and generalizability, allowing for replication by others in order to assess reliability of the findings (Wiersma 1986). In critical science (Carr and Kemmis 1983; McCutcheon 1981), reflection upon thought is viewed as a means to improve the human condition, with researchers seeking to uncover tacit or hidden assumptions, motives, perspectives, and implications for action. Contrasting these orientations is the field research orientation.

Theoretical Underpinnings

Field research may be considered a generic term for observing events in the natural setting (Schatzman and Strauss 1973). It draws from a wide array of philosophical, anthropological and sociological ideas such as phenomenology, symbolic interactionism, ethnomethodology, linguistic philosophy, and hermeneutics. Each area of inquiry centrally deals with the social meanings embedded within intentions, beliefs, motives, and attitudes. Therefore, field research methods include approaches that allow for access to the meanings that guide individual behavior.

Phenomenology, for instance, is the study of phenomena, which seeks to place qualitative meaning on all events and interactions affecting the people under study. Phenomenologists do not assume they know what things mean to the people they are studying, but rather, they attempt to understand the conceptual world of their subjects in order to interpret the meaning constructed around events in their everyday lives (Geertz 1973).

Compatible with phenomenology is the tradition of symbolic interactionism (Blumer 1969). Both assume that human experience is mediated by interpretation, with participants assigning meaning to people, objects, events, and situations. Since humans are actively engaged in creating their own meaning, researchers must choose to be participant observers in order regularly to interact with or observe the subject as an expression of self and as a member of several subcultures within society. Interactionists are concerned with how individuals construct meaning from interaction with others. In particular, individuals define themselves as a result of social interaction, enabling people to change and grow as they move through an interactive process.

Many anthropologists use a phenomenological perspective to describe a given culture, otherwise known as ethnography (Spindler 1982; Wolcott 1973). A true ethnography is considered a description of cultural meanings given to all the settings, objects, events, informants, and their experiences within a particular culture foreign to the researcher, whereas an ethnology uses an ethnography as a foundation for further classification, comparison and explanation (Spradley and McCurdy 1972). It is important to clarify that an ethnography is not a research strategy, although ethnographic techniques may be used in field research. This is especially true since many researchers use these techniques in cultures common to them. Robert C. Bogden, and Sara K. Biklen (1982) suggest a series of research strategies that may be viewed as ethnographic: participant-observation, documentary evidence, and in-depth, structured and semi-structured interviews. Using these techniques, the field researcher tries to unfold the "emic" cultural knowledge (view from within the culture) in its most natural form (Spindler 1982, p. 6)

Five traits tend to characterize field research (Bogden and Biklen 1982). First of all, the natural setting is considered to be the direct source of data with the researcher acting as the key instrument. Countless studies have found researchers "shadowing" main actors. Harry Wolcott, for example, chose to shadow an elementary school principal for a two year period (1973). However, other researchers have described and interpreted life-worlds anywhere from primitive societies (Wax 1971) to students in medical schools (Becker, Geer, Hughes, et al., 1961) to the induction of a beginning teacher of art (Hawke 1980). This also reinforces the second trait: meaning is the essential concern. Researchers are primarily concerned with discovering the ways different people make sense of their lives.

Third, "qualitative researchers are concerned with process rather than simply with outcomes or products" (Bogden and Biklen 1982, p. 28). Understanding how it is that people create meaning from social situations is predominantly a process of coming to appreciate the insider's viewpoint through contextualization (Wiersma 1986, p. 234).

Fourth, field research is descriptive, perhaps even obsessively so. Taken-for-grantedness becomes important if the researcher is going to unlock a deeper and more comprehensive understanding of the person, event, or situation under study.

Finally, researchers in this tradition tend to analyze their data inductively. Since they are not out to prove or disprove hypotheses held before entering the study, abstractions are categorized to develop theory that develops from the bottom up, or what Barney Glaser, and Anselm L. Strauss have coined as "grounded theory" (1967). As data collection ensues and initial analysis is undertaken, theories begin to emerge. The researcher uses this process of induction continuously to focus ever more specifically toward underlying meanings.

In drawing together all of these perspectives and traits, the field researcher begins to realize the variety of viewpoints available as research strategies. In essence:

The field researcher is a methodological pragmatist. He sees any method of inquiry as a system of strategies and operations designed—at any time—for getting answers to certain questions about events which interest him (Schatzman and Strauss 1973, p. 7).

Field researchers often proceed based on a combination of the above theoretical perspectives. These areas of inquiry provide the necessary parameters, direction, and methods in which to proceed flexibly, or if desirable, in a manner faithful to a single perspective. Though a basic understanding may initially direct the research, data-gathering design decisions are made throughout the study. Indeed decisions about design and analysis proceed hand in hand. Research always begins with some problem or issue, or what Malinowski referred to as "foreshadowed problems" (cited in Hammersley and Atkinson 1983, p. 28), though some research seeks to develop theories inductively through systematic data collection (Glaser and Strauss 1967).

Foreshadowed problems for this study were presented earlier as I discussed the conflicts that emerged for me when I was a consultant. Further to this, the research study is grounded in the literature of personal practical knowledge. The model developed by Elbaz (1981) and further elaborated by Clandinin (1983), and Connelly and Clandinin (n.d.) was used as a structure from which to begin characterizing the practical knowledge of the supervisor. After a six week period of collecting and analyzing data inductively, I compared my analysis with the structure defined by the above authors and found overlapping categories. However, no attempt was made to limit the research categories to those referred to in the model and adaptations were made as a result of analyzing the data inductively in response to the unique nature of the supervisor's practical knowledge. These adaptations are illustrated at the appropriate points later in the document.

Case Study Research

Case studies are often described in field research. The single case study is the detailed examination of one setting, subject, set of documents or events. It offers the researcher an opportunity to probe in-depth. Bogden and Biklen (1982) suggest there are several types of case studies: historical, observational, and life history. Researchers using this concentration scout for possible places and people that might be the subject or the source of the data. Robert K. Yin suggests (1984) that the rationale for a single case study design has to do with representing: (1) the critical case; (2) the extreme case; or (3) the revelatory case (p. 42–43). The studies being reported here most appropriately fall into an extreme case category since Ruth is considered an exemplar in her field.

When researchers study two or more settings, subjects, or events, they are doing multiple-case studies. Bogden and Biklen (1982) suggest that some multiple-case studies begin with a single case study, which later becomes the first in a series of studies, while some researchers do comparative case studies. With the latter, two or more studies are done and then compared or contrasted.

In conceptualizing the original study, I listed all the consultants and supervisors of art or fine arts I knew in Western Canada. Through careful attention to the possible participants, I considered either a multiple-case study or a single case study approach. Having reviewed the literature on supervisors and its critical neglect of the role of a single supervisor within a school district setting, particularly in a research study employing ethnographic techniques, it became obvious that a single case study would be beneficial to the field. This became even more evident as I realized the study might be used to describe one particular supervisor who was considered an exemplar in the field. On the basis of professional and personal knowledge of Ruth, prior to conceptualizing the study, I joined with other consultants, supervisors, teachers, and principals in Western Canada, in admiring her supervisory abilities. Seldom if ever, did anyone speak against Ruth. For the most part, she had acquired many friends at all levels of the workforce and had been instrumental in many change efforts. To provide her colleagues with the opportunity to analyze and reflect upon the knowledge of such a leader in the field of art education, and as a role model for fellow consultants and supervisors in their pursuit of significant and meaningful educational change, would be of significant value to the field. The breadth of understanding that might have been gained through a multiple-case study was set aside in favor of the depth that would be attained in a single case study of an exceptional supervisor.

Gaining Entry

Negotiating access into research settings is a common problem in field research. The researcher usually needs to sell herself as a credible person doing a worthwhile project (Woods 1986, p. 22). Prior to the studies reported here, Ruth and I had known one another previously on a purely professional level. After following university protocol for gaining entry into her School Board, I phoned to confirm her participation in the study. I spoke to her about how she might benefit from the experience as well as I, especially since I would be a participant-observer and would be able to do some things with or for her. On my one pre-research visit, Ruth remarked that she would not have participated in this study if it had been anyone else as the researcher (Pre-Field diary 2, 1). Gaining entry was contingent upon my standing as a person in the eyes of Ruth. She viewed me as a credible individual with similar interests, goals, and notions regarding the arts, education, and consulting. And though I was credible in her eyes, I was distanced enough to allow for reliable data collection. However, as the research study progressed, gaining access into other people's domains often took extra patience and care. Peter Woods suggests that negotiating access "is not just about getting into an institution or group in the sense of crossing the threshold that marks it off from the outside world, but proceeding across several thresholds that mark the way to the heart of a culture" (1986, p. 24).

John M. Johnson (1975) agrees with Woods when he says "all entrees are progressive in that a researcher gets to know more and more people as his research proceeds" (p. 64). In this sense, negotiating access and data collection are not separate phases in the research design and may overlap significantly (Hammersley and Atkinson 1983). Often, gatekeepers guard access into certain settings and become the field researcher's initial contact with the research setting. These people are primarily concerned about the image of the setting the researcher will uncover and may therefore attempt to control the line of inquiry exercised by the researcher (Bogden and Biklen 1982, p. 121). Whatever problems are encountered as an attempt to gaining access, the emphasis remains upon building trust and rapport (Junker 1960, p. 32). In this study, one specialist teacher at the Fine Arts Centre acted as a gatekeeper. Throughout the study, even until the last day, she would tell me things about Ruth, albeit more as time went along, but they were nearly always couched with a statement asking me not to record it in my little book. She was obviously very concerned about the image I would portray. She was not going to be responsible for drawing any attention to flaws in the operation of the Centre, and she was certainly always faithful to Ruth. Another individual who was a critical gatekeeper was Ruth's secretary. As she came to accept my presence, she offered to share more information verbally and through written documents. Everything she typed for Ruth for instance was photocopied and given to me.

Unfortunately, throughout the single case study, I was never granted entry into any one-on-one meetings between Ruth and her superiors. She felt these few meetings were too critical to jeopardize. She had approximately five of these meetings during the fifteen week time period I spent with her.

The Researcher as Participant-Observer

As researchers enter the field they must be conscious of the participant-observer continuum (Burgess 1984). At one extreme is the complete observer doing covert research from a firmly rooted sociological stance. Although these researchers believe they uncover valid knowledge due primarily to lack of researcher effect or bias of the culture under study, there are concerns associated with non-reciprocity because of the lack of contact with the participants. The researcher having no overt relationship, can never cross-check perceptions with those of the participants. At the other extreme, we have complete participation, an overt method deriving from anthropology. Again, this appears to be advantageous until one realizes that over-participation could lead to "going native": becoming so involved with the subjects that the original intention gets lost (Bogden and Biklen 1982, p. 128). Between these two extremes lie the viewpoints of participant-as-observer and observer-as-participant, assuming these perspectives offers the researcher maximum freedom to adopt or avoid participating in a given situation. Frequently, these last two stances ask the researcher to assume the attitude of the respectable incompetent or novice, acting as a stranger and as a friend. In fact, research roles are constantly negotiated and renegotiated with different informants throughout the research project (Schatzman and Strauss 1973).

For the original study, I essentially "shadowed" Ruth for approximately 80 to 85 percent of a four month research period—September through December. The remaining time reflected the few days she had at meetings in other cities, or the few days I spent on academic matters away from the research site.

For the extended study, I interviewed each woman twice for approximately one to three hours each time. I also met informally with them on a number of occasions. My work with each of them in the original study was also used in the extended study as a means of grounding the work concerning what I had learned about Ruth's practical knowledge.

I characterized my role as primarily a participant-as-observer during the original study because of the shadowing aspect. This did not mean that Ruth and I never talked, for often during the day she would stop and talk to me about certain situations. This was important for her since she believed knowledge was contextual. So that I might be perceived as more of a participant than an observer, I helped out around the Centre gathering materials for lessons, preparing music for choir rehearsals, collecting ticket money for upcoming concerts, and several other secretarial tasks. In this way, I was perceived as providing some of the operating assistance the Centre had lost during the previous budget cutbacks. I felt tugged at times to go "native" especially during the first month of the study, but gradually a balance was found and everyone seemed to understand my placement in the organization. As time passed and my involvement and perceptions increased, so did the amount of data I was developing increase.

Qualitative Data Collection and Ongoing Analysis

Data collection in field research may be obtained in several ways. This section describes those most commonly used and implemented in the study.

Field notes.   Field notes are the primary source of data in this form of research. Everything that is perceived or reflected upon is actively gathered into this data bank. Substantive field notes are a continuous record of the situations, events, and conversations in which the researcher is involved. Occasionally, field notes are gathered with particular categories in mind, while at other times they may be more concerned with conceptual issues (Burgess 1984).

Field notes are obtained by observing participants in their own culture. James P. Spradley (1980) suggests three types of observation: descriptive, focused, and selective observations. Descriptive observations aim to describe the setting, the people, and the events that take place. Spradley suggests that in doing descriptive observations, nine features need to be identified: space, actors, activities, objects, acts, events, time, goals, and feelings. Once these are described in field notes, questions can begin to uncover more focused areas for observation, and thus focused observation is attempted. As more detailed portraits of a given situation are portrayed, finer and more distinct selections become important for continuing analysis and thus selective observation emerges.

Several types of field notes should be carefully maintained. Methodological field notes are kept in conjunction with substantive field notes. These notes consist of personal reflections, impressions, and problems encountered in the field. This form of note taking allows the observer to be reflective as a form of analysis throughout the research (Burgess 1984).

Barney Glaser and Anselm L. Strauss (1967), and Leonard Schatzman and Anselm L. Strauss (1973) emphasize the importance of analytic notes. As preliminary analyses develop during the research, analytic notes help pose questions, hypotheses or propositions in order to develop models or theories.

These various forms of field notes were kept throughout the study and totalled sixty-three entries, or in other words, represented data collected over a total of sixty-three days. Quotations made from these notes are referred to by FD, followed by the number of the entry (number of consecutive days to date), and the page number. For example, (FD 3, 20), stands for Field Diary entry #3, page 20.

Formal and informal observations.   Another type of field notes are formal and informal observations. The only differences between these and the field notes mentioned above are reflected in the researcher's overt note taking during a particular event. Formal observations are collected for short periods of time, such as a half an hour, in which the researcher gathers as much detail as possible. Due to the intensity of the writing, the researcher should be inconspicuously situated so as not to draw any attention. Informal observations are a more relaxed form of overt note taking of a specific event over a longer period of time, such as two hours. Spradley's (1980) nine categories need to be attended to, unless certain predetermined parameters define the data collection. For this study, four formal observations were gathered during a one-on-one teacher visit with Ruth, as well as a demonstration lesson, and two speeches given at conferences. Quotations made from formal observations are referred to as FO, followed by the number of the entry, and the page number. For example, (FO 4, 17), stands for Formal Observation #4, page 17.

Eleven informal observations were made during this research. Two were during small group meetings with teachers, three with Fine Arts Centre staff meetings, one of a demonstration lesson, two with arts council meetings, one with a supervisor's meeting, one with the fine arts school extension into junior high meeting, and one with a one-on-one meeting with a principal. Quotations made from informal observations are referred to as IO, followed by the number of the entry, and the page number. For example, (IO 11, 4), stands for Informal Observation #11, page 4.

Interviews.   An interviewer should endeavor to strike a balance between two extremes on an interview continuum. One end seeks to provide a conversation, done in an informal, open, unstructured and reflexive fashion. On the other, interrogation is conducted in a formal, closed, structured and standardized manner. Only a balance will provide validity and reliability from an intense interview capturing the respondent's perspective.

During both studies, I was able to develop rapport with Ruth and her colleagues by showing interest, understanding and sympathy for their lives. In this way Robert G. Burgess (1984) suggests interviews complement participant-observation. To begin, I had prepared aides-memoirs to ensure the coverage of certain topics. However, these were left open enough to allow Ruth to expand on those things of interest. Finally, I tried to accommodate different questioning techniques, as recommended by Burgess.

> First, descriptive questions which allow informants to provide statements about their activities. Secondly, structural questions which attempt to find out how informants organize their knowledge and, finally, contrast questions which allow informants to discuss the meanings of situations and provide an opportunity for comparisons to take place between situations and events in the informant's world. (Burgess 1984, pp.111–112)

Questions should always be conceived as "triggers" aiming to pull out new, more focused, or more precise responses from the respondents. Generally, the researcher moves through setting the tone with the respondent in an informal way, then recalls something both have experienced in order to form a consensus, and proceeds directly into theme questions. Language used by the respondent is critically important and the interviewer should not attempt to interpret but should have the respondent interpret what is being said. These technical aspects of interviewing were observed throughout the study.

Fourteen interviews were given during the course of the original study. Five were with Ruth at approximately three week intervals throughout the study. Of the nine remaining, one each was held with: an art specialist, drama specialist, music consultant, secretary, junior high art teacher, university art education professor, modern languages supervisor, senior high principal, and the associate superintendent of curriculum. Quotations made from any interviews in the original study are referred to as Inter, followed by the number of the entry, and the page number. For example, (Inter 1, 8), represents Interview #1, page 8. Quotations in the second study are referred to by the name (pseudonym) of the respondent.

Documents.   Personal documents produced by Ruth were collected because they described particular actions, experiences, and beliefs, often revealing her personal viewpoint. Collected as well, were documents influencing her practice such as memorandums, letters, and records. Many of these documents were readily available but some were solicited.

To analyze the documents, content analysis was essential. To begin, it was necessary to consider the authenticity of the documents, the possibility of distortion and deception on the part of the author of the document, and the availability and sampling of the documentary evidence (Burgess 1984). As each of these points was considered, I looked for structures, themes or categories. Consideration was given to determining if the intent was consistent with the content, and in fact, what effect the content had on its intended audience.

Triangulation.   As the data collection and ongoing analyses ensued, it became important to consider what Norman K. Denzin (1978) suggested as several forms of cross-validation or triangulation. Essentially, triangulation is a comparison of different forms of information to determine whether or not there is corroboration. To the extent that this procedure is carried out during the study, the researcher can assess if a sufficient amount of data has been collected in a given area in order to determine the validity across sources. Different sources were used singularly or in combination to form triangulation. Data triangulation refers to time, space, or person triangulation as they related to the study. Methodological triangulation was also used and refers to one method used on different occasions or different methods used on the same subject.

Data analysis.   Data analysis was undertaken throughout the data collection process. I began by recognizing what sensitizers were guiding the research. Sensitizers are any recurring words, ideas, or images found within the data or the theoretical literature guiding the research. For example, early on Ruth used the word "community" to describe such situations as working with teachers and peers, and later as her experience as a nun. As the studies progressed this was found to be a major image guiding her practical knowledge. Having acknowledged this sensitizer and others, coding of all the material ensued according to key words or terminology used by Ruth. Model building began and through constant comparison and triangulation, categories emerged. I was careful to look for contradictions or negative evidence in order to further focus my reflections upon her practical knowledge. Finally, a theoretical model was considered deductively according to the literature of practical knowledge, but inductively in order to question the differences between teacher and supervisor practical knowledge. Though it is outlined as a linear process here, it was in fact dynamic, and perhaps more like a circular process.

Validity and reliability.   Field research tries to bring together the unique and the general, focusing on the subjective and the objective. As with all research, validity and reliability are crucial elements. Internal validity is quite high for field research since it uses the setting as its source for data collection. Internal validity is strengthened with the researcher acting as the instrument, the device, and the measure. The degree to which this validity is sound lies in the correspondence between what is measured and what was intended to be measured. External validity can be claimed if the results are generalizable to other settings. In this study, that can be determined only by other supervisors or consultants who feel their practical knowledge has some similarity to what is portrayed here. Finally, reliability is achieved when the data collection and analysis procedures are so carefully documented that another researcher could follow the data collection and analysis and determine the same results (Yin 1984, p. 36).

Endnotes

CHAPTER 2: CHARISMATIC AND TRANSFORMATIONAL LEADERSHIP

1. An earlier version of this chapter appears in the *Canadian Review of Art Education* (1993) 20(2): 80–98, entitled "Charismatic and transformational leadership within a community of women arts educators.". The author is grateful to the editors of that journal for giving their permission to reprint the article with adaptation here.

CHAPTER 3: THE BASIS AND CONTENT OF RUTH'S
PERSONAL PRACTICAL KNOWLEDGE

1. Interview quotes previously published in *Studies in Art Education* (1992) 33(2): 110–121, entitled "A Profile of an Arts Supervisor" are reprinted in chapters 3 and 4 with permission of the editor.

CHAPTER 4: THE CONTEXTS OF RUTH'S PRACTICAL KNOWLEDGE

1. Werner (1987) has used this spelling. For the purposes of this study, the term "colleagual" (defined as a member of a profession), rather than "collegial" (defined as belonging to a college), is used for it better describes the intent of Ruth's model of change.

CHAPTER 5: RUTH IN EDUCATIONAL CHANGE

1. The sections entitled "Power and empowerment in teacher change," "Bureaucratic control and educational stability," "The interface between teachers and administration," and "Image as a conceptual tool" are reprinted with permission from: Rita L. Irwin. (1989). "A Fine Arts Supervisor's Practical Knowledge: A Case Study." *Visual Arts Research*, 15(1), 21–35.

References

Aburdene, Patricia, and John Naisbitt. 1992. *Megatrends for women*. New York: Villard Books.

Aisenberg, Nadya, and Mona Harringtona. 1988. *Women of the academe: Outsiders in the sacred grove*. Amherst: The University of Massachusetts Press.

Al-Khalifa, Elisabeth. 1989. Management by halves: Women teachers and school management. In Hilary DeLyon, and Frances Widdowson Migniuolo Eds. *Women teachers: Issues and experiences*. pp. 83–96. Philadelphia: Open University Press.

Aoki, T. Tetsuo. 1984. *Curriculum implementation as instrumental action and as situational praxis*. Curriculum praxis monograph series no. 9, pp. 4–17. Edmonton: University of Alberta, Department of Secondary Education.

———. 1978. Toward curriculum inquiry in a new key. In James J. Victoria and Elizabeth J. Sacca Eds. *Presentations on art education research: Phenomenological description*, pp. 47–69. Montreal: Concordia University, 1(2).

———. 1983. Towards a dialectic between the conceptual world: Transcending instrumentalism in curriculum orientation. *Journal of Curriculum Theorizing* 5(4): 4–21.

Aoki, T. Tetsuo, Carol Langford, David M. Williams, and Donald C. Wilson. 1977. *British Columbia social studies assessment*. Vol 1–3. Victoria, B.C.: British Columbia Ministry of Education.

Astin, Helen S., and Carole Leland. 1991. *Women of influence, Women of vision: A cross-generational study of leaders and social change*. San Francisco, CA: Jossey-Bass.

Avolio, Bruce J., and Bernard M. Bass. 1988. Transformational leadership, charisma, and beyond. In James G. Hunt Eds., *Emerging leadership vistas*, pp. 29–49. Toronto, ONT: Lexington Books.

Bandura, Albert. 1978. The self system in reciprocal determinism. *American Psychologist* April: 344–357.

Barth, R. 1990. *Improving schools from within: Teachers, parents, and principals can make a difference*. San Francisco: Jossey-Bass.

Barton, Len, and Martin Lawn Eds. 1980. *Self and structure*. Birmingham, U.K.: Westhill College.

Bass, Bernard M. 1990. *Bass and Stogdill's handbook of leadership: Theory, research and managerial application*. New York: Free Press: Collier MacMillan.

———. 1985. *Leadership and performance beyond expectations*. New York: Free Press.

Bass, Bernard M., David A. Waldman, Bruce J. Avolio, and Michael Bebb. 1987. Transformational leadership and the falling dominoes effect. *Group and Organizational Studies* 12(1): 73–87.

Becker, Howard S., Blanche Geer, Everett C. Hughes, and Anselm Strauss. 1961. *Boys in white: Student culture in medical school*. Chicago: University of Chicago Press.

Becker, Howard. 1970. *Sociological Work*. Chicago: Aldine.

Belenky, Mary F., Blythe M. Clinchy, Nancy R. Goldberger, and Jill M. Tarule. 1986. *Women's ways of knowing: The development of self, voice, and mind*. New York: Basic Books.

Bennis, Warren G., Kenneth Benne, and Robert Chin Eds. 1961. *The Planning of change*. New York: Holt, Rinehart and Winston.

Bennis, Warren, and Burt Nanus. 1985 *Leaders*. New York: Harper and Row.

Bensimon, Estela Mara. 1993. A Feminist reinterpretation of President's definitions of leadership. *Peabody Journal of Education* 68(3): 143–156.

Berman, Louise M. 1984. *Understanding situational meanings of curriculum in-service acts: A response*. Curriculum praxis monograph series no. 9: 56–63. Edmonton: University of Alberta, Department of Secondary Education.

Berman, Paul, and Milbrey McLaughlin. 1975. *Federal programs supporting educational change: A findings in review*. Vol. 4. Santa Monica, CA: Rand Corporation.

———. 1978. *Federal programs supporting educational change: Implementing and sustaining innovations*. Vol. 8. Santa Monica, CA: Rand Corporation.

Bevan, Mary H. 1989. *Leadership, charisma, personality, and power*. Paper presented at the Annual Meeting of the National Women's Studies Association, Towson, MD.

Blackmore, Jill. 1989a. Changes from within: Feminist educators and educational leadership. *Peabody Journal of Education* 66(3): 19–40.

———. 1989b. Educational leadership: A feminist critique and reconstruction. In John Smyth Ed. *Critical perspectives on educational leadership*, pp. 91–129. Philadelphia: The Falmer Press.

Blumer, Herbert. 1976. The Methodological position of symbolic interactionism. In Martyn Hammersley and Peter Woods Eds. *The process of schooling: A sociological reader*, pp. 12–18. London: Routledge and Kegan Paul.

Blumer. Herbert. 1969. *Symbolic interactionism: Perspective and method.* Englewood Cliffs, N.J.: Prentice-Hall.

Boal, Kimberly B., and John M. Bryson. 1988. Charismatic leadership: A phenomenological and structural approach. In James G. Hunt, B. Rajaram Baliga, H. Peter Dachler, and Chester A. Schriesheim Eds. *Emerging leadership vistas*, pp. 11–28. Toronto, Ont: Lexington Books.

Bogden, Robert C., and Sara K. Biklen. 1982. *Qualitative research for education: An introduction to theory and methods.* Toronto: Allyn and Bacon.

Bowes, D., J. Chomas, I. Hall, G. Illaszewicz, R. Loder, A. Shepherd, and B. Skaalid. 1983. Implementing curriculum: The role of the principal. *Saskatchewan Education Administrator* 15(2): 13–26.

Brisken, Linda. n.d.. *Feminist pedagogy: Teaching and learning liberation.* Toronto, Ontario: York University.

Brown, Jean. 1993. Leadership for school improvement. *Emergency Librarian* 20(3): 8–20.

Burgess, Robert. G. 1984. *In the field: An introduction to field research.* London: George Allen and Unwin.

Burns, James M. 1978. *Leadership.* New York: Harper and Row.

Butler, Matilda, and William Paisley. 1978. *Factors determining roles and functions of educational linking agents.* San Francisco: Far West Laboratory.

Butterfield, D. Anthony. 1988. Chapter 2 commentary: Welcome back charisma. In James G. Hunt , B. Rajaram Baliga, H. Peter Dachler, and Chester A. Schriesheim Eds. *Emerging leadership vistas*, pp. 67–72. Toronto, Ont: Lexington Books.

Cantor, Dorothy W., and Toni Bernay. 1992. *Women in power: The secrets of leadership.* Boston: Houghton Mifflin.

Carr, Wilfred, and Stephen Kemmis. 1983. *Becoming critical: Knowing through action research.* Victoria, Australia: Deakin University.

Carson, Terrence R. 1984. *Conversations with participants about curriculum implementation.* Curriculum praxis monograph series no. 9: 18–42. Edmonton: University of Alberta, Department of Education.

———. 1985. *Curriculum implementation as school improvement: What are the possibilities for praxis?* Curriculum praxis occasional paper series no. 36. Edmonton: University of Alberta, Department of Secondary Education.

Cavers, Lloyd. 1988. *Teacher efficacy: Its relationship to school level organizational conditions and teacher demographic characteristics.* Ph.D. diss., University of British Columbia, Vancouver, Canada.

Cawelti, Gordon Ed. 1993. *Challenges and achievements of American education.* 1993 Yearbook of the Association for Supervision and Curriculum Development. Alexandria, VA: Edwards Bros. Inc.

Clandinin, D. Jean. 1983. *A Conceptualization of image as a component of teacher personal practical knowledge in primary teachers' reading and language programs.* Ph.D. diss., University of Toronto, Ontario.

———. 1986. *Classroom practice: Teacher images in action.* Falmer Press: London.

Conger, Jay A. 1989. *The charismatic leader: Behind the mystique of exceptional leadership.* San Francisco: Jossey-Bass.

Conger, Jay A., and Rabinda N. Kanungo. 1988. The Empowerment process: Integrating theory and practice. *Academy of Management Review* 13(3): 471–482.

Connelly, F. Michael, and D. Jean Clandinin. 1985. Personal practical knowledge and the modes of knowing: Relevance for teaching and learning. In Elliot Eisner Ed. *Learning and teaching: Ways of knowing,* pp. 174–198. Chicago: University of Chicago Press. 84th Yearbook of the National Society for the Study of Education.

———. 1990. Stories of experience and narrative inquiry. *Educational Researcher* 19(5): 2–14.

———. n.d.. *Teachers' personal practical knowledge: Image and narrative unity.* Calgary and Toronto: The University of Calgary, and the Ontario Institute for Studies in Education and the University of Toronto.

Corbett, H. Dickson, and Bruce Wilson. 1990. *Testing, reform and rebellion.* Norwood, NY: Ablex.

Crandall, David P. 1977. Training and supporting linking agents. In Nicholas Nash and Jack Culbertson Eds. *Linking processes in educational improvement,* pp. 189–267. Columbus, Ohio: University Council for Educational Administration.

Crandall, David P., and Susan F. Loucks. 1983. *A Roadmap for school improvement: Executive summary of the study of dissemination efforts supporting school improvement.* Vol 10. Androver, Mass.: The Network Inc.

DeLyon, Hilary, and Frances Widdowson Migniuolo Eds. 1989. *Women teachers: Issues and experiences.* Philadelphia: Open University Press.

Denzin, Norman K. 1978. *The Research act: A theoretical introduction to sociological methods. 2d ed.* New York: McGraw Hill Book Co.

Desjardins, Carolyn. 1989. The Meaning of Carol Gilligan's concept of "different voice" for the learning environment. In Carol Pearson, Donna Shavlik, and Judith Touchton Eds. *Educating the majority: Women challenging tradition in higher education,* pp. 134–146. New York: MacMillan.

Dewey, John. 1938. *Experience and education.* New York: Collier Books.

Donovan, J. 1990. *Feminist theory: The intellectual traditions of American feminism.* New York: Continuum.

Dow, Ian I., Ruth L. Whitehead, and Ruth L. Wright. 1984. *Curriculum implementation: A framework for action.* Ontario Public School Teachers' Federation.

Dunlap, Diane M., and Paul Goldman. 1991. Rethinking power in schools. *Educational Administration Quarterly* 27(1): 5–29.

Efland, Arthur D. 1976. The School art style: A functional analysis. *Studies in Art Education* 32(4): 21–33.

Eisner, Elliot W. 1972. *Educating artistic vision.* New York: MacMillan.

———. Ed. 1985. *Learning and teaching: The ways of knowing.* 84th Yearbook of the National Society for the Study of Education, Part II. Chicago: University of Chicago Press.

———. 1988. The Principal's role in arts education. *Principal,* 67(3): 6–9.

———. 1987. *The Role of discipline-based art education in America's schools.* Los Angeles, CA: Getty Center for Education in the Arts.

Elbaz, Freema. 1981. The Teacher's "practical knowledge:" Report of a case study. *Curriculum Inquiry* 11(1): 43–71.

———. 1983. *Teacher thinking: A study of practical knowledge.* London: Croom Helm.

English, Fenwick W. Ed. 1982. *Fundamental curriculum decisions.* Alexandria, Virginia: Association for Supervision and Curriculum Development.

Favaro, Basil Joseph. 1984. *Re-searching the meaning of consulting in teacher inservice education.* Curriculum praxis monograph series no. 9: 43–55. Edmonton: University of Alberta, Department of Secondary Education.

Ferguson, Kathy E. 1984. *The Feminist case against bureaucracy.* Philadelphia: Temple University Press.

Fisher, Berenice. 1988. Wandering in the wilderness: The search for women role models. *Signs: Journal of Women in Culture and Society* 13(2): 211–233.

Forman, Bernard I. 1973. Currents and countercurrents in art education. *Art Education* 26(9): 10–13.

Foster, William. 1993. The Administrator as a transformative intellectual. *Peabody Journal of Education* 68(3): 5–18.

———. 1989. Towards a critical practice of leadership. In John Smyth Ed. *Critical perspectives on educational leadership,* pp. 39–62. London: Falmer Press.

Friedman, Susan. 1985. Authority in the feminist classroom: A contradiction in terms? In Margo Culley and Catherine Portuges Eds. *Gendered subject,* pp. 203–208. Boston: Routledge and Kegan Paul.

Freire, Paulo. 1973. *Education for critical consciousness*. New York: The Seabury Press.

――. 1970. *Pedagogy of the oppressed*. New York: The Seabury Press.

Fullan, Michael. 1979. Conceptualizing problems of curriculum implementation. In Walter Werner Ed. *Curriculum Canada: Perceptions, practices, prospects*, pp. 40–50. Vancouver: Canadian Association for Curriculum Studies and Centre for the Study of Curriculum and Instruction, University of British Columbia.

――. 1993. Innovation, reform, and restructuring strategies. In Gordon Cawelti Ed. *Challenges and achievements in American education*, pp. 117–133. Alexandria, VA: Association for Supervision and Curriculum Development.

――. 1981. School district and school personnel in knowledge utilization. In Rolf Lehming and Michael Kane Eds. *Improving schools: Using what we know*, pp. 212–251. Beverly Hills: Sage Publications.

――. 1982. *The Meaning of educational change*. Toronto: OISE Press.

――. 1992. Visions that blind. *Educational Leadership*, February, 19–20.

Fullan, Michael., Stephen Anderson, and Earle Newton. 1986. *Support systems for implementing curriculum in school boards*. Toronto, ONT: OISE Press and Ontario Government Bookstore.

Fullan, Michael., and Suzanne Stiegelbauer. 1991. *The new meaning of educational change*. 2d. ed. New York, NY: Teachers College Press.

Gardner, Howard. 1983. *Frames of mind: The theory of multiple intelligences*. New York: Basic Books.

Gardner, John. 1990. *On leadership*. New York: The Free Press, MacMillan.

Geertz, Clifford. 1973. *The Interpretation of cultures*. New York: Basic Books.

Gilligan, Carol. 1982. *In a different voice*. Cambridge, MA: Harvard University Press.

Gilligan, Carol., Nona P. Lyons, and Trudy J. Hanmer Eds. 1990. *Making connections: The relational worlds of adolescent girls at Emma Willard School*. Cambridge, MA: Harvard University Press.

Giroux, Henry A. 1989. Rethinking education reform in the age of George Bush. *Phi Delta Kappan* 70(9): 728–730.

――. 1991. *Postmodernism, feminism, and cultural politics: Redefining educational boundaries*. Albany: State University of New York Press.

Glaser, Barney and Anselm L. Strauss. 1967. *The Discovery of grounded theory: Strategies for qualitative research*. Chicago: Aldine.

Graham, Jill. 1988. Chapter 3 commentary: Transformational leadership: Fostering follower autonomy, not automatic followership. In James G.Hunt, B. Rajaram Baliga, H. Peter Dachler, and Chester A. Schriesheim Eds. *Emerging leadership vistas*, pp. 73–79. Toronto, Ont: Lexington Books.

Hall, Gene F., and Susan F. Loucks. 1977. A Developmental model for determining whether the treatment is actually implemented. *American Educational Research Journal* 14(3): 263–276.

Hall, Gene F., Susan F. Loucks, William L. Rutherford, and Bevlan W. Newlove. 1975. Levels of use of the innovation: A framework for analyzing innovation adoption. *Journal of Teacher Education.* Vol 26, (Spring): 52–56.

Hall, Gene E., William L. Rutherford, Shirley H. Hord, and Leslie L. Huling. 1983 Effects of three principal styles on school improvement. *Educational Leadership* 41(5): 22–29.

Hamblen, Karen A. 1984. An Art education chronology: A process of selection and interpretation. *Studies in Art Education* 26(2): 111–120.

Hammersley, Martyn, and Paul Atkinson. 1983. *Ethnography: Principles in practice.* London: Tavistock.

Hammersley, Martyn, and Peter Woods Eds. 1976. *The Process of schooling: A sociological reader.* London: Routledge and Kegan Paul.

Harding, Sandra. 1986. *The Science question in feminism.* Ithaca, NY: Cornell University Press.

Hargreaves, Andy, and Ruth Dawe. 1989. *Coaching as unreflective practice: Contrived collegiality or collaborative culture.* Paper presented at American Educational Research Association annual meeting, March, San Francisco, CA.

Hart, Florence M. 1984. Art education in the primary division. In Ronald N. MacGregor Ed. *Readings in Canadian art education*, pp. 25–35. Vancouver, BC: WEDGE, University of British Columbia.

Harvey, Glen., and David P. Crandall. 1988. *A Beginning look at the what and how of restructuring.* Andover, MA: The Network, and Regional Laboratory for Educational Improvement of the Northeast and the Islands.

Havelock, Ronald G. 1973. *The Change agent's guide to innovation in education.* Englewood Cliffs, N.J.: Educational Technology Publications.

Hawke, David M. 1980. *The Life-world of a beginning teacher of art.* Ph.D. diss., University of Alberta, Edmonton, Alberta, Canada.

Hearn, Jeff, and Wendy Parkin. 1983. Gender and organisations. *Organisation Studies* 4(3): 219–242.

Helgeson, Sally. 1990. *The Female advantage: Women's ways of leadership.* Toronto: Doubleday Currency.

Holland, Patricia E. 1989. Stories of supervison: Tutorials in a transformative practice of supervision. *Peabody Journal of Education* 66(3): 61–77.

Holy Bible. n.d. *Holy Bible: Authorized King James Version.* Cambridge, UK: Cambridge University Press.

House, Robert J. 1977. A 1976 theory of charismatic leadership. In James G. Hunt and Lars L. Larson Eds. *Leadership: The cutting edge*, pp. 186–207. Carbondale: Southern Illinois Press.

House, Ernest. 1981. Three perspectives on innovation: Technological, political and cultural. In Rolf Lehming and Michael Kane Eds. *Improving schools: Using what we know*, pp. 17–21. Beverly Hills, CA: Sage.

Hoy, Wayne K., and Cecil G. Miskel. 1978. *Educational administration: Theory, research and practice*. 2d ed. New York: Random House.

Huberman, A. Michael, and Matthew Miles. 1984. *Innovation up close*. New York: Plenum.

Huling-Astin, Leslie L. 1990. Mentoring is squishy business. In Theresa M. Bey and C. Thomas Holmes Eds. *Mentoring: Developing successful new teachers*, pp. 39–50. Reston, VA: Association of Teacher Educators.

Hunt, James G., B. Rajaram, Baliga, H. Peter Dachler, and Chester A. Schriesheim. 1988. Charismatic and transformational leadership, In James G. Hunt, B. Rajaram Baliga, H. Peter Dachler, and Chester A. Schriesheim, Eds. *Emerging leadership vistas*, pp. 5–9. Toronto, Ont: Lexington Books.

———. 1988. *Emerging leadership vistas*. Toronto, Ont: Lexington Books.

Hurwitz, Al. 1967. The Art supervisor as agent for curriculum change. *Studies in Art Education* 9(3): 69–77.

Irwin, Rita L. 1989. A Fine arts supervisor's practical knowledge: A case study. *Visual Arts Research* 15(1): 21–35.

———. 1992. A Profile of an arts supervisor: A political image. *Studies in Art Education* 33(2): 110–121.

———. 1993. Charismatic and transformational leadership within a community of women arts educators. *Canadian Review of Art Education*, 20(2): 80–98.

———. 1992. *Charismatic leadership for women arts educators*. A paper presented at the Canadian Society for Studies in Education Conference, June, at Charlottetown, Prince Edward Island.

———. 1993. The Dialectical nature of supervisory practical knowledge: An ethical dilemma. In Debra Court and Ted Riecken Eds. *Culture and ethics: Dilemmas in educational change*, pp. 25–30. Calgary, Alta: Dietsleg.

———. 1988. *The Practical knowledge of a fine arts supervisor in educational change: A case study*. Ed.D. diss., University of British Columbia, Vancouver, B.C., Canada.

Jaggar, Allison M. 1989. Love and knowledge: Emotion in feminist epistemology. In Allison M. Jaggar and Susan Bordo Eds. *Gender, body/knowledge: Feminist reconstructing of being and knowledge*, pp. 145–171. New Brunswick: Rutgers University Press.

Jaggar, Allison M., and Susan Bordo Eds. *Gender, body/knowledge: Feminist reconstructing of being and knowledge.* New Brunswick: Rutgers University Press.

Johnson, John M. 1975. *Doing field research.* London: Collier Macmillan.

Johnson, Mark. 1984. Review of teacher thinking: A study of practical knowledge. *Curriculum Inquiry* 14(4): 465–468.

Jordon, Debra J. 1992. Effective leadership for girls and women in outdoor recreation. *Journal of Physical Education, Recreation, and Dance,* 63(2): 61–64.

Joyce, Bruce., and Beverly Showers. 1980. Improving inservice training: The messages of research. *Educational Leadership,* 3(7): 379–385.

Junker, Buford Helmholz. 1960. *Field work: An introduction to the social sciences.* Chicago: University of Chicago Press.

Kirby, Peggy C., Louis V. Paradise, and Margaret I. King. 1992. Extraordinary leaders in education: Understanding transformational leadership. *Journal of Educational Research,* 85(5): 303–311.

Knoop, Robert. 1992. Leaderless groups. *The Canadian School Executive,* September, 21–23.

Kormos, Jim and Robin Enns. 1979. *Professional development through curriculum development.* Toronto: Ontario Teachers' Federation.

Kreisberg, Seth. 1992. *Transforming power: Domination, empowerment, and education.* Albany, NY: State University of New York Press.

Kuhnert, Karl W., and Philip Lewis. 1989. Transactional and transformational leadership: A constructive/developmental analysis. In William E. Rosenbach and Robert L. Taylor Eds. *Contemporary issues in leadership.* 2d ed., pp. 192–205. Boulder: Westview Press.

Kushnell, Elliot., and Rae Newton. 1986. Gender, leadership style, and subordinate satisfaction: An experiment. *Sex Roles,* 14(3/4): 203–209.

La Tour, Richard M. 1985. *District art supervisors: Selected linking agent roles and functions in educational change.* Ph.D. diss., Eugene, OR: University of Oregon.

Lather, Patti. 1991. *Getting smart.* New York: Routledge.

Lehming, Rolf and Michael Kane Eds. 1981. *Improving schools: Using what we know.* Beverly Hills, CA: Sage.

Leithwood, Kenneth A. 1982. *Studies in curriculum decision-making.* Toronto: OISE Press.

———. 1992. The Move toward transformational leadership. *Educational Leadership* 45(5): 8–12.

Lincoln, Yvonna S. 1989. Critical requisites for transformational leadership: Needed research and discourse. *Peabody Journal of Education* 66(3): 176–181.

Little, Judith W. 1990. The persistence of privacy: Autonomy and initiative in teachers' professional relations. *Teachers College Record*, 91(4): 509–36.

Lippitt, Ronald. 1961. Dimensions of the consultants' job. In Warren G. Bennis and Robert Chin Eds. *The Planning of change*, pp. 156–167. New York: Holt, Rinehart and Winston.

Loucks, Susan. F., and Ann Lieberman. 1982. Curriculum implementation. In Fenwick W. English Ed. *Fundamental curriculum decisions*, pp. 126–141. Alexandria, Virginia: Association for Supervision and Curriculum Development.

Lowenfeld, Viktor. 1947. *Creative and mental growth: A textbook in art education.* New York: MacMillan.

Luke, Carmen, and Jennifer Gore Eds. 1992. *Feminisms and critical pedagogy.* New York: Routledge.

Lyons, Nona., Jane Forbes Saltonstall, and Trudy J. Hanmer. 1990. Competencies and vision: Emma Willard girls talk about being leaders. In Carol Gilligan, Nona P. Lyons, and Trudy J. Hanmer, Eds. *Making connections: The relational worlds of adolescent girls at Emma Willard School.* pp.183–214. Cambridge, MA: Harvard University Press.

MacGregor, Ronald N. Ed. 1984. *Readings in Canadian art education.* Vancouver, BC: WEDGE, University of British Columbia.

MacIntyre, Alasdair. 1981. *After virtue: A study in moral theory.* London: Gerald Duckworth.

Madey, Doren Louise. 1980. *A Study of the relationships among educational linker roles and selected linker function.* Ph.D. diss., Duke University, 1979. Dissertation Abstracts International, 40, 6247A.

Malin, Nigel., and Kevin Teasdale. 1991. Caring versus empowerment: Considerations for nursing practice. *Journal of Advanced Nursing*, 16: 667–662.

Mann, Margaret L. W. 1982. *Linking agents and state-mandated educational projects: A study of the role and functions of facilitators during the year-one phase of implementing project basic within the local school systems of Marylan.* Ph.D. diss., University of Maryland, 1981. Dissertation Abstracts International, 42, 3573A.

Manuel, Ann. 1988. *The influence of principals in art program promotion in Newfoundland secondary schools.* Master's thesis, University of British Columbia, Vancouver, Canada.

Martin, Jane Roland. 1984. Bringing women into educational thought. *Educational Theory* 34(4): 341–353.

Martin, William J., and David J. Willower. 1981. The Managerial behavior of high school principals. *Educational Administration Quarterly*, 17(1): 69–90.

Matlin, Margaret W. 1987. *The Psychology of women.* New York: Holt, Rinehart and Winston.

McCutcheon, Gail. 1981, On the interpretation of classroom observations. *Educational Researcher*, May: 5–10.

McKeon, Richard. 1952. Philosophy and action. *Ethics.* 62(2): 79–100.

Miller, Jean Baker. 1976. *Toward a new psychology of women.* Boston: Beacon Press.

———. 1982. Women and power. *Work in progress* #82–01. Wellesley, MA: Stone Center Working Papers Series.

Miller, John P., and Wayne Seller. 1985. *Curriculum perspectives and practice.* New York: Longman.

Miles, Matthew., Ellen R. Saxl, and Ann Lieberman. 1988. What skills do educational "change agents" need? An empirical view. *Curriculum Inquiry* 18(2): 157–193.

Morgan, Gareth. 1986. *Images in organization.* Beverly Hills: SAGE.

Murray, Margo. 1991. *Beyond the myths and magic of mentoring: How to facilitate an effective mentoring program.* San Francisco: Jossey-Bass.

Nash, Nicholas, and Jack Culbertson Eds. 1977. *Linking processes in educational improvement.* Columbus, Ohio: University Council for Educational Administration, 189–267.

Noddings, Nel. 1984. *Caring: The feminine approach to ethics and moral education.* Berkeley, CA: University of California Press.

Nyberg, David. 1981. *Power over power.* Ithaca, NY: Cornell University Press.

Oliver, Donald, and Kathleen Waldron Gershman. 1989. *Education, modernity, and fractured meaning: Toward a process theory of teaching and learning.* Albany, NY: State University of New York Press.

Orlich, Donald. 1976. Stalking curriculum; Or where do principals learn about new programs? *Educational Leadership* 33(1): 614–621.

Pajak, Edward. 1993. Change and continuity in supervision and leadership. In Gordon Cawelti Ed. *Challenges and achievements of American education.* Aleaxandria, VA: Edwards Bros Inc.

Pinar, William F., and Madeleine R. Grumet. 1980. Theory and practice in the recon-ceptualization of curriculum studies. In Len Barton and Martin Lawn Eds. *Self and structure.* Birmingham, U.K.: Westhill College.

Polanyi, Michael. 1958. *Personal knowledge.* Chicago: University of Chicago Press.

Polkinghorne, Donald E. 1988. *Narrative knowing and the human sciences*. Albany, NY: State University of New York Press.

Powell, Gary N. 1988. *Women and men in management*. Newbury Park: SAGE.

Rafferty, Pat. 1987. *An interpretive study of elementary school teachers' descriptive accounts of the art teaching task*. Ph.D. diss., University of British Columbia, Vancouver, Canada.

Regan, Ellen M., and Carol F. Winter. 1982. The influence of consultants. In Kenneth A. Leithwood. *Studies in curriculum decision-making*, pp. 68–86. Toronto: OISE Press.

Riordan, Robert C., Ed. 1976. *Education, participation, power: Essays in theory and practice*. Cambridge, MA: Harvard Educational Review Reprint Series No. 10.

Rich, Adrienne. 1976. *Of woman born*. New York: Norton.

Roberts, Nancy. 1985. Transforming leadership: A process of collective action. *Human Relations* 38(11): 1023–1046.

Rosenbach, William E., and Sharon Hayman. 1989. In William E. Rosenbach and R. L. Taylor, 1989. *Contemporary issues in leadership*. 2d. ed., pp. 210–221. Boulder, CO: Westview Press.

Rosenbach William E., and Robert L. Taylor. 1989. *Contemporary issues in leadership*. 2d. ed. Boulder, CO: Westview Press.

Rosener, Judy B. 1990. Ways women lead. *Harvard Business Review*, (November/December): 119–125.

Ross, John A., and Ellen M. Reagan. 1990. Self-reported strategies of experienced and inexperienced curriculum consultants: Exploring differences. *The Alberta Journal of Educational Research* 36(2) 157–180.

Sagaria, Mary Ann D. 1985. The Managerial skills and experiences of men and women administrators: Similarities and differences. *Journal of Educational Equity and Leadership* 5(1): 19-30.

Sarason, Seymour. 1981. *The Culture of the school and the problem of change*. 2d ed. Boston: Allyn and Bacon Inc.

Schatzman, Leonard, and Anselm L. Strauss. 1973. *Field research: Strategies for a natural sociology*. Englewood Cliffs: Prentice-Hall.

Schlecty, P. 1990. Schools for the 21st century: The conditions for intervention. In Ann Lieberman Ed. *Schools as collaborative cultures: Creating the future no,* pp. 233–256. New York: Falmer Press.

Schon, Donald A. 1983. *The Reflective practitioner: How professionals think in action*. New York: Basic Books.

——. Ed. 1991. *The reflective turn: Case studies in and on educational practice*. New York: Teachers College Press.

Schubert, William H. 1993. Curriculum reform. In Gordon Cawelti Ed. *Challenges and achievements in American education*, pp. 81–115. Alexandria VA: Association for Supervision and Curriculum Development.

———. 1990. On mentorship: Examples from J. Harlan Shores and others through the lenses provided by James B. Macdonald. *JCT* 9(3): 47–69.

Schutz, Alfred. 1962–1973. *Collected papers. Vols. 1–3.* The Hague, Netherlands: Martinus Nijhoff.

Schutz, Alfred, and Tristram Luckmann. 1974. *The Structures of the life-world.* London: Heinemann.

Schwab, Joseph J. 1969. The Practical: A language for curriculum. *School Review* 78(1): 1–23.

Schweitzer, Arthur. 1984. *The Age of charisma.* Chicago: Nelson-Hall.

Senge, Peter M. 1990a. *The Fifth discipline: The art and practice of the learning organization.* New York: Doubleday/Currency.

———. 1990b. The Leader's new work: Building learning organizations. *Sloan Management Review* (Fall): 7–23.

Sergiovanni, Thomas J. 1990. Adding value to leadership gets extraordinary results. *Educational Leadership* 47(8) 23–27.

Sergiovanni, Thomas J., and F. Carver. 1980. *The New school executive: A theory of administration.* New York: Harper and Row.

Sergiovanni, Thomas J. and Robert J. StarrattJ. 1983. *Supervision: Human perspectives.* New York: McGraw Hill.

Shakeshaft, Charol. 1987. *Women in educational administration.* Newbury Park: SAGE.

Shrewsbury, Carolyn. 1987. What is feminist pedagogy? *Women's Studies Quarterly* 15 (3/4).

Smyth, John. 1989. A 'Pedagogical' and 'educative' view of leadership. In John Smyth Ed. *Critical perspectives on educational leadership*, pp. 179–204. Philadelphia: The Falmer Press.

Sotirin, Patty. 1987. *The good man speaks: A rhetorical analysis of the charismatic organizational leader.* A paper presented at the Western Speech Communication Association, February, at Salt Lake City, Utah.

Spindler, George. 1982. *Doing the ethnography of schooling: Educational anthropology in action.* New York: Holt, Rinehart and Winston.

Spradley, James P., and David W. McCurdy. 1972. *The Cultural experience: Ethnography in complex society.* Toronto: Science Research Associates.

Spradley, James P. 1980. *Participant observation*. New York: Holt, Rinehart and Winston.

Spretnak, Charlene Ed. 1982. *The Politics of women's spirituality: Essays on the rise of spiritual power within the feminist movement*. New York: Anchor Books/Doubleday.

Starrett, Barbara. 1982. The Metaphors of power. In Charlene Spretnak Ed. *The politics of women's spirituality: Essays on the rise of spiritual power within the feminist movement*, pp. 185–193. New York: Anchor Books/Doubleday.

Statham, Anne. 1987. The Gender model revisited: Differences in the management styles of men and women. *Sex Roles*: (16) 7–8.

Sternberg, Robert J., and David R. Caruso. 1985. Practical modes of knowing. In Elliot W. Eisner Ed. *Learning and teaching: The ways of knowing*, pp. 133–158. 84th Yearbook of the National Society for the Study of Education, Part 2. Chicago: University of Chicago Press.

Strodl, Peter. 1992. *A model of teacher leadership*. A paper presented at the Eastern Educational Research Association Annual Meeting, March, at Hilton Head, SC.

Surrey, Janet L. 1987. Relationship and empowerment. *Work in progress*. Wellesley, MA: Stone Center Working Papers Series.

Swoboda, Marian, and Marian Vanderbosch. 1989. The Society of outsiders: Women in administration. *Journal of NAWDAC* (Spring): 3–6.

The Milan Bookstore Collective. 1990. *Sexual difference: A theory of social-symbolic practice*. Bloomington: Indiana University Press.

Tierney, William G. 1989. Advancing democracy: A critical interpretation of leadership. *Peabody Journal of Education* 66(3): 157–175.

Torbert, William R. 1991. *The Power of balance*. Newbury Park: SAGE Publications.

Tyler, Ralph. 1949. *Basic principles of curriculum and instruction*. Chicago: Chicago University Press.

Van Nostrand, Catherine Herr. 1993. *Gender-responsible leadership: Detecting bias, implementing interventions*. Newbury Park: SAGE.

Victoria, James J. and Elizabeth J. Sacca. Eds. 1978. *Presentations on art education research: Phenomenological description*. Montreal: Concordia University, 12.

Wax, Rosalie. 1971. *Doing fieldwork: Warning and advice*. Chicago: University Press.

Weber, Max. 1947. *The theory of social and economic organization*. New York: Free Press.

Werner, Walter Ed. 1979. *Curriculum Canada: Perceptions, practices, prospects*. Vancouver: Canadian Association for Curriculum Studies and Centre for the Study of Curriculum and Instruction, University of British Columbia, Vancouver, Canada.

Werner, Walter. 1987. Training for curriculum implementation. *Pacific Education* 1(1): 40–53.

Wiersma, William. 1986. *Research methods in education: An introduction. 4th ed.* Toronto: Allyn and Bacon.

Wise, Arthur E. 1988. The Two conflicting trends in school reform: Legislative learning revisited. *Phi Delta Kappan* 69(5): 328–333.

Wojtyla, Karol. 1981. *Toward a philosophy of praxis.* New York: The Crossroad Publishing Company.

Wolcott, Harry. 1973. *The Man in the principals office: An ethnography.* Toronto: Holt, Rinehart and Winston.

Woods, Peter. 1986. *Inside schools: Ethnography in educational research.* London: Routledge and Kegan Paul.

Yin, Robert K. 1984. *Case study research: Design and methods.* Beverly Hills: Sage.

Index